Cultural Guidance in the Development of the Human Mind

Cultural Guidance in the Development of the Human Mind

Edited by
Aaro Toomela

**Advances in Child Development Within
Culturally Structured Environments**
Jaan Valsiner, Series Editor

Ablex Publishing
Westport, Connecticut • London

British Library Cataloguing in Publication Data is available.

Library of Congress Catalog Card Number: 2002066581
ISBN: 1-56750-572-4
        1-56750-573-2 (pbk.)

First published in 2003

Ablex Publishing, 88 Post Road West, Westport, CT 06881
An imprint of Greenwood Publishing Group, Inc.
www.ablexbooks.com

Printed in the United States of America

∞™

The paper used in this book complies with the
Permanent Paper Standard issued by the National
Information Standards Organization (Z39.48-1984).

10 9 8 7 6 5 4 3 2 1

Contents

Contributors

Tabassum Ahmed, University of Pennsylvania, School of Medicine, Philadelphia, Pennsylvania.

Alfredo Ardila, Instituto Colombiano de Neuropsicologia, Bogota, Colombia.

John W. Berry, Psychology Department, Queen's University, Kingston, Ontario, Canada.

Kathleen R. Gibson, Department of Basic Sciences, University of Texas Houston, Dental Branch, Houston, Texas.

Eve Kikas, Department of Psychology, University of Tartu, Tartu, Estonia.

Ivana Marková, Department of Psychology, University of Stirling, Stirling, Scotland.

Bruce L. Miller, University of California at San Francisco, School of Medicine, San Francisco, California.

Katherine Nelson, Developmental Psychology, City University of New York, New York, New York.

Aaro Toomela, Department of Special Education, University of Tartu, Tartu, Estonia.

Jaan Valsiner, Frances Hiatt School of Psychology, Department of Psychology, Clark University, Worcester, Massachusetts.

Jacques Vauclair, UFR de Psychologie & PsyCLE (Centre for Research in Psychology of Cognition, Language & Emotion), Université de Provence, Aix-en-Provence Cedex, France.

Introduction: Culture as an Explanation of the Human Mind

Aaro Toomela

BACKGROUND

This volume tries, from different perspectives, to answer the same question: What role do culture and socially structured environment play in the development of the human mind? The question, of course, is not whether cultural environment is important. The answer "yes" would be accepted by most, if not all, developmentalists. Rather, the question is qualitative: Does culture introduce something entirely novel into the structure of the developing mind? The most obvious way to approach this last question would seem to be to carefully study child development. This edited volume as a whole, however, proceeds from the position that one single perspective is not sufficient for understanding the role of culture in the developing human mind. That position reflects my long-standing fascination with Vygotsky's theory. Very few in the history of psychology have dared to approach the study of the human mind in all main perspectives—evolution of the mind, evolution of culture, retrogression after brain damage, child development—as complementary. Vygotsky and his followers, especially Luria, were among those few (e.g., Luria, 1979; Vygotsky, 1983; Vygotsky & Luria, 1930, 1994).

So the question is why only one perspective is insufficient. In principle, the answer lies in the concept that for understanding a phenomenon it is insufficient to describe only what the phenomenon is. Rather, it is as necessary to understand what the phenomenon is not. The study of child development can tell a lot about how a child develops, but there is knowledge that cannot be constructed in child studies. First, only human children in the human social–cultural environment are able to appropriate human culture. No other animal can do that. Thus, the brain of a human child must be special. Studies of child development cannot give us an understanding of what makes the human brain special. The development of the mind is determined by both neural and environmental factors. And if we want to understand child development, we need to understand what characteristics of the brain allow children—only human children—to develop into cultural human beings. To understand the unique characteristics of the human brain, it must be compared with that of nonhumans. These are questions for comparative psychology.

Second, the study of child development cannot sufficiently inform us about what makes the human social–cultural environment special. Even healthy human children do not develop into cultural human beings in nonhuman (and inhuman) environments. The result of mental development embeds the contribution of developing neural systems and the environment in such a complex web that it is not possible to determine what the role of the brain is and what specific role the environment has (see Baldwin, 1906, for an explanation of why such contributions cannot be separated). The specific characteristics of the brain are studied in neuropsychology. The specific characteristics of the social–cultural environment also need to be studied separately. That is done in cultural psychology.

The history of psychology has demonstrated that it is not easy to answer the questions studied in different subfields of psychology—comparative, developmental, cultural, or neuropsychology. Naturally, it is even more intricate to understand how these fragments should be put together. At the same time it seems obvious that it is not only useful but also absolutely necessary to create such a "big picture." If our goal is to understand child development, we must know what is specifically human in the nervous system, what makes the human environment special, what is "inborn" to the brain and what is environmental, and what emerges as a qualitatively novel result of the interaction of both.

With this volume we, of course, did not start with the attempt to look at the "big picture" from an empty space. Actually, we are proceeding from an overcrowded field of knowledge. That field is loosely organized into independent or competing camps who either ignore the existence of the others or claim their truth is better than that of the others. For example, many scholars believe that the social–cultural nature of the human environment is the clue to understanding individual human development. Many in this field, however, have forgotten to tell us what exactly they mean by *culture* and why. Too often the main or only defining attribute of culture is a political border between geographic areas. Apparently the imaginary political border is a marker for something else. If so, then it would be much more appropriate to define and measure that "something else" instead of using an indirect correlate of culture. Many others have to choose among hundreds of definitions of culture or create new ones. Usually such choices remain implicit.

To proceed meaningfully, the choices have to be made explicit. Otherwise it is too easy to fall into a trap of very hot and absolutely useless debates over the relationships among essentially unrelated fragments of knowledge. An example would be the question of whether animals "have" culture or whether culture is unique to humans. Since there certainly are both similarities and differences between humans and other animals, the "yes" or "no" depends solely on what specific definition of culture has been chosen. To be involved in any kind of useful discussion it is imperative at least to make explicit how the battlefield is marked; "apples" and "oranges" can be put together only in the "fruits" battlefield. So the least we should do is to state explicitly what we are looking for. If we are looking for culture in animals or cross-cultural differences between humans or the role of culture in child development, we must define what we mean by culture. And it is even better when we can answer *the question* why we made that particular choice or why we prefer to define culture in one or another way.

This volume can give answers or possible answers to many questions. Directly or indirectly, however, the main axis around which the ideas revolve is language and its role in the human mind. Does language make humans unique or not? If yes, then how? If no, then how can we tell that? Again, these questions are old and have many different ways and different justifications to give "yes" or "no" answers that we would like. As an editor I asked myself whether we could agree with F. Max Müller, who a long time ago wrote that "Language is our Rubicon, and no brute will dare to cross it" (Müller, 1887, p. 173). Maybe we can go further and suggest, together with Lev Vygotsky or Grace Andrus de Laguna, among others, that language is *the* clue, in addition to human uniqueness, to understanding the differences between cultures and the differences between cultural individuals, and the mechanisms of human child development. Perhaps we can go even further and declare that culture is best defined as language.

If I want to be coherent and follow the rules I myself mentioned above, I should also have an answer to the why-question. Why should language be that important? I have argued elsewhere (e.g., Toomela, 1996) that language seems to be the only mental tool that allows us to perceive the world in a way that is not available to our direct senses—visual, auditory, tactile, olfactory, gustatory, or visceral. We cannot perceive directly things or phenomena that are too big/too far from us (e.g., a solar system), that are too small (e.g., electrons), or that are unavailable to our senses (e.g., electrical field). We seem to know about such things and phenomena only because of our verbalized theories about them. Such theories are our eyes to see the invisible and our fingers to touch the untouchable. It also seems that no animals other than humans and only sufficiently old humans with certain cultural experiences are able to construct and understand such theories. Thus, maybe language is *the* answer. Maybe it is not at all.

That was from where I started as an editor. Every potential contributor to this volume was provided with the following information:

Basic ideas on which the book will focus are presented below.

1. Human environment is structured in a way that qualitatively differs from the environments of all other animals. These qualitative differences constitute "culture."

   Possible views to defend:

   a. There are no qualitative differences between structures of human and nonhuman (animal, primate, ape) environments; or

   b. There are qualitative differences—in defending that view the difference(s) should be defined. (That view *does not* imply that the structures of human and nonhuman environments differ in all respects. There is continuity from nonhuman to human environment that introduces similarities.)

2. The specifically human characteristics of environment (i.e., culture) allow humans to achieve psychological processes/systems qualitatively different from those of all animals.

Possible views to defend:

a. The human mind does not qualitatively differ from the minds of animals (or only primates or apes): or

b. The human mind is qualitatively different from animal minds. In defending that view, at least some specific examples of qualitative differences should be proposed and discussed. In addition, (possible) mechanisms of how culture enters the mind and allows achieving qualitatively new psychological functions should be proposed.

3. It is (primarily) language that makes the difference between human and nonhuman environments and, correspondingly, between human and nonhuman minds. (Language should be taken broadly as any system for communication: speech, sign language, written language, etc.)

Possible views to defend:

a. Language does not make the difference, or language is not enough.

b. Language does make the difference—analysis of specific processes should be used as examples.

The authors were not constrained in their answers to these questions. Even more, if the contributor chose an approach where these ideas were not directly addressed, the contribution still remained acceptable. For some "camps" in our scattered field of "knowledge about the human mind and its development," even asking certain questions may make no sense.[1] It will appear in the end whether we can go beyond "camps" and approach a bigger picture. If we do not succeed, either we are not ready (should be read: "the editor is not smart enough") or there is no coherent big picture at all.

STRUCTURE OF THE BOOK

This book is divided into four parts. Part I, Human Development from the Perspective of Comparative Psychology, is dedicated to questions regarding the evolution of the (human) mind and possible similarities and differences between the minds of humans and those of other animals. In the first chapter, Jacques Vauclair discusses developmental relationships between animal and human minds. Vauclair argues that it is possible to observe both continuities and non-continuities in the evolution of the human mind. Kathleen R. Gibson approaches the same questions from a slightly different angle. She shows that the differences between humans and animals cannot be fine grained. Rather, growth in brain size and asymmetry may be responsible for most differences. In the last chapter in Part I, Jaan Valsiner directs attention to basic theoretical questions that have not been taken seriously in comparative and developmental psychology. Instead of asking what mental operations or characteristics animals or children "have," researchers should focus on the questions of emergence and development of novel forms. Development can be understood quite differently, and research questions that follow from usually implicit understanding of the nature of development are constrained by that implicit theoretical background. This, in turn, has led most of the mainstream psychology to answer questions that do not help to understand the phenomena under study.

Part II, Culture in the Developing or Regressing Brain, includes two chapters. Both chapters ask what characteristics of the human mind are related to basic, biologically determined construction of the brain and what characteristics/operations result from the interaction with (social–cultural) environment. In Chapter 4, Alfredo Ardila develops two ideas: First, the human brain possesses certain basic capabilities, that is, ways of processing information, and second, culture provides content to these capabilities. In Chapter 5, Tabassum Ahmed and Bruce L. Miller analyze the relationships between the brain and visual arts. They propose that certain brain regions are responsible for artistic abilities. These artistic abilities, according to them, are independent of culture; art is processed and produced by specific brain regions that emerged in the evolution of the anatomically modern humans.

Part III, Cultural Perspective on Human Development, is dedicated to the study of culture. John Berry describes ecocultural perspective on human diversity according to which human activity can be understood only within the context in which it develops and takes place. Ecocultural perspective has two roots. First, all human societies exhibit commonalities, and second, behavior that is based on these commonalities is differentially developed and expressed in response to ecological and cultural contexts. In Chapter 7, Ivana Markova discusses competing theories on how to understand culture and human activity in cultural context. Bakhtinian "dialogical," simultaneous nature of cultural mechanisms is opposed to Lotmanian sequential and relatively stable understanding of culture. Markova also demonstrates that theoretical ideas developed by scholars are shaped by culture and ideology; sometimes scientific ideas may be shadowed by politically correct ways of expressing them.

Part IV, The Role of Culture in Child Development, discusses relationships between culture and child development. All three authors' chapters in this part, by Katherine Nelson, Aaro Toomela, and Eve Kikas, argue that child development is a much more complex process than it is usually understood. Acquisition of cultural tools for the mind—language—is a complex hierarchical process. Children first acquire words, or symbols in general, that only externally resemble adult symbols. Internally, these symbols may have a structure that is different from that of adults. All three authors' chapters also propose that symbol development seems to proceed over general stages. Development of symbols, in turn, leads to changes in other psychological processes, perhaps even to the emergence of qualitatively novel mental structures and corresponding operations. All three authors also suggest that child development and cultural development are in many respects similar and that individual mental development can be understood better by studying evolution of human culture and vice versa.

Finally, in the afterword I have tried to synthesize ideas from all different perspectives on the human mind, discussed in the four parts of this book. That emerging synthesis, indeed, seems to be a productive way for going further in the study of the human mind. Different perspectives can be taken as complementary; each of the perspectives has something to say that other perspectives alone cannot.

NOTE

1. Indeed, sometimes researchers have been quite explicit in questioning the relevance of some questions. Esther Thelen, the leading scholar in the "Dynamic Systems Approach" to child development, for example, declared that "from a dynamic point of view, therefore, the developmental questions are not what abilities or core knowledge infants and children really have or what parts of their behavior are truly organic or genetic but how the parts cooperate to produce stability or engender change (Thelen, 1995, p. 94)."

REFERENCES

Baldwin, J. M. (1906). *Thought and things. A study of the development and meaning of thought or genetic logic.* London: Swan Sonneschein & Co.

Luria, A. R. (1979). *Jazyk i soznanije.* Moscow: Izdatel'stvo Moskovskogo Universiteta.

Müller, F. M. (1887). *The science of thought. Vol. 1.* New York: Charles Scribner's Sons.

Thelen, E. (1995). Motor development. A new synthesis. *American Psychologist, 50*(2), 79–95.

Toomela, A. (1996). How culture transforms mind: A process of internalization. *Culture and Psychology, 2*(3), 285–305.

Vygotsky, L. S. (1983). Istorija razvitija vyshikh psikhicheskih funkcii. (Originally written in 1931.) In A. M. Matjushkina (Ed.), *L. S. Vygotsky. Sobranije sochinenii. Tom 3. Problemy razvitija psikhiki.* (pp. 5–328). Moscow: Pedagogika.

Vygotsky, L. S., & Luria, A. R. (1930.) *Etjudy po istorii povedenija. Obezjana. Primitiv. Rebjonok.* Moscow-Leningrad: Gosudarstvennoje Izdatel'stvo.

Vygotsky, L., & Luria, A. (1994.) Tool and symbol in child development. (Originally written in 1930.) In R. van der Veer & J. Valsiner (Eds.), *The Vygotsky reader.* (pp. 99–174.) Oxford, UK: Blackwell.

Part I: Human Development from the Perspective of Comparative Psychology

1. Would Humans Without Language Be Apes?

Jacques Vauclair

THE POSTULATE OF MENTAL CONTINUITY

The bedrock of comparative psychology of cognition, especially where non-human primates are concerned, rests on Darwin's famous account according to which continuity would be the main trait leading from the animal to the human mind. This idea was popularized through the statement in which Darwin postulated only quantitative differences between humans and the other species, namely "the difference in mind between man and the higher animals, great as it is, certainly is one of degree and not of kind" (Darwin, 1871, p. 128).

We can only agree with Darwin's continuity position as concerns the existence of some kind of mental organizations in animals, in particular in nonhuman primates, as a necessary part of the perception of objects and their localization and interrelationships in space and time (Walker, 1983) and in many adaptive functions, including problem solving and memory (e.g., Vauclair, 1996). In effect, human and animal brain functions show sufficient similarity to allow comparisons if one assumes that animal brains are devices for selecting and organizing perceived information, and that the neural systems that accomplish perception and memory exhibit evolutionary continuity. It thus appears that these global functions are performed by the animal in ways that are basically similar to human performance, that is, through the construction and use of representations of various degrees of schematization and abstraction (Roitblat, 1982).

One of the main assignments of comparative psychology of cognition is to attempt to describe similarities between animals and between animals and humans. But its task is also to uncover possible differences between two or more species. Primate communication and language (including the attribution of mental states to others: Povinelli & Edy, 1996) are obviously good candidates for revealing such differences. However, a close inspection of the available literature in relation to other aspects of general human cognition (e.g., spatial behavior, coordination of movements in hand usage) can also help to shed light on the issue of resemblance and difference between human and nonhuman primates.

THE LANGUAGE ISSUE: A CASE OF DISCONTINUITY

I plan to show that animal communication and human language differ in some crucial ways that are related both to the structure of these communicative systems and to their functional use. This demonstration will be made by borrowing examples from natural and spontaneous communications among primates as well as from experiments that attempted to train ape species to use some of the features of human language.

To return to evolutionary theory, Darwin also considered that some characteristics of human behavior were clearly more on the discontinuous side than on the continuous one. The following excerpt illustrates such a view: "The development of the moral qualities is a more interesting problem [. . .]. A moral being is one who is capable of reflecting on his past actions and their motives—of approving of some and disapproving of others; and the fact that man is the one being who certainly deserves this designation, is the greatest of all distinctions between him and the lower animals" (Darwin, 1871, pp. 426–427). Furthermore, Darwin also proposed that the universal belief in "spiritual agencies" represented "the most complete of all the distinctions between man and the lower animals" (Darwin, 1871, p. 430).

Considerations about beliefs and intentions in ethology and in animal psychology have been tackled more recently within the field of "cognitive ethology" (e.g., Griffin, 1984; Allen & Bekoff, 1997) and with the concept of "theory of mind," proposed by Premack and Woodruff (1978). As concerns moral issues, these questions have been addressed only indirectly, for example by Lorenz (1970). The attribution of moral attitudes to animals (de Waal, 1996) has been challenged, however, notably by Kummer (1978).

It seems that the issue of the importance of the discontinuities in the mind introduced by the human specificity of language, moral qualities, and beliefs in some kinds of transcendental values ultimately refers to language understood as a system of exchanges and values (Bronckart, Parot, & Vauclair, 1987; Vauclair, 1990, 1995).

About Some Structural Differences Between Animal Communication and Human Language

It is necessary first to characterize the structure of human language with respect to the communicatory systems of animals. The well-known system of alarm calls emitted by vervet monkeys is probably a good example that illustrates some of the differences between the two organizations. Vervet monkeys have three classes of predators—leopards, snakes (pythons), and eagles—the presence of which is signaled by three different alarm calls (Strushaker, 1967). The production of each type of alarm calls evokes a different and appropriate response in conspecifics, which (1) look up and run into dense bush in response to eagle's alarms; (2) flee up to the trees in response to leopard's alarms; (3) look at the ground around them in response to python's alarms.

Even though these calls could be considered arbitrary with respect to the predators they designate, such arbitrariness is different from that of linguistic signs for at least two main reasons (see Figure 1.1). First, this arbitrariness in the vervet

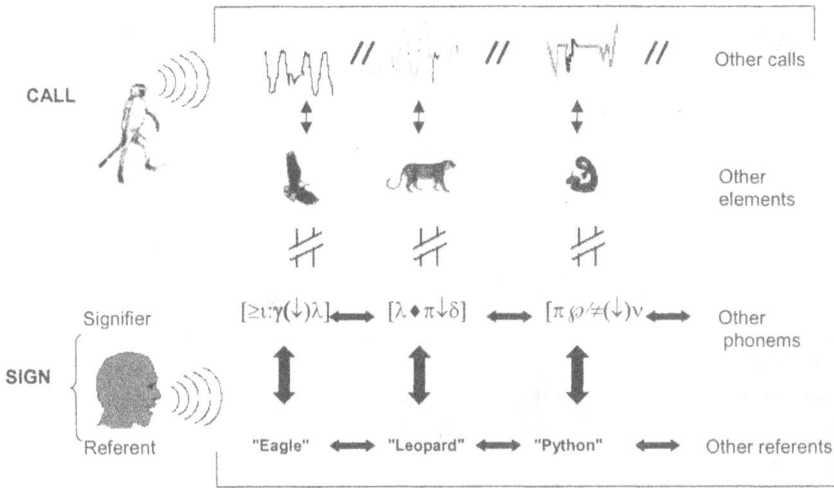

Legend:

//   Absence of articulation

   Signs secondarily related to objects

↕   Reciprocal relations between signifiers and referents

⬌   Oppositions and contrasts with all signs

Figure 1.1
Differences between Animal Calls and Linguistic Signs

monkey does not imply the intervention of a duality of patterning between a sound, or a phonemic level, and a concept or a semantic level (Hockett, 1960; Bickerton, 1990). Second, the arbitrariness implied in the vervet's alarm system is not related to a conventionalization that ties together the level of phonemic and semantic representations. If young vervets have to learn to produce more specific calls in response to a given class of predators, they do not have to learn a conventional rule associating such or such a call to such or such a predator (Cheney & Seyfarth, 1990). Finally, each category of the vervet's alarm calls appears to be strictly linked to the predator (or category of predators) to which it refers. Thus, its specific meaning is not the result of oppositions to other categories of calls produced in the species (Figure 1.1).

Briefly, what the vervet's alarm calls might send is information about a global configuration. This proposition has also been made by Bickerton (1990), for whom animal communication is holistic because it is concerned with the communication of whole situations. For example, the units of animal communication convey whole chunks. These chunks as they are expressed, for example, in the vervet alarm calls are roughly equivalent to "A predator just appeared!" or "Look out! A leopard's coming!" By contrast, language deals mainly with entities, that is, other creatures, objects, or ideas to which states or actions are attributed.

An additional property of the linguistic sign, the feature of displacement (e.g., Hockett, 1960), also seems to be lacking in animal communicatory systems. This feature concerns the fact that a linguistic sign can be detached or decontextualized from the element (object, event, or state) to which it relates or that its meaning is available regardless of the contextual situation in which it appears (Gärdenfors, 1996). Following this concept, a sign might become a symbol equivalent to a verbal sign when it can be used without direct connection to an experimental context. Von Glaserfeld (1977) has argued that animals' communicatory signals fail to achieve this transformation, because a mere delay (distance in time and space) does not change the one-to-one correspondence between the sign and the situation. In brief, a linguistic entity connects not only an object with a sign, but signs themselves.

To summarize, one could say that the mastery of signs in human language can be mostly characterized as an activity that consists of detaching the sounds and the words (i.e., phonemes and morphemes) from the configuration of the objects they represent and to conventionally relate these signs together, according to structures of phonemic and semantic equivalences and oppositions. These structures can be defined as "paradigmatic" because each item (sound or word) takes sense by distinction and by opposition to all other items that can commute in a given position, like linguistic units can commute in any position in a sentence (Saussure, 1966). For example, in the sentence "this animal is an eagle," the item "animal" takes sense by opposition to the other expressions that could come to the same place ("moving object," "organism," "being," "thing," "bird," etc.). Within the same logic, the item "is" takes its meaning by opposition to "has been," "will be," "looks like," etc.; and the meaning of "eagle" is specified by its opposition to "leopard," "python," "predator," or "vulture" (see Figure 1.1).

In language, the relation between referent and signifier is qualified as arbitrary, because there is no physical or analogical resemblance between the sequence of sounds and the content that is represented. In this respect, most of Washoe's gestures (Gardner & Gardner, 1969), Sarah's tokens (Premack, 1971), and the lexigrams operated by Austin, Sherman, and other language-trained chimpanzees (e.g., Savage-Rumbaugh, Rumbaugh, & McDonald, 1985) indeed entertain an arbitrary relation with the various aspects of the reality they represent. For linguists (Saussure, 1966), however, the "radical arbitrariness" that characterizes verbal units is of a higher level of difficulty than the simple relation between two realities (see also Bickerton, 1990, and Vauclair, 1990). In fact, two types of material reality need to be processed by the subject in order to comprehend or to produce a verbal sign: there is, on the one hand, the acoustic property of the sign and, on the other hand, the material property corresponding to the content expressed by the sign. Thus, a verbal sign is not simply a relation between material elements (sounds) and the content to which they refer (objects or actions). It is, rather, the product of two representations, one built on the acoustic material and the other built on the meaning (conceptual image). The relation between the two images is said to be arbitrary because all natural languages have selected a sequence of sounds to stand for a particular concept in an arbitrary manner and through social convention. It is precisely this conventional and arbitrary relation between a signifier and its referent that is called *radical arbitrariness*. Although the construction of conceptual and acoustic images is typically an individual activity, the basic operation of language, that is, the designation or creation of signs, is nevertheless performed through social convention.

How can this analysis based on human languages help to clarify the issue of the linguistic nature of the chimpanzee's production of symbols? In order to demonstrate that an ape (or any other animal) uses symbols that are equivalent to verbal signs, one should, from the present perspective, be able to show (1) that the ape possesses an individual representation of the signifier (e.g., of a gesture) and of its content or meaning; (2) that a social convention has made the analysis of the representation possible; and (3) that the representation can be grasped by opposition to other signs. Clearly, such requirements await demonstration in the field of comparative investigations of "linguistic" abilities of nonhuman primates.

About Some Functional Differences Between Animal Communication and Human Language

It could be argued that the structural differences mentioned earlier between human language and animal communication are somewhat trivial because they compare a very sophisticated medium for conveying information and intentions (i.e., language) to a phylogenetically less advanced system (i.e., animal communication). In this respect, the comparison might appear somewhat unfair because it is likely (also still not proved) that contemporary languages represent a rather recent form of expression that could have evolved from simpler modes of social exchanges (either gesturally or acoustically based). This notwithstanding, it appears that typically human communicatory systems (including gestural and spoken language but also prelinguistic manifestations) have specific modalities that are apparently not shared by any animal communicatory system.

Following the pioneering work of Bühler (1934), two principal modalities can be distinguished in the linguistic as well as in the prelinguistic communication among humans (Bates, 1979). The primary function of language is to exchange information about the world. Such an *informative function* takes two forms: a declarative form that serves for representing states of the world (e.g., "John comes") and an interrogative form. The other function is *injunctive* (imperative) and *exclamatory* and mostly expresses itself with requests and demands (e.g., "Come!"). Developmental studies with young children have shown that the use of declaratives (e.g., Wetherby et al., 1988; Bassano & Maillochon, 1994) becomes the dominant mode of communication between 1 and 2 years of age (about 60% of all utterances).

It happens that a major difference between humans and nonhuman primates is that the use of a signal or a learned symbol by the latter is restricted largely to its imperative function, whereas humans will use a word predominantly as a declarative. Declaratives (Bates, Camaioni, & Volterra, 1975) can be words or gestures, and they function not primarily to obtain a result in the physical world, but to direct another individual's attention (its mental state) to an object or event, as an end in itself. Thus, a human toddler might say "Plane!" apparently to mean "It's a plane!" or "Look, a plane," and so on. In such cases, the child communicates simply to share interest in something that he or she sees, that this object is a plane, and that the child has identified it and finally that he or she wants the partner to look at it.

It can be asserted with some confidence that the use of protoimperative signals is the exclusive mode of communication by animals of different phyla. When, for example, your cat vocalizes at you in the vicinity of the window and at the same time glances back and forth from the window to you, the cat is using a protoimperative signal that can be interpreted as "I want to go out." But it is very unlikely that your cat would use these same communicative signals to let you know that it has noticed something interesting in the garden.

This imperative function also appears to be the predominant (if not exclusive) mode used by "linguistically" trained apes. To illustrate this question, the case of the bonobo Kanzi studied by Savage-Rumbaugh (e.g., Savage-Rumbaugh et al., 1986) can be used. Studies reveal that (1) Kanzi had more or less spontaneously learned the symbolic function of a visual signal and (2) could (at the age of 8 years) comprehend English sentences at a level similar to that of a two-year-old child (Savage-Rumbaugh et al., 1993). But interestingly, and contrary to human children who use language to make indicative or declarative statements, 96 percent of Kanzi's productions were requests (Savage-Rumbaugh, Rumbaugh, & McDonald, 1985). Thus, the difference between Kanzi's modality of communication and the typical declarative mode observed by humans is striking. In effect, communication in the apes has essentially an imperative function (this appears to be the rule for all animal species, and this mode is sufficient to fulfill the biological requirements as, for example, to warn again predators; see above the case of vervet monkeys' alarm calls). By contrast, humans use not only linguistic signs but also prelinguistic means of communication such as gestures (e.g., pointing) for both imperative and declarative purposes (e.g., two persons sharing an interest toward a third person, object, or event: Bard & Vauclair, 1984; Vauclair, 1984).

The Future of the Study of Linguistic Skills in Apes

I have tried to point out in this section both the structural and functional differences in the spontaneous communicative signals as well as trained symbols used by nonhuman primates as compared to human language. The conclusion that two chief achievements of human language are lacking in animals does not imply that research on this issue with nonhuman primates or any other animal species must be abandoned. It is quite the reverse, because a proper identification of the main features of a given system should help in defining a better program for further studies. Three directions for such investigations can be briefly mentioned: (1) It is likely that the limitation in the types of productions made by trained animals might be due in part to constraints inherent to the experimental environment. For example, this environment has strongly encouraged Kanzi and other trained apes to formulate mostly requests for activities or objects. Thus, an environment that would facilitate more spontaneous expressions on the subject's part could better reveal its real accomplishments (Bodamer et al., 1994). (2) It is possible that deficits in the informative modality in apes could be due to their difficulty to express attention-related demands. This constituent of the declarative mode could thus be studied along with the ability of nonhuman primates to emit emotions (e.g., exclamatory function) through the symbolic system they are exposed to. (3) Focusing on the use of declaratives in nonhuman primates (in natural communication and in the lab) and the capacity for joint attention to objects (Bruner, 1983) could help to recognize the antecedents of these possibly unique features of human language and could set a framework that allows the development of mental attribution of beliefs, knowledge, desires, and intentions to social partners (e.g., Vauclair, 1982; Tomasello, 1998). After all, gestural and spoken declaratives constitute an elaborate form of joint attention, by which a given speaker attempts to affect the listener's mind. In this same line of thinking, protodeclarative and declarative behaviors may be precursors to the development of a theory of mind (Baron-Cohen, 1992).

Another remark is in order. The fact that nonhuman primates lack language does not mean that these species cannot show peculiarities in their behavior that bring them closer to humans compared to any other animal species. A series of investigations on spatial representations recently carried out in our laboratory clearly shows this. These investigations were based on the work of Hermer and Spelke (1994, 1996), which has examined the abilities of 18- to 24-month-old human children to combine geometric with nongeometric information in order to properly reorient in space. These authors found that toddlers were limited in their spatial behaviors in that they used only the shape of the experimental environment to reorient, even when more salient nongeometric information was available. In this sense, young children behaved like rats or chicks (e.g., Cheng, 1986), whereas human adults reoriented in a more flexible way. To explain this source of flexibility, Hermer and Spelke (1996) have argued that language is necessary to combine geometric and landmark-based information. More precisely, these authors propose that the age at which children begin to successfully locate a target using geometric and nongeometric information (at about 6 to 6.5 years of age) approximately corresponds to the age at which they begin producing sentences that would uniquely specify object location and orientation, such as "near" or "to the right/left" (MacWhinney, 1995).

We have recently demonstrated (Gouteux, Thinus-Blanc, & Vauclair, 2001), however, that rhesus macaques were able to jointly use geometric and landmark-based cues when presented with the same set-up as the one used with young children. These findings tend to demonstrate that spatial processing became more flexible with evolution; and we have hypothesized that such a flexibility could have evolved in nonhuman primates independently of specifically human cognitive features such as symbolic representation and language (a different example requiring representation of spatial relations by monkeys can be found in Vauclair, Fagot, & Hopkins, 1993).

HAND COLLABORATION AND THE REPRESENTATION OF VISUO-GESTURAL MOVEMENTS

The comparison of human and nonhuman primates has too often been exclusively based on language because the latter is more or less implicitly assumed to represent the hallmark of the species *homo sapiens*. I believe that this view is reductive and neglects other important features that seem to be as important as linguistic signs for a proper characterization of the human nature. The following sections will therefore be devoted to considering two of these (related) features. The first one concerns the apparently original way (division of labor between hands) humans act on objects; the second one is related to the existence in humans of genuine visuo-gestural representations that are manifested in the use of specific techniques such as weaving. Finally, a third section will contrast the developmental pathways of human and nonhuman primates in the acquisition of manipulatory behaviors, including the use of tools, by stressing the role of the social context in these acquisitions.

Differences in Laterality and Hand Use in Primates

A domain that is rarely considered in the comparative approach of cognition between human and other primates concerns the patterns of coordination required to perform food processing and other related activities. This field is interesting because it shows that at some point in the process of hominization, forces have acted on the way the brain machinery (and thus the behavioral outputs) perform in order to fill new demands for adapted actions on the environment.

To discuss this question properly, it is necessary first to summarize the current state of knowledge concerning manual organization and hemispheric lateralization in nonhuman primates. Contrary to humans who show a strong bias for using the right hand, nonhuman primates express individual patterns of laterality but no bias toward the left or toward the right at the population level (Ward & Hopkins, 1993). However, hand laterality in these species was shown to depend on the nature of the task as well as on postural constraints related to hand usage (Fagot & Vauclair, 1991). Thus, manual activities requiring strong visuospatial demands induce a preferential use of the left hand both in gorillas and baboons (Vauclair & Fagot, 1987, 1993). With the exception of chimpanzees, which, as a species, show a weak preference for the right hand (60%: Hopkins, 1994; for a review see Hopkins, 1996), nonhuman primates do not display, at the group or population levels, any systematic predominance of one hand over the other.

The above patterns of nonhuman primate lateralization are mostly obtained from the investigations of unimanual actions. But interspecies differences in hand use are also apparent when the overlapping manual activity in the manipulation of objects by human and ape infants is considered. An instance of overlap is counted when manipulatory events involving both right and left hands occur concurrently. In such cases, human infants exhibited greater variety and differentiation than did ape infants (Vauclair & Bard, 1983). Furthermore, this flexibility in the activity of the human infant appeared in the many instances where objects were transferred from one hand to the other during active manipulation. No case of such transfer was reported for the young apes.

Other differences between nonhuman primates and humans can be observed in the ways hands are used to handle tools. With respect to hand coordination in humans, Guiard (1987) has identified three basic models (orthogonal, parallel, or in series) describing hand coordination in right-handed subjects. The two hands of an operator of a milling machine can serve to illustrate the orthogonal assemblage. In this case, the operator moves a piece in a horizontal plane by acting on the crank with one hand (the left) according to the Y-axis, whereas the other hand (the right) acts on the crank to move the object on the X-axis. In parallel assemblages, both motors act in a synergistic fashion, essentially by adding their respective efforts (an example is provided by the weightlifter or by a child with a skipping rope). In the model of serial assemblage, the action of one hand produces a frame of reference upon which the second hand will act. Sewing activities and writing offer examples of such an assemblage. In the case of hand-sewing, for example, the left hand (of a right-handed person) manipulates the fabric relative to the body or to the table, while the other hand manipulates the needle relative to the fabric.

Interestingly, only the serial model implies differentiation in the role of each hand and thus an asymmetrical organization. It might thus be stated that this last kind of assemblage could explain lateral specialization among humans. We know that such a division of labor between hands appears early in ontogeny. For example, by 6 months of age, the human infant reaches for objects with bimanual coordination: a hand lands on the support near the object and then the other hand comes into contact and grasps it. This bimanual behavior (in right-handed subjects) is conceived of as one hand (the left) providing the spatial conditions necessary for reaching by the other hand (de Schonen, 1977).

Although the literature on ape tool use is extensive, few reports have focused on the ways hands are employed during complex manipulations (McGrew & Marchant, 1997). A survey of this literature suggests the following picture regarding hand use and hand collaboration. It appears that most tool use behaviors performed by nonhuman primates are realized unimanually. One study on ant fishing by chimpanzees (Nishida & Hiraiwa, 1982) has provided data with respect to hand use during tool use behavior. The authors observed that 65 percent of the feeding bouts involved the use of only one hand. In bouts where both hands participated in the activity of inserting the probe into the nest, there is no evidence that the hands were used in accordance with the serial model.

When force is required, as when chimpanzees crack hard-shell nuts (Hannah & McGrew, 1987), movements are bimanual but bilateral; that is, both hands act together in parallel. I am not aware of any case of spontaneous tool use that is realized according to an asymmetrical division of labor between the hands that is so common for most complex human activities. Some kind of division of labor can appear between both hands acting symmetrically and the mouth or the foot performing a specific action (generally in food processing). This organization can already be seen among marsupials and several other mammals (e.g., rodents, squirrels) and, of course, monkeys and apes. Most forms of nonhuman primate tool use appear thus to be predominantly performed unimanually (ant dipping by chimpanzees is a notable exception, McGrew, 1992), whereas human tool use activities almost always imply the collaboration of both hands. It happens that none of the manual behaviors realized by nonhuman primates have ever achieved the functional complexity and potential variability found in the asymmetrical lateralized hands of humans (Vauclair, 1993). From this perspective, serial assemblage must represent a uniquely human feature that appears early during human ontogeny (Connolly & Dalgleish, 1989) and that reflects a hierarchical division of labor between the hands for coordinated actions.

Visual Imagery and Visuo-spatial Expressions

For those interested in the phylogeny of cognitive processes between human and nonhuman primates, interspecies comparisons cannot be limited to language but must encompass the whole range of achievements that appear to develop somewhat independently from language. If, as I have postulated elsewhere (Vauclair, 1996), following Vygotsky (1962; see also Zivin, 1979), language is a system that is both communicatory and representational and that most of the representations we use are of linguistic support, it is also necessary to consider the existence in humans of nonverbal representational capacities. Among those abilities, we can mention the capacity to envision possible alternatives or to use references that do not exist *in situ*. Such competencies can be seen in visual gestural expressions used, for example, in tapestry and weaving and which require highly elaborated spatial representations that can neither be reduced to language nor be explained by it (Bresson, 1976). They express themselves in the use of spatial frameworks in the above-mentioned gesturo-visual activities. In these behaviors, hand movement coordinations in space do not rest on concrete supports but are framed by the complementary roles of the two hands, where one hand (the left hand in right-handed subjects) provides the spatial conditions necessary for the manipulations performed by the other, so called dominant, hand. Interestingly, the manual coordinations required by these complex spatial activities (e.g., in tapestry) develop and are taught in a way that is, to a great extent, independent of language, namely via direct observation and/or motor imitation. The fact that these activities cannot be taught by verbal means does not imply that verbal commentaries cannot be useful in attracting attention or scanning the operations involved in the complex coordinations of actions required in the above-mentioned tasks. Because they can be taught to blind people, they cannot be considered to be purely visually guided activities (Bresson, 1976). Another interesting feature of these activities is that that they have been found in all human societies. But, and this is my main point, it is worth noticing that such activities with the corresponding levels of difficulty seen in humans are lacking in the repertoire of animal species.[1] For example, no report is available showing that chimpanzees can be trained to make a knot (an ability found in 2- to 3-year-old human children)!

It thus seems that humans in the course of their recent evolution (it is likely that crafts appeared at the dawn of the Neolithic period) have developed sets of spatial representational abilities that are independent of language. Indeed, the fact that these skills are independent of language does not preclude the possibility that they develop, similarly to language, in children after the age of two years in accordance with increasing complexity of thinking during human development (e.g., Siegler, 1998). This raises the important question concerning the prerequisites for object manipulation and mastery of communicative skills (including language for humans) during early development. In this respect, it is necessary to consider comparative studies of nonhuman primates concerning the development of patterns of actions on objects and their relations with the development of cognitive capacities and referential communication.

Developmental Issues in Relation to Object Manipulations

Several studies have been carried out on the development of object manipulation in nonhuman primates (for reviews, see Vauclair, 1996; Tomasello & Call, 1997). This question can be illustrated by reporting the case of the development of object-directed behaviors as compared in three groups of primates (capuchin monkeys, chimpanzees, and humans), with special reference to the role of the social context in the acquisition of tool use (Vauclair & Anderson, 1995). Given the prime role of the social environment for simian primates, it is important to bear in mind that many of the manipulatory skills necessary for finding and preparing food, including the use of tools, originate and are perfected in a social milieu. From a comparative and evolutionary point of view, therefore, it is valuable to compare the relationships between the social context of object manipulation and tool use (i.e., technology) in human and nonhuman primates (Vauclair, 1982).

For example, with the goal of analyzing the communicatory behavior of adults in relation to infants' object manipulation, Bard and Vauclair (1984) asked: (1) whether adults acted on objects so as to engage the infants' attention with those objects, and (2) whether object manipulation by the adults influenced the infants' behavior with the objects. The results indicated that adult apes rarely acted on objects with the apparent intent of engaging an infant's attention, whereas adult humans manipulated objects primarily with the intent of stimulating, sustaining, or enhancing the infant's actions on the objects. Infant apes responded differentially; although they did not attend to the manipulations by adult apes, one of them did attend to, and even manipulated, objects when interacting with an adult human. More specifically, this infant ape (the famous bonobo Kanzi, who was later "linguistically" trained: see Savage-Rumbaugh et al., 1985, 1986) typically did not attend to the adult ape's actions. When he did attend, the mother was acting neutrally. This bonobo infant showed similar object-oriented responses to those of both the bonobo mother and the human caretaker, although these two adults acted differently. The human often attempted to engage the infant's attention with objects, but the bonobo infant typically did not attend to the adult's actions. The common chimpanzee infant, when in the presence of a human caretaker, showed object-oriented responses that were very similar to those observed in the human infant, including high frequencies of appropriate (i.e., infant attend) responses to the adult's attempts to engage, and a high proportion of instances in which the infant did not attend when the adult acted neutrally (Bard & Vauclair, 1984; Vauclair, 1984). Other data have confirmed that human-reared chimpanzee infants showed some early behavioral patterns more similar to those of humans than of mother-reared conspecifics (Bard & Gardner, 1996).

By considering different tool use behaviors (e.g., spoon use by humans, use of hammers by capuchin monkeys and chimpanzees), Vauclair and Anderson (1995) have described some of the resemblances and differences between human and nonhuman primates in the ontogeny of object manipulation and tool use, and the role of the social context in transmission of basic technological skills. The example of human infants learning to use a spoon illustrates the need to master the motor skills and the spatial and temporal components of tool use (see above). Similarly, young nonhuman primates have to master the movement constraints for efficient tool use, as well as the quality of the material to be used, whether it be a stick or twig for probing or a stone or piece of wood for nut-cracking.

The main difference between the two best-studied, tool-using nonhuman primate species (capuchin monkeys and chimpanzees) and humans is related to the social context in which object-oriented behaviors develop. A typical form of communication between the infant and a competent adult (e.g., the mother) arises in humans during object manipulation. This form is characterized by the mutual exchange between mother and infant regarding a large variety of discrete, moveable objects; for example, the mother encourages and sustains the infant's engagement with objects (Bard & Vauclair, 1983). By contrast, the nonhuman primate mother does not appear to intervene directly in the infant's object manipulations (but see Boesch, 1991, for exceptions in chimpanzees). In capuchin monkeys as well as in chimpanzees, the prolonged dependency of the infant on the mother results in the infant receiving selective exposure to environmental stimuli, in particular those instances of object–object combinations leading to food. This prolonged relationship, backed up by trial-and-error learning, is probably sufficient to ensure the social transmission of tool behaviors (McGrew, 1977). The relative contributions of different mechanisms (local or stimulus enhancement, observational learning, and imitation) in the development of tool use remain to be clarified, but it is difficult to determine how this issue could be resolved in the wild. The apparent absence of a real capacity to imitate in capuchin monkeys and the presence of such a capacity in chimpanzees (see Custance, Whiten, & Bard, 1995) make it more likely that true imitation may play some role in the ontogeny of tool use in the latter species. In this context, as pointed out by McGrew (1992), negative findings regarding imitative skills in contrived laboratory conditions need to be taken with caution. Rehabilitant orangutans in free-ranging conditions show a number of tool-using acts that appear to have been imitated from humans (Russon & Galdikas, 1993), and the bonobo Kanzi, with an extensive history of rich and positive interactions with humans, learned how to flake stones and use the resulting cutting tools through observing humans (Toth et al., 1993).

As concerns social transmission techniques in objet manipulation and tool use, an interesting perspective consists in looking for correlation between these behaviors and the possession of some "mind-reading" skills. The apparent absence of the capacity for self-recognition in capuchin monkeys (Anderson & Roeder, 1989) and its presence in chimpanzees (Gallup, 1970) suggest that chimpanzees but not capuchins may possess the necessary skills to be able to engage in at least occasional rudimentary forms of teaching of tool use, as was reported by Boesch (1991) for chimpanzees' nut-cracking. In this context, teaching is held to indicate that individual A (the teacher) is aware of the lack of skill (mental or motor) in individual B (the learner), that is, individual A engages in theory of mind. As stated by Cheney and Seyfarth, "to teach, one must recognize a difference between one's own knowledge and someone else's knowledge and then take explicit steps to redress this imbalance" (Cheney & Seyfarth, 1990, p. 306). It is precisely this limitation in the mind-reading skills or attribution of mental states to others (Premack & Woodruff, 1978) that precludes the emergence of teaching attempts: "Without attribution, instruction cannot even begin, because those with knowledge do not realize that the information possessed by others can be quite different from their own" (Cheney & Seyfarth, 1990, p. 306). Of course, both imitation and theory of mind skills are much more developed in humans, and it is in this species that imitation and teaching of tool use techniques, enhanced through linguistically based information transfer and other nonverbal means, are most important, at least once the earliest forms have been mastered.

CONCLUSION

Given our present state of knowledge, the answer to the question posed in the title of this chapter can be neither a definitive "yes" nor a definitive "no." If language and its associated competencies, as I have listed them above, are the obvious apanage of humans, the human specificity is clearly not limited to linguistic features. Other forms of nonverbal behaviors linked to bimanual coordinations and gesturo-spatial representations also seem to be lacking in nonhuman primates, including apes. These behaviors constitute some of the primary ingredients of our human cultural heritage. But, both linguistic and nonlinguistic competencies indeed rest on one another and perhaps on the more fundamental peculiarity of the human nature, namely the fact that our cognitive achievements are grounded and, in large part, determined by social constraints. These constraints will shape the way we interact with each other as well as our actions systems (and their forms) on physical objects. Thus, our communicative behaviors are performed within triadic systems of interaction, whereas social interactions between animals have a dyadic structure. Triangularity characterizes exchanges within the linguistic system and links objects, symbols, and concepts. This feature is also evident in other expressions of nonlinguistic behaviors, such as in pretend play when the child not only plays with objects as if they were other objects, but also happens to treat them as companions (see the concept of *transitional object* proposed by Winnicott, 1971). In animals, communication is apparently performed within dyadic systems of relations. Situations in which one animal appears to show attention to a triadic relationship involving itself, another animal, and some third party appear in fact to be remarkably rare (Bard & Vauclair, 1984), and only a few cases have been reported in the primate literature, such as in the formation of coalitions by chimpanzees (de Waal, 1982). In other words, contrary to humans, animals do not seem to confront the other of the other.

If our nearest primate relatives like the chimpanzees display some aspects of these human forms of behaving and interacting, it appears that they have never expressed them in their full range, neither during their development nor after long training periods.

To finish, a word of caution must be made concerning the approach chosen by ethologists and comparative psychologists when they deal with comparisons between humans and other animal species. Most of the time, these comparisons are made with respect to the finality of the main biological functions. With this perspective, they may miss, as was eloquently observed by the French sociologist Edgar Morin (1973) "that *Homo sapiens* is also *Homo demens* which is recognizable not only for its brain and its tool making abilities as we used to say, not only for its language as we now say, but also for the magic, for the myths and the traumas that death inflicts to the most intimate parts of its consciousness."

NOTE

1. Animals in all phyla (mostly insects, birds, and primates) build nests of varying spatial structures and complexity. If nest building behaviors are often driven by preprogrammed schemas, it is also obvious that they are flexible with individual variations and

adjustments to changing conditions in the environment (Gould & Gould, 1994). However, the nature of action programs required in nest building is different from those involved in the visual and gestural organizations that underlie the human techniques we are dealing with.

REFERENCES

Allen, C., & Bekoff, M. (1997). *Species of mind: The philosophy and biology of cognitive ethology*. Cambridge, Mass.: MIT Press.

Anderson, J. R., & Roeder, J.-J. (1989). Responses of capuchin monkeys (*Cebus apella*) to different conditions of mirror-image stimulation. *Primates; 30*, 581–587.

Bard, K. A., & Gardner, K. H. (1996). Influences on development in infant chimpanzees: Enculturation, temperament, and cognition. In A. E. Russon, K. A. Bard, & S. Taylor Parker (Eds.), *Reaching into thought. The mind of the great apes* (pp. 235–256). Cambridge: Cambridge University Press.

Bard, K. A., & Vauclair, J. (1984). The communicative context of object manipulation in ape and human adult-infant pairs. *Journal of Human Evolution, 13*, 181–190.

Baron-Cohen, S. (1992). How monkeys do things with "words". *The Behavioral and Brain Sciences, 15*, 148–149.

Bassano, D., & Maillochon, I. (1994). Early grammatical and prosodic marking of utterance modality in French. A longitudinal case study. *Journal of Child Language, 21*, 649–675.

Bates, E. (1979). *The emergence of symbols. Cognition and communication in infancy.* New York: Academic Press.

Bates, E., Camaioni, L., & Volterra, V. (1975). The acquisition of performatives prior to speech. *Merril-Palmer Quarterly, 21*, 205–226.

Bickerton, D. (1990). *Language & Species.* Chicago: University of Chicago Press.

Bodamer, M. D., Fouts, D. H, Fouts, R. S., & Jensvold, M. L. A. (1994). Functional analysis of chimpanzee (*Pan troglodytes*) private signing. *Human Evolution, 9*, 281–296.

Boesch, C. (1991). Teaching among wild chimpanzees. *Animal Behaviour, 41*, 530–532.

Bresson, F. (1976). Inferences from animal to man: Identifying functions. In M. von Cranach (Ed.), *Methods of Inference from Animal to Human Behaviour* (pp. 319–342). Paris: Mouthon.

Bronckart, J.-P., Parot, F., & Vauclair, J. (1987). Les fonctions de communication et de représentation chez l'animal. In *La Psychologie* (pp. 92–122). Paris: Gallimard (Encyclopédie de la Pléiade).

Bruner, J. S. (1983). *Child'Talk.* New York: W. W. Norton.

Bühler, K. (1934). *Sprachtheorie.* Jena: Fischer.

Cheney, D. L., & Seyfarth, R. M. (1990). *How monkeys see the world. Inside the mind of Another species.* Chicago: University of Chicago Press.

Cheng, K. (1986). A purely geometric module in the rat's spatial memory. *Cognition, 23*, 149–178.

Connolly, K., & Dalgleish, M. (1989). The emergence of a tool-using skill in infancy. *Developmental Psychology, 25*, 894–912.

Custance, D. M., Whiten, A., & Bard, K. A. (1995). Can young chimpanzees imitate arbitrary actions? *Behaviour, 132*, 839–858.

Darwin, C. (1871). *The Descent of Man and Selection in Relation to Sex.* Murray: London.

Fagot, J., & Vauclair, J. (1991). Manual laterality in nonhuman primates: A distinction between handedness and manual specialization. *Psychological Bulletin, 109,* 76–89.

Gallup, G. G. (1970). Chimpanzees: Self-recognition. *Science, 167,* 86–87.

Gärdenfors, P. (1996). Cue and detached representations in animal cognition. *Behavioural Processes, 35,* 263–273.

Gardner, R. A., & Gardner, B. T. (1969). Teaching sign language to a chimpanzee. *Science, 165,* 664–672.

Glaserfeld, E. Von (1977). The development of language as purposive behavior. In S. R. Harnad, H. D. Stecklis, & J. Lancaster (Eds.), *Origins and evolution of language and speech* (pp. 212–226). New York: New York Academy of Sciences.

Gould, J. L., & Gould, C. G. (1994). *The animal mind.* New York: Freeman.

Gouteux, S., Thinus-Blanc, C., & Vauclair, J. (2001). Rhesus monkeys use geometric and non geometric information during a reorientation task. *Journal of Experimental Psychology: General* (in press).

Griffin, D. R. (1984). *Animal Thinking.* Cambridge, Mass.: Harvard University Press.

Guiard, Y. (1987). Asymmetric division of labor in human skilled bimanual action: The kinematic chain as a model. *The Journal of Motor Behavior, 19,* 486–517.

Hannah, A. C., & McGrew, W. C. (1987). Chimpanzees using stones to crack open oil palm nuts in Liberia. *Primates, 28,* 31–46.

Hermer, L., & Spelke, E. (1994). A geometric process for spatial reorientation in young children. *Nature, 370,* 57–59.

Hermer, L., & Spelke, E. (1996). Modularity and development: The case of spatial reorientation. *Cognition, 61,* 195–232.

Hockett, C. F. (1960). The origin of speech. *Scientific American, 203,* 88–96.

Hopkins, W. D. (1994). Hand preference for bimanual feeding in a sample of 140 chimpanzees. *Developmental Psychobiology, 31,* 619–625.

Hopkins, W. D. (1996). Hand preferences for coordinated bimanual task in 110 chimpanzees (Pan troglodytes): Cross-sectional analysis. *Journal of Comparative Psychology, 109,* 291–297.

Kummer, H. (1978). Analogs of morality among nonhuman primates. In G. S. Stent (Ed.), *Morality as a biological phenomenon.* Life Research Report 9 (pp. 35–52). Berlin: Dahlem Konferenzen Verlag Chemie.

Lorenz, K. (1970). *Studies in animal and human behaviour.* London: Methuen.

MacWhinney, B. (1995). *The CHILDES Project: tools for analyzing talk.* Hillsdale, N.J.: Erlbaum.

McGrew, W. C. (1977). Socialization and object manipulation of wild chimpanzees. In S. Chevalier-Skolnikoff & F. E. Poirier (Eds.), *Primate bio-social development: Biological, social, and ecological determinants* (pp. 261–288). New York: Garland.

McGrew, W. C. (1992). *Chimpanzee material culture.* Cambridge: Cambridge University Press.

McGrew, W. C., & Marchant, L. F. (1997). On the other hand: current issues in and meta-analysis of behavioral laterality of hand function in nonhuman primates. *Yearbook of Physical Anthropology, 40,* 211–232.

Morin, E. (1973). *Le Paradigme perdu: la nature humaine.* Paris: Seuil.

Nishida, T., & Hiraiwa, M. (1982). Natural history of a tool-using behavior by wild chimpanzees in feeding upon wood-boring ants. *Primates, 11,* 73–99.

Povinelli, D. J., & Eddy, T. J. (1996). What young chimpanzees know about seeing? *Monographs of the Society for Research in Child Development, 63.*

Premack, D. (1971). Language in chimpanzees? *Science, 172,* 808–822.

Premack, D., & Woodruff, G. (1978). Does the chimpanzee have a theory of mind? *The Behavioral and Brain Sciences, 3,* 615–636.

Roitblat, H. L. (1982). The meaning of representation in animal memory. *The Behavioral and Brain Sciences, 5,* 353–406.

Russon, A. E., & Galdikas, B. M. F. (1993). Imitation in free-ranging rehabilitant orangutans *(Pongo pygmaeus). Journal of Comparative Psychology, 197,* 147–161.

Saussure, F. De (1966). *Course in general Linguistics.* New York: McGraw-Hill. (First published in French in 1916).

Savage-Rumbaugh, E. S., Rumbaugh, D. M., & McDonald, K. (1985). Language learning in two species of apes. *Neuroscience and Biobehavioral Reviews, 9,* 653–665.

Savage-Rumbaugh, E. S., McDonald, K., Sevcik, R. A., Hopkins, W. D., & Rupert, E. (1986). Spontaneous symbol acquisition and communicative use by pygmy chimpanzees *(Pan paniscus). Journal of Experimental Psychology: General, 115,* 211–235.

Savage-Rumbaugh, E. S., Murphy, J., Sevcik, R. A., Brakke, K. E., Williams, S. L., & Rumbaugh, D. M. (1993). Language comprehension in ape and child. *Monographs of the Society for Research in Child Development, 58,* 3–4.

Schonen de, S. (1977). Functional asymmetries in the development of bimanual coordinations in human infants. *Journal of Human Movement Studies, 3,* 144–156.

Siegler, R. S. (1998). Children's thinking. Upper Saddler River, N.J.: Prentice-Hall.

Strushaker, T. T. (1967). Auditory communication among vervet monkeys *(Cercopithecus aethiops).* In S. A. Altman (Ed.), *Social communication among primates* (pp. 281–324). Chicago: University of Chicago Press.

Tomasello, M. (1998). Uniquely primate, uniquely human. *Developmental Science, 1,* 1–16.

Tomasello, M., & Call, J. (1997). *Primate cognition.* New York: Oxford University Press.

Toth, N., Schick, K. D., Savage-Rumbaugh, E. S., Sevcik, R. A., & Rumbaugh, D. M. (1993). Pan the tool-maker: Investigations into the stone tool-making and tool-using capabilities of a bonobo *(Pan paniscus). Journal of Archaelogical Science, 20,* 81–91.

Vauclair, J. (1982). Sensorimotor intelligence in human and nonhuman primates. *Journal of Human Evolution, 11,* 757–764.

Vauclair, J. (1984). A phylogenetic approach to object manipulation in human and non-human primates. *Human Development, 27,* 321–328.

Vauclair, J. (1990). Primate cognition: from representation to language. In S. T. Parker & K. R. Gibson (Eds.), *"Language" and intelligence in monkeys and apes: Comparative developmental perspectives* (pp. 312–329). New York: Cambridge University Press.

Vauclair, J. (1993). Tool use, hand cooperation and the development of object manipulation in human and non-human primates. In A. F. Kalverboer, B. Hopkins, & R. Geuze (Eds.), *Motor development in early and later childhood: Longitudinal approaches* (pp. 205–216). Cambridge: Cambridge University Press.

Vauclair, J. (1995). *L'intelligence de l'animal.* Paris: Seuil (Point Sciences).

Vauclair, J. (1996). *Animal cognition: Recent developments in modern comparative psychology.* Cambridge, Mass.: Harvard University Press.

Vauclair, J., & Anderson, J. R. (1995). Object manipulation, tool use, and the social context in human and non-human primates. *Techniques & Culture, 23–24,* 121–136.

Vauclair, J., & Bard, K. A. (1983). Development of manipulations with objects in ape and human Infants. *Journal of Human Evolution, 12,* 631–645.

Vauclair, J., & Fagot, J. (1987). Spontaneous hand usage and handedness in a troop of baboons. *Cortex, 23,* 265–274.

Vauclair, J., & Fagot, J. (1993). Manual specialization in gorillas and baboons. In J. P. Ward & W. D. Hopkins (Eds.), *Primate laterality: Current behavioral evidence of primate asymmetries* (pp. 193–205). New York: Springer Verlag.

Vauclair, J., Fagot, J., & Hopkins, W. D. (1993). Rotation of mental images in baboons when the visual input is directed to the left cerebral hemisphere. *Psychological Science, 4,* 99–103.

Vygotsky, L. S. (1962). *Thought and Language.* Cambridge, Mass.: MIT Press.

Ward, J. P., & Hopkins, W. D. (Eds.) (1993). *Primate laterality: Current behavioral evidence of primate asymmetries.* New York: Springer Verlag.

Waal, F. B. M. de (1996). *Good natured.* Cambridge, Mass.: Harvard University Press.

Waal, F. B. M. de (1982). *Chimpanzee politics.* London: Jonathan Cape.

Walker, S. (1983). *Animal thought.* London: Routledge & Kegan.

Wetherby, A., Cain, D. H., Yonclas, D. G., & Walker, V. G. (1988). Analysis of intentional communication of normal children from the prelinguistic to the multiword usage. *Journal of Speech and Hearing Research, 31,* 240–252.

Winnicott, D. W. (1971). *Playing and Reality.* New York: Basic Books.

Zivin, G. (Ed.) (1979). *Development of self-regulation through speech.* New York: Wiley.

2. Continuities Between Great Ape and Human Behaviors

Kathleen R. Gibson

In his 1872 volume, *The Expression of Emotions in Man and Animals*, Charles Darwin postulated that the emotional and behavioral differences between animals and humans were matters of degree rather than of kind. In so doing, he broke with the dominant Western philosophical tradition that human minds are qualitatively different from and superior to those of other animals. In particular, Darwin's postulate stood in stark contrast to the dominant Cartesian view that animal behavior is instinctive but human behavior is rational (Descartes, 1980).

Darwin's concept that the behavioral differences between animals and humans are matters of degree rather than of kind had little immediate impact on the Cartesian paradigm and has not been fully accepted even among psychologists, anthropologists, and others who focus on the origin of human mental capacities. Thus, some twenty years after the publication of *The Expression of the Emotions in Man and Animals*, C. Lloyd Morgan proposed what has come to be known as Morgan's Canon—that animal behavior must always be explained by the simplest possible mechanism (Morgan, 1894). The Canon, which has long dominated some branches of psychology, had the positive effects of limiting anthropomorphism and introducing more scientific rigor into the interpretations of animal behavior. Morgan's Canon, however, has not usually been applied to interpretations of human behavior. This has resulted in a double standard. When animal and human behaviors appear quite similar, the human behavior is often interpreted to reflect advanced mental capacities while the animal behavior is assumed to be mediated by simpler mechanisms. This result is a self-reinforcing, anti-Darwinian view of strong qualitative gaps between animal and human minds that may better reflect the differing standards of behavioral interpretation than the actual extent of human–animal behavioral differences.

Morgan's Canon primarily influenced behaviorist psychologists and had little impact on other fields. Nonetheless, many twentieth-century anthropologists, archaeologists, linguists, and others continued to espouse Cartesian rather than Darwinian views of animal versus human minds. As a consequence, much of literature reads as a search for *the* qualitative animal–human distinctions that many scholars assume must exist and must serve as the defining characteristics of humanity. Mid-twentieth century anthropologists thus assured us that humans were the only animals with culture, symbolic language, and tool-making capacities (White, 1959). When, in the 1960s, it became apparent that wild chimpanzees made tools (Goodall, 1964) and captive chimpanzees could symbolize (Gardner & Gardner, 1969), definitions of humanity changed. We became the only animals with syntactic language (Terrace, 1979) and the only animals with the ability to use a tool to make a tool. At various times, humans were also defined as the only animals with self-awareness, consciousness, deceptive capacities, theory of mind, and imitative skills. Given this loud chorus of support for human uniqueness models, it is easy to assume that Darwin's concepts of behavioral continuity have been proven wrong and have no support among modern scholars. Not so. Each time a behavioral characteristic is defined as uniquely human, some animal behaviorists assert that similar behaviors can be found in one or more of the great apes and/or in other animals. Continuity theories thus continue to remain alive and well in the field of human evolution, and it now seems clear that the rudiments of nearly all behaviors once thought to be uniquely human can be found in great apes (Gibson, 1996; Gibson & Ingold, 1993; Gibson & Jessee, 1999; Russon, Bard, & Parker, 1996).

Qualitative uniqueness versus continuity controversies remain alive in large part because, even though great apes exhibit the rudiments of many behaviors previously thought to be uniquely human, human behavioral capacities do obviously exceed those of other animals in numerous domains. Some animals, for example, do make tools, symbolize, and use syntax, but no animal begins to match human capacities in these areas. Those scholars who report the existence of human-like capacities in other animals often fail to provide models that can explain both the similarities and the differences between animal and human behaviors. Their claims about animal abilities thus often seem counterintuitive. This chapter attempts to remedy this gap, both by providing the case for continuities between humans and great apes in the domains of language, tool-making, social intelligence, and advanced motor skills and by suggesting a mechanism that can account for the differences between great apes and humans in these behavioral domains.

THE HUMAN GENOME PROJECT: IMPLICATIONS

The human genome contains approximately 30,000 genes, and, of these, close to 99% are shared with chimpanzees (Svante, 2001). Hence, humans and chimpanzees differ by about 300 to 400 genes. These provide all of the genetic information underlying the behavioral, neurological, anatomical, physiological, and biochemical differences between the species. The small number of genes differentiating the chimpanzees and humans implies that some discontinuities based on the influence of single, uniquely human, genes may exist. It appears, however, to rule out overly fine-grained models that assume that each discernible human–chimpanzee physical or behavioral difference is controlled by a unique gene. It has also long been known that most genes have pleiotropic effects (i.e., affect many traits). Hence, the genetic evidence favors epigenetic models that assume that a limited number of genetic changes in combination with environmental influences produce existing behavioral and neurological differences between apes and humans.

NEUROANATOMICAL EVIDENCE

The most obvious differences between ape and human brains are quantitative. The average human brain is three to four times as large as the average great ape brain, and in absolute terms, most structural components of the brain are larger in humans than in great apes. In primates, absolute brain size correlates strongly with the sizes of individual brain structures, with the exception of olfactory structures. In particular, very strong correlations (.96–.99) exist between absolute brain size and the size of those higher processing centers that have exhibited the greatest expansion in human evolution, including the neocortex, striatum, and cerebellum (Gibson & Jessee, 1999; Finlay & Darlington, 1995). Sizes of neural areas thought to mediate advanced mental abilities are, thus, largely predictable from overall brain size. Other differences between ape and human brains may also be predictable consequences of increased brain size. These include increased ratios of glial cells and neuronal connections with respect to neurons in the human neocortex and increases in the numbers of fissures and gyri in the human brain (Jerison, 1980). The overall expansion of the human brain in comparison to great ape brains requires only a very few additional mitotic divisions of neuronal precursor cells during the embryonic period (Rakic, 2001), and the most highly expanded neural structures are those that experience the latest maturation dates in the embryonic period (Finlay & Darlington, 1995). Hence, differential expansion of the human brain and of its higher neural processing centers may primarily reflect changes in embryonic developmental timing that demand minimal genetic changes.

Not all quantitative changes in brain proportions, however, are merely by-products of increased brain size (Barton & Harvey, 2000; de Winter & Oxnard, 2001). Some systems, such as the cerebellar system, have experienced quantitative changes that do not strictly reflect expanded neural tissue (MacLeod, 2000). Views of major qualitative dichotomies between human and animal behaviors would also suggest the presence of qualitatively, as opposed to quantitatively, unique human brain structures. No major brain structures are known to exist in the human brain, however, that cannot be found in the brains of other primates. Indeed, current evidence suggests that, for the most part, human brain structure is remarkably similar to that of the great apes, even at the level of fairly small anatomical details such as the relative enlargement of the left, as compared to the right, temporal lobe (Gannon et al., 1998). Recent evidence does, however, suggest the presence of unique cytoarchtectonic features of the human visual cortex (Preuss, Qi, & Kaas, 1999). It is likely that similar fine-grained cytoarchitectonical differences will be found in other brain areas. What will prob-ably remain unclear in the immediate future is whether these differences are pre-dictable consequences of expanded brain size or represent genetically determined qualitative distinctions of the human brain. Given the limited number of unique human genes and the overall pleiotropic nature of genetic control, however, the first research imperative is to determine whether unique cytoarchitectonic features of the human brain can be explained by more general phenomena such as increased brain size, rather than by an accumulation of large numbers of unique genes.

In sum, most of the known unique aspects of human brain organization appear to reflect predictable consequences of increased brain size that may require changes in only a few genes. Additional genetic changes, however, may be necessary to account for some quantitative and cytoarchitectonic human brain distinctions. Taken together, the neurological and genetic evidence suggest that a very few genetic changes leading to greatly expanded overall human brain size may account for most, but probably not all, animal–human behavioral dichotomies. The remainder of this chapter focuses on those aspects of human behavior that may reflect increased human brain size.

HUMAN BEHAVIORAL AND COGNITIVE UNIQUENESS IN RELATION TO INCREASED BRAIN SIZE

Current behavioral and neurological evidence indicates that the increased information-processing capacities accompanying human brain size expansion are likely to have provided our species with advances in two general capacities: fine sensorimotor discrimination and mental construction (Gibson, 1990). Taken together, these increased capacities can account for many of the enhanced linguistic, technical, social, and motor capacities of the human species.

That the quantity of nervous tissue devoted to specific sensorimotor modalities relates to sensorimotor capacity is well documented both within and between species. For example, animals with especially fine manual sensorimotor dexterity, such as raccoons and primates, have expanded manual neocortical motor and somatosensory representations (Welker & Seidenstein, 1959). Spider monkeys, who have especially dexterous tails, also have expanded tail regions of the neocortex (Pubols & Pubols, 1972), and herbivores with well-developed lips and tongues exhibit expanded neuronal representation of those body regions (Welker et al., 1976). Within the human brain, the motor and somatosensory areas controlling the hands and the oral cavity are differentially enlarged in comparison to those controlling other body parts. These neural enlargements provide us with the manual dexterity to use tools and with the oral dexterity needed to precisely distinguish tongue and lip movements such as those needed to produce "t" versus "d" or "b" versus "p" sounds. As such these neural enlarge-ments account, in part, for expansions in human vocal, musical, technical, and artistic capacity.

The ability to make precise movements and distinguish fine sensory discriminations is the first step toward higher manual, vocal, and cognitive skills, but much more is needed. Movements, perceptions, and thoughts must also be organized into effective simultaneous and sequential constructs. The pronunciation of any phoneme, for example, requires the simultaneous coordination of lip, tongue, palate, and laryngeal movements. The pronunciation of words and sentences requires that these individual simultaneous constructions be strung together in logical sequences that can be produced rapidly and automatically. Sentence construction also demands the mental flexibility to create novel sound and meaning sequences. Native adult speakers of any verbal language do this proficiently and automatically. Handwriting, typing, playing a musical instrument, singing, gymnastics, and dance require similar abilities to create rapid, automatic, and highly variable motor sequences.

Mental constructional abilities similar to those needed to produce skilled movements also underlie the higher cognitive aspects of varied behavioral domains, including language, understanding the minds of others, imitation, tool-making, architecture, art, and music. In each domain, human mental construction is hierarchical in nature in that humans first construct subroutines that are later embedded in still more complex routines by processes of combination and recombination. For example, an individual may construct individual dance steps that are combined and recombined into differing dance routines that are then further combined, recombined, and embedded in larger choreographed dance performances. Human mental construction is also flexible in nature in that individual constructed routines can be used in multiple contexts and embedded into multiple higher-order schemes. For example, a phrase can be incorporated into numerous diverse sentences.

The hierarchical and constructed nature of human understandings of each other's intentions is evident from Dennett's descriptions of orders of intentionality in which each higher order incorporates greater amounts of information and embeds information into more complex units (Dennett, 1988, p. 185). For instance, in Dennett's system, "x believes that p" represents first-order intentionality; "x wants y to believe that x is hungry" represents second-order intentionality; and "x wants y to believe that x believes he is all alone" represents third-order intentionality (Dennett, 1988, p. 185). Evidence indicates that nonhuman primates possess some concepts of intentionality, but only humans demonstrate third and higher orders of intentionality.

In the domain of vocal language, humans construct individual words from sequences of phonemes, phrases from words and sentences from words and phrases. They do so hierarchically in the sense that phonemes, words, and phrases are subordinated to larger units. They do so in a flexible manner in that individual constructions can be combined and recombined in diverse patterns. Hierarchical and flexible mental construction is also evident within human gestural and written languages. Some captive great apes have mastered components of gestural and visual languages, but in all cases the extent to which they can apply mental constructional skills to their linguistic capacities falls far short of that of humans. At most, great apes have demonstrated capacities to combine two to three gestures or visual lexigrams in a structured, meaningful way (Greenfield & Savage-Rumbaugh, 1990), whereas by $2^1/_2$ to 3 years of age, human children are composing complex sentences.

Within the domains of tool making and architecture, humans manufacture individual objects that are then combined and recombined with other individually manufactured objects to create "constructed" tools and/or other "constructed" objects. For instance, humans manufacture stone points, binding materials, and wooden shafts and join them together to make spears. Individual components of the spear, such as the binding materials and wooden shafts, can be combined in other ways to make alternate objects: e.g., to provide the foundations of teepees or rafts. Great apes, in contrast, make tools by processes of subtraction: e.g., by removing side twigs to make straight probes or by removing chips from stones to create sharp-edged points. They do not construct tools from two or more distinct components. Great apes construct nests from branches, but they do not construct human-like dwellings from separately manufactured subcomponents, such as poles, hide, and binding materials.

Great apes do exceed humans in their abilities to locomote in the trees. To some extent, this reflects species anatomical differences such as the grasping feet and long arms possessed by apes. Some forms of arboreal locomotion such as moving through the canopy from one tree to another also require advanced planning of motor actions and sequences of actions. Hence, it is possible that great apes equal or exceed humans in the mental constructional skills involved in their routine locomotor activities. On the other hand, the diversity and creativity of human locomotor patterns greatly exceed those demonstrated by great apes. Only humans, for example, have invented swimming techniques, complex forms of dance and gymnastics, horseback riding, skating, and group-coordinated motor routines such as marching. In general, except for the intense interest in the origins of human bipedalism, anthropologists and primatologists have shown little interest in the origins of human locomotor capacities. Hence, the extent to which humans may fall behind, match, or exceed great apes in their capacities to invent new locomotor routines and to subordinate newly invented motor routines into still higher order motor sequences remains unknown. The evidence of modern ballet and Olympic competitions in areas such as gymnastics and ice-skating suggests, however, that human abilities to apply mental constructional skills to locomotor realms are extraordinary.

That these mental constructional skills depend in large part on increased brain size is evident from theoretical considerations. Neuronal network theories, for instance, suggest that while individual neuronal nets may be capable of perceiving many different items or of eliciting different kinds of movements, individual nets cannot handle multiple perceptions or movements simultaneously (Hinton, McClelland, & Rumelhart, 1986). This requires multiple nets. For example, in Hinton's model, an individual neuronal network could perceive a chimpanzee or an onion, but in order to perceive a chimpanzee eating an onion, at least two separate nets would be needed, one to perceive the onion and the other to perceive the chimpanzee. Similarly, given the slow speed of neuronal feedback, the rapid generation of skilled motor sequences demands that a series of actions be recruited prior to the actual initiation of the first movement (Rumelhart & Mc-Clelland, 1986). This requires the simultaneous action of multiple networks controlling the separate movements.

One regular result of brain size enlargement in mammals is increases in the numbers of neocortical areas devoted to specific sensorimotor modalities, and it is now known that areas of the neocortex that have shown the greatest size increases in human evolution, the association areas, actually contain multiple sensory and motor areas (Kaas, 1987). Patients with damage to the neocortical association areas display behavioral deficits that have been interpreted to result from abilities to synthesize diverse perceptions into higher-order mental constructs (Luria, 1966). The multiplication of neocortical areas devoted to specific sensory and motor modalities may help provide the multiple neural nets needed for these synthetic capacities. The enlargement of other neural structures is also likely to have contributed to enhanced human mental constructional skills. The cerebellum plays an essential role in allowing rapid attention shifts and in the smooth coordination of motor actions and is now known to also have cognitive functions (MacLeod, 2000). The basal ganglia play a critical role in procedural learning, that is, in learning to generate movements and acquired information automatically and with little conscious thought (Mishkin, Malamut, & Bachavelier, 1984). Finally, the enlarged human frontal lobes enhance mental constructional skills by providing mental flexibility and increases in the number of items that can be held in short-term memory.

In sum, one major cognitive capacity, mental construction, appears to cross-cut numerous human behavioral and motor domains and to be integral to those behaviors that are clearly expanded in humans as compared to great apes, including language, tool-making, and the ability to understand the minds of others. As noted above, these expansions in mental construction of a flexible and hierarchical nature may result, at least in part, from the increased size of the brain and higher neural processing areas.

INFANTILE CHANNELING BEHAVIORS, NEURAL PLASTICITY, AND THE DEVELOPMENT OF HUMAN-LIKE BEHAVIORS

Mental constructional capacities in both great apes and humans increase during growth and maturation (Case, 1985; Gibson, 1990). Most comparative studies of great ape versus human capacities focus on the highest adult capacities attained rather than on less developed infantile capacities. Species differ profoundly, however, in their spontaneous infantile behaviors (Gibson, 1990, 1991). In particular, human infants manifest a variety of behaviors that appear as precursors to adult cognitive capacities, including babbling, facial imitation, social smiling, vocal interchanges with caretakers, playing with causative physical relationships between two or more objects (tertiary circular reactions), rhythmic pounding and counting actions, and arranging objects in classificatory sets according to color, size, shape, or other properties. Some of these behaviors, such as babbling, are missing from the repertoire of great ape behaviors. Some, such as tertiary circular reactions and arranging objects into classificatory sets, develop much later in great ape ontogeny than in human ontogeny (Gibson, 1991; Langer, 2000).

Species differences in infantile behaviors have two potential implications for understanding human behavioral evolution. First, by analyzing what babies do, we can gain insight into possible genetically determined species differences. It is possible, for instance, that those genes that specifically code for human, as compared to great ape, behavioral capacities manifest themselves early, rather than late, in ontogeny. If so, comparisons that limit themselves to adult capacities may miss critical species distinctions. Second, it is now known that many mammalian brains, including rat, mouse, monkey, and human brains, exhibit considerable neural plasticity depending on environmental inputs (Diamond, 1988). This plasticity continues into adulthood but is strongest during periods of growth and maturation. As a result of neural plasticity, differing environmental inputs can produce major functional differences in adult brains. For example, portions of the temporal lobe that have auditory functions in humans with normal hearing acquire visual functions in the congenitally deaf (Neville, 1991). Thus, environmental input during infancy and youth, including that input resulting from the infant's and child's own behaviors, may have critical effects on the cognitive capacities of mature human brains.

These considerations suggest that adult linguistic, tool-making, social, and other abilities reflect the channeling of brain-size–mediated mental constructional capacities in species-specific directions by behavioral and environmental inputs during infancy and youth. That language, imitative capacities, and other human-like capacities may, in part, reflect youthful environmental input is also evident from studies of apes reared in captivity versus those reared in the wild. The former group appears to exhibit more human-like behaviors in language and mirror self-recognition domains (Greenfield & Savage-Rumbaugh, 1990; Parker, Mitchell, & Boccia, 1994). That great apes exhibit some human-like behaviors, such as language, in captivity but not in the wild has always presented an interpretive paradox. The mental constructional paradigm presented here suggests that great apes do, indeed, have the cognitive capacities to develop rudiments of these human-like behaviors, but their natural environments and spontaneous infantile and childhood behaviors usually channel the development of their cognitive capacities in other directions.

CONCLUSIONS

Great apes exhibit the rudiments of many behaviors sometimes thought to be uniquely human, including language, imitation, tool-making, mirror self-recognition, and social intelligence. In this sense, major continuities exist between the behaviors of great apes and humans, and none of these capacities can be said to be uniquely human. Humans, however, exceed apes in each of these domains in that they apply greater amounts of mental construction to their behaviors than do the great apes. This mental construction is of both a hierarchical and a flexible nature and appears to depend in large part on expansion of brain size, including expansions of the neocortical association areas, the cerebellum, and the basal ganglia. To a large extent, expansion of human brain size and the increased mental constructional capacity that it provides may reflect a very few genetic changes that influence developmental timing during the embryonic period. If so, major behavioral differences between great apes and humans may reflect minimal genetic change. A relatively unexplored area, however, is that of comparative infantile behaviors. To the extent that infantile behaviors channel the development of adult brains and behaviors, a full understanding of the evolution of human behavioral capacities demands that greater attention be paid to infants. It is also possible that analyses of infantile behaviors will reveal species differences in behavior that cannot be accounted for by the more general increases in brain size and in mental constructional capacity, and that thus require the postulation of additional genetic change beyond those that lead to increases in amounts of neural tissue.

REFERENCES

Barton, R. A., & Harvey, P. H. (2000). Mosaic evolution of brain structure in mammals. *Nature, 405*, 1055–1058.

Case, R. (1985). *Intellectual development from birth to adulthood.* New York: Academic Press.

Darwin, C. (1872). *The expression of emotions in man and animals.* Chicago: University of Chicago Press.

Dennett, D. C. (1988). The intentional stance in theory and practice. In R. Byrne & A. Whiten (Eds.), *Machiavellian Intelligence* (pp. 180–201). Oxford: Oxford University Press.

Descartes, R. (1980). *Discourse on method and meditations on first philosophy.* Originally published in 1641. Translated by D. A. Cress. Indianapolis: Hackett Publishing.

de Winter, W., & Oxnard, C. (2001). Evolutionary radiations and convergences in the structural organization of mammalian brains. *Nature, 409*, 710–714.

Diamond, M. C. (1988). *Enriching heredity.* New York: The Free Press.

Finlay, B. L., & Darlington, R. B. (1995). Linked regularities in the development and evolution of mammalian brains. *Science, 168*, 1578–1584.

Gannon, P. J., Holloway, R. L., Broadfield, D. C., & Braun, A. R. (1998). Asymmetry of the chimpanzee planum temporale: humanlike pattern of Wernicke's brain language area homolog. *Science, 279*, 220–222.

Gardner, R. A., & Gardner, B. T. (1969). Teaching sign language to a chimpanzee. *Science, 187*, 752–753.

Gibson, K. R. (1990). New perspectives on instincts and intelligence: Brain size and the emergence of hierarchical mental constructional skills. In S. T. Parker & K. R.

Gibson (Eds.), *"Language" and intelligence in monkeys and apes: Comparative developmental perspectives* (pp. 97–128). Cambridge: Cambridge University Press.

Gibson, K. R. (1991). Myelination and behavioral development: A comparative perspective on questions of neoteny, altriciality, and intelligence. In K. R. Gibson & A. C. Petersen (Eds.), *Brain maturation and cognitive development: Comparative and cross-cultural perspectives* (pp. 29–64). Hawthorne, N.Y.: Aldine De Gruyter.

Gibson, K. R., & Ingold, T. (Eds.) (1993). *Tools, language, and cognition in human evolution.* Cambridge: Cambridge University Press.

Gibson, K. R. (1996). The biocultural human brain, seasonal migrations, and the emergence of the Upper Paleolithic. In P. Mellars & K. Gibson (Eds.), *Modelling the early human mind* (pp. 33–47). Cambridge: McDonald Institute for Archaeological Research.

Gibson, K. R., & Jessee, S. (1999). Language evolution and the expansion of multiple neurological processing areas. In B. King (Ed.), *The origins of language: What nonhuman primates can tell us* (pp. 189–228). Santa Fe: School of American Research Press.

Goodall, J. (1964). Tool-use and aimed throwing in a community of free-ranging chimpanzees. *Nature, 201,* 1264–1266.

Greenfield, P. M., & Savage-Rumbaugh, E. S. (1990). Grammatical combination in *Pan paniscus:* process of learning and invention in the evolution and development of language. In S. T. Parker & K. R. Gibson (Eds.), *"Language" and intelligence in monkeys and apes: Comparative developmental perspectives* (pp. 540–578). Cambridge: Cambridge University Press.

Hinton, G., McClelland, J. L., & Rumelhart, D. E. (1986). Distributed representations. In D. E. Rumelhart & J. L. McClelland (Eds.), *Parallel distributed processing* (pp. 77–109). Cambridge, Mass.: MIT Press.

Jerison, H. J. (1980). Allometry, brain size, cortical surface, and convolutedness. In E. Armstrong & B. King (Eds.), *Primate Brain Evolution: Methods and Concepts* (pp. 77–84). New York: Plenum Press.

Kaas, J. H. (1987). The organization of neocortex in mammals: Implications for theories of brain function. *Annual Review of Psychology, 38,* 129–151.

Langer, J. (2000). The descent of cognitive development. *Developmental Science, 3,* 361–378.

Luria, A. (1966). *Higher cortical functions in man.* New York: Basic Books.

MacLeod, C. E. (2000) *The Cerebellum and Its Part in the Evolution of the Human Brain.* Ph.D. Dissertation, Simon Frazer University.

Mishkin, M., Malamut, B., & Bachavelier, J. (1984). Memories and habits: two neural systems. In G. Lynch, J. L. McGaugh, & N. M. Weinberger (Eds.), *Neurobiology of learning and memory* (pp. 65–77). New York: Guilford Press.

Morgan, C. L. (1894). *An introduction to comparative psychology.* London: Walter Scott.

Neville, H. J. (1991). Neurobiology of cognitive and language processing: Effects of early experience. In K. R. Gibson & A. C. Peterson (Eds.), *Brain maturation and cognitive development: Comparative and cross-cultural perspectives* (pp. 355–380), Hawthorne, N.Y.: Aldine de Gruyter.

Parker, S. T., Mitchell, R. W., & Boccia, M. L. (Eds.) (1994). *Self-awareness in animals and humans: Developmental perspectives.* Cambridge: Cambridge University Press.

Preuss, T. M., Qi, H.-X., & Kaas, J. H. (1999). Distinctive compartmental organization of human primary visual cortex. *Proceedings of the National Academy of Sciences USA, 96*, 11601–11606.

Pubols, B. H., & Pubols, L. M. (1972). Neural organization of somatosensory representation in the spider monkey. *Brain, Behavior, and Evolution, 5*, 342–346.

Rakic, P., & Kornack, D. (2001). Neocortical expansion and elaboration during primate brain evolution: a view from neuroembryology. In D. Falk & K. R. Gibson (Eds.), *Evolutionary Anatomy of the Primate Cerebral Cortex* (pp. 30–56). Cambridge: Cambridge University Press.

Rumelhart, D., & McClelland, J. (Eds.) (1986). *Parallel distributed processing, vol 1.* Cambridge, Mass.: MIT Press.

Russon, A. E., Bard, K., & Parker, S. T. (Eds.) (1996). *Reaching into thought: The minds of great apes.* Cambridge: Cambridge University Press.

Svante, P. (2001). The human genome and our view of ourselves. *Science, 16*, 1219–1220.

Terrace, H. S. (1979). *Nim: A chimpanzee who learned sign language.* New York: Knopf.

Welker, W. K., Adrain, H. O., Lifschutz, W., Kaulen, R., Caviedes, E., & Gutman, W. (1976). Somatic sensory cortex of llama (*Lama glama*). *Brain, Behavior and Evolution, 13*, 184–193.

Welker, W. K., & Seidenstein, S. (1959). Somatic sensory representation in the cerebral cortex of the raccoon (*Procyon lotor*). *Journal of Comparative Neurology, 111*, 469–501.

White, L. A. (1959). *The evolution of culture: The development of civilization to the fall of Rome.* Cambridge: Cambridge University Press.

3. Assumptions and Knowledge Construction: What Can Science Learn from Primate Languages and Cultures?

Jaan Valsiner

When some questions in science are asked over and over again—and not answered—then there must be some good reasons for such intellectual idioadaptation (to borrow the term from Severtzoff, 1929). The questions "Can apes learn a language?" "Are they intelligent?" "Do they 'have culture?" are of the kind that are repeatedly asked in psychology and anthropology. These questions force interested scientists and laypersons to take sides between different viewpoints. Some may believe that chimpanzees indeed "have culture," whereas others would deny that species (or any other nonhuman species) such privilege. A legitimate scientific question—"Under what conditions can (at least some) representatives of a species develop a particular new way of functioning?"—is replaced by a diagnostic inclusion/exclusion game: "they" (e.g., chimpanzees) are "like us" (humans) in "culture" (or "language capacity") versus "they" are "not like us" (as "we" are "humans" and "they" are "animals"). The question here is simple: Why is that question (of distinction) a question at all?

THE "TALKING APES" AND PSEUDOEMPIRICISM IN PSYCHOLOGY: THE NON-NORMALITY OF "NORMAL SCIENCE"

Psychologists are often enamored by the game of empiricism—they let the empirical evidence "prove" which of the opposite viewpoints fits. The empirical evidence is supposed to "prove" whether chimpanzees "have" (or "do not have") language. Yet the issue of whether the other species are "haves" (of our precious human characteristics) or "have-nots" (being on their evolutionarily established locus in the natural world) can be viewed as a good example of pseudoempiricism (Smedslund, 1995)—trying empirically to demonstrate what logically follows from the researcher's axiomatic standpoint.

The problem with pseudoempiricism is not its "pseudo" nature, but rather its redirection of the research questions asked from those scientifically productive to others that ignite episodic disputes, without productive solutions. The phrasing of the issue of higher primates' "culture" or "language" in terms of the "have"/"have-not" opposition is one of the many dead-end streets into which scientific disciplines at times wander. Of course, behind these intellectual impasses proliferates the practice of "normal science" (Kuhn, 1962) in which it is consensually accepted not to question the premises of ongoing empirical research programs.

There is a disturbing quality to normality, even in science. "Normality" is solid and self-satisfied and develops by small increments of empirical contributions to the "democracy of the literature" in the given area (Valsiner, 2000a). It is unimaginative because it is afraid to be proven wrong in general ideas or in the uses of methodologies. It may accept discrepancies within the empirical evidence. Through that it looks eternally intelligent—the same questions are repeated, with different stylistic niceties and with the belief in the beneficial accumulation of data. Yet the questions asked are themselves not questioned. Neither are the socially accepted ("received") methods for answering these questions. Everything is accomplished "correctly"—and without surprises that would demonstrate the lack of creativity in the science itself.

The Driving Force: Social Representations of the Mind

Research projects of primate mental functions have undergone a process of "normalization" almost from their outset. Popular scientific questions have taken over from the substantive, and highly technical, issues of what innovations in ape action patterns can tell us about their species-specific adaptation reserves and about human evolution. After being out of touch with the research on primate language instruction and development for about two decades (Valsiner & Allik, 1982), I am uncomfortably surprised to find the very same questions asked in the first decade of the twenty-first century as were asked in the 1970s. Do laboratory-trained apes "have" language? Is it "really" language that all the highly educated research participants—Kanzi, Austin, Koko, Sherman, Lana, and Washoer, to name a few—"have"? Do higher primates in the wild "have culture"? Opinions differ on that issue (e.g., McGrew, 1998; Tomasello & Call, 1997), yet there is the basic question to be answered: What does it (culture or no culture) mean for understanding human phylogeny? The persistence of such questions seems to indicate that the problem is not a "lack of crucial data." No doubt there can be another clever experimental project with at least one capable *bonobo*, followed by an equally ingenious refutation with another *bonobo*, about some feature of human cognitive and semiotic capacities that was previously thought (by humans) to belong only to their species but that emerges in a primate under some influences. The frontiers of human-ness may thus be renegotiated, yet what it is that makes such evidence possible remains uncovered. In the middle of discussions about the nature ("language" or "not language") of the new adaptations of higher primates, researchers move away from the fundamental question of how evolution (and history) are progressively being made up by the active organisms within their environments.

The problem is with our misplaced research questions, which pay tribute to the needs of the laypersons (the question "do apes have language?" makes a nice dinner-table conversation topic for many), rather than theoretically make sense of what the successes in teaching different representatives of higher primates different new instrumental action strategies mean for our understanding of human *development*—both phylogenetically and ontogenetically. Whether apes (or humans, for that matter) are "haves" ("have" language, culture, laptops, cellular phones, etc.) or "have-nots" (i.e., do not "have" these and other nice "things") is largely irrelevant for the study of basic processes of development (Cairns, 1979, Valsiner, 1997, 1998). Instead, the issue of basic process through which development of novel psychological phenomena can happen under specific circumstances is the main question for developmental cultural psychology (Valsiner, 2000b, 2001a). It is the generative focus in general, rather than mere documentation of the already emerged forms, that is the core of developmental science.

Three issues stand at the foundation of phylogeny of semiotic systems. First, the notion of development in general (and its auxiliary concepts, such as learning and imitation) needs to be clarified. Recent controversies about imitation (Tomasello & Call, 1997; Whiten & Ham, 1992) have largely taken the issue in a behavioral (common-sense) direction, rather than giving full coverage to the developmental take on the notion. Second, the unity of discrete and continuous transformations in development needs to be elaborated. Finally, the logic of reconstruction of prospective accounts of human phylogeny (rather than retrospective causal attributions of higher psychological functions to selected events—bipedalism, tool-making, or gesture language) needs to be developed.

NOVELTY-GENERATING PROCESSES

A major problem is inherited by the research on phylogeny of semiotic capabilities from the uncertainty about development in developmental psychology. Despite clear specification of how novelty is created on the basis of the previous history and under current task demands (e.g., the notion of circular reaction—see Baldwin, 1902, 1906, 1915), our contemporary psychology has managed to ward off the developmental perspective from its theoretical core.[1]

Nature of Development

Psychology has had difficulties with integrating the notion of development into its theoretical core ever since its separation from philosophy. The latter root of psychology let the new discipline loose in asking questions about the being (ontology) of psychological phenomena, rather than about their becoming. The latter focus was central in some parts of biology (e.g., embryology) that provided the impetus for the emergence of developmental science.

Outcomes and Processes

As a result of a compromise between the foci on "being" and "becoming," development is often viewed as merely sequential change over childhood (e.g., stage accounts) or over the whole life course. Each stage (or state) is an ontologically defined entity—each has its own "being." The "becoming" focus becomes satisfied as acceptance of the transition from one state of "being" to another. The depiction of *outcomes* of development— sequence of stages— becomes an account of development in general. Surely these outcomes, or stages, can be described in their stable states and ordered on the life-course time-scale of the organism. This is a description rather than an explanation of the course of development.

The actual course of development is a process of construction of new forms of functioning in irreversible time (Valsiner, 2002). If a science such as psychology, biology, or anthropology claims to study development,[2] it is precisely the general principles of that process which (Valsiner, 1997) need to be formulated through the help of empirical investigation. Yet such investigation is first and foremost built on the axiomatic basis of developmental science.

FROM "BEING" TO "BECOMING": AN OUTLINE OF DEVELOPMENTAL AXIOMATICS

Any scientific enterprise depends on general assumptions (axioms) that are presumed to be appropriate for the given preferred (by the researcher) look at the object of investigation. The crucial feature for any scientific perspective is that these general assumptions are made explicit and that all of the rest of the scientific knowledge construction is consistent with that explicit axiomatic base. The empirical work can lead to the change of some of that axiomatic base (hence the importance of learning from the phenomena).

Assumptions of Identity

The nondevelopmental and developmental perspectives are clearly differentiated by the basic assumption of identity. The identity axiom is the basis for ontological ("as is") perspectives in psychology.

In its generic form, the identity axiom is:

$$\{X \text{ is } X\} \text{ and } \{X \text{ is not } [\text{not-}X]\}$$
$$\text{or}$$
$$\{X \text{ is } Y\} \text{ and } \{X \text{ is not } [\text{not-}Y]\}$$

These versions indicate that some identity of being is implied in its existing form. The boundaries of the identified objects are maintained as determinate (i.e., there is no doubt that X and non-X are two clearly separable, mutually exclusive entities). This axiomatic set-up makes it in principle impossible to conceptualize any change and development. Thus, a move from {**X is X**} to {**X is Y**} is not here viewable as change but as a discovery of a mere difference (e.g., "we thought that X is X but it turns out it is Y" or "we thought that newborns were passive but now we know that they are active"). This displacement of some believed-in characteristic by its opposite is not in itself an example of development. It is merely a substitution of one identity by another. The identity axiom guides the investigation process to time-free classification and re-classification of given, fixed notions of the phenomena.

Assumption of Identity-As-Change Potential

In contrast, if a researcher is interested in issues of change and development, the identity axiom above is of no help. It can be transformed into a three-part view on the issue:

{**X is X**} and [**something between X and** {**other-than-X**}]

and

[**X is not** {**other-than-X**}]

Here the determinacy of distinction is maintained for other-than-X (which X is not), but eliminated for the boundary region of X (as X) by introducing the notion of "something between." Here the stable identity (X) and the fuzzy realm of potential change (X is "something between" X itself and "other-than"-X) are parts of the same whole.

That "something between" has fuzzy status—it is no longer X, nor is it yet other-than-X. Consider a cloudy day after a rainfall, with still a few raindrops falling. Although the rainfall would constitute a clearly identifiable state of affairs (falling rain is rainfall), the few drops falling are an example of "something in between." It is *no longer raining*, nor is it *not yet* completely not raining. In a similar vein, a child is clearly a child (X) but simultaneously s/he is also "something between" child and adult. Yet surely the child is not adult (yet). When phrased in terms of classic (nondevelopmental) experimental terminology, development can be defined as eternal movement from a "floor effect" toward a "ceiling effect."

The unity of X and "something between" X and "other-than-X" provides the axiomatic basis for systemic, dialogical theoretical efforts (e.g., Hermans, 2001; Markova, this volume). The "in-between"-ness can be viewed as the potential for emergence of new forms—the fuzzy playground for the actual development to take place (Valsiner, 1994).

Assumption of Change

The assumption of change introduces temporal order. It itself is not yet an axiom for emergence. It indicates the de-differentiation of a previously known phenomenon—an entrance into a state of "chaos" or uncertainty:

$$\{X \text{ becomes [something between X and (other-than-X)]}$$
$$\text{but}$$
$$[X \text{ is not (other-than-X)]}\}$$

Starting from this axiom makes it possible to guide one's investigative focus toward expecting some change—in time—while observing a (still) distinguishable object. For example, while observing a primate's pointing toward a faraway object, a human observer can view this act (from the identity standpoint) as an outstretched finger (relative to other fingers) and nothing beyond this. But when the interpreter utilizes the change axiom, that finger begins to belong to both being an outstretched finger and the implied act of pointing (toward something "out there" and for reasons implied to be present in the person who points). Thus, *the outstretched finger becomes something between the finger* per se, *and the object-world*. Yet it is clearly not the objecte-world itself. It indicates the directionality of effort and serves as informational basis for intentionality estimation.

The axiom of change leads investigators to view all phenomena currently in a steady state in terms of their potential or actual changes. In fact, it biases them toward assuming that change happens, and that a moment of stability is temporary in the inevitable dynamic of the system. In some cases this need not be the case; for instance, observing the change of a physical object, even if possible (e.g., that of a rock in the sea, constantly being washed by the water), may not be scientifically productive (except when the science is that of rock formation). How adequate is a particular axiomatic stance depends on the goals of the investigators rather than on the nature of the objects of investigation.

The Core of Developmental Science

In case of developmental science, the change axiom is the basis for *axiom of emergence*:

$$\{X \text{ becomes (other-than-X)}\}$$

The latter includes an orientation to the process of becoming, yet does not capture a focus on developmental phenomena. Disappearance of X is focused on, but not the reappearance of a new state. The latter is characterized by *emerging identity* axiom:

$$\{[X \text{ becomes (other-than-X)] becomes Y}\}$$

This axiom includes the transition from the previous identifiable state (X) to a new identifiable (relatively permanent) state Y. It is here that development—as it entails nonreversible change—comes to the focus of investigators' attention. It also entails the "orthogenetic principle" (Werner & Kaplan, 1956) since it is assumed that development takes place through de-differentiation of the previous whole (X) into a semiorganized state (as was outlined above for axiom of change), and the new hierarchical integration of the "intermediary flux" into a new whole (Y). That new whole undergoes de-differentiation again and becomes reintegrated in yet another new form. Complexity of phenomena increases through hierarchical integration.

The higher level of complexity of the phenomena also leads to greater interpersonal variability within a population. Each individual organism develops by its own unique life course, governed by hierarchical integration. As a result, the variation between individuals is particularly enhanced at the highest level of their psychological forms. Among the latter, the ones that entail semiotic mediation are thus likely to be variable at the most. This general feature of complex forms may explain the interindividual variability between apes in their adaptation to the language laboratory environments.

HISTORICAL ROOTS OF DEVELOPMENTAL SCIENCE

The formalistic examples given above may look new in their logic-like form, yet they are not new by any means. Developmental science has a long history in the domain of embryology and developmental biology (Cairns, 1998). Most of the major ideas of development were clearly formulated at the turn of the twentieth century.

For example, the emerging identity axiom has been recognized in developmental science since its first formulation by James Mark Baldwin in his two "postulates of method." The first (or "negative") postulate emphasized the irreversibility of time in development:

The logic of genesis is not expressed in convertible propositions. Genetically, A → (that is, *becomes*, for which the sign → is now used) B; but it does not follow that B → (becomes) A. (Baldwin, 1906, p. 21)

The first postulate specifies the realm of possible relations that are allowable among the formulas of "genetic logic"—namely, each proposition includes a temporal directionality vector. Thus, the reversal (i.e., B → A) is not implied by the notion of A becoming B. The symmetry of transformation between A and B is broken by irreversibility of time, and of the very transformation.

Such symmetry-breaking process is a general feature of living systems (Prigogine, 1973). Of course, the focus on irreversibility of biological growth processes was known in biology and philosophy, through the synthesizing efforts of Henri Bergson (1907), long before it became popular through the social prestige of physics and the titillating "order-out-of-chaos" metaphor that has captured public minds since 1980s.

Baldwin specified how access to developmental phenomena is possible in his second ("positive") postulate:

... that series of events is truly genetic which cannot be constructed before it has happened, and which cannot be exhausted backwards, after it has happened. (Baldwin, 1906, p. 21)

The "positive" nature of this postulate is in its focusing of the study of development on that of the unfolding novel processes, rather than their prediction or retrospective explanation of different outcomes. The phenomena of *emergence, becoming,* and *transformation* become the objects of investigation. Such investigation would entail *preserving the irreversible time sequence* in the data.

The Microgenetic Perspective

One example of the kinds of investigation is that of microgenesis. Its empirical focus is on sequences of *intermediate new forms* that are emerging and decaying when the person faces a new situation. Friedrich Sander, one of the originators of the microgenetic perspective remarked:

The formation of the successive stages [of visual percept], which usually emanate one from the other by sudden jerks, has a certain shading of non-finality; the intermediaries lack the relative stability and composure of the final forms; they are restless, agitated, and full of tensions, as though in a plastic state of becoming. . . . The peculiar mode of presentation of these pre-figurations that are simplified relative to some final form is in no wise comparable to that of the final forms of similar outline; it is considerably richer in quality. (Sander, 1930, p. 194)

The feeling-tone of tension detected in the sequence of intermediate forms is an indicator of the process of development. The intermediate forms grow into one another in ways that allow for branching at every junction; for example:

A–**ab**–B–**bc**–C → leads to final → X

The uncertainty as well as openness to new emergence would be located at the binding of the adjacent intermediate forms (**ab, bc**). The microgenetic process entails the unity of the multilinear potential of the developmental construction (as given by the variety of directions in which the genesis process can go—at **ab** or **bc**), and the unilinear actualization of that potential (as only C, followed by X, emerges in the sequence).

Potential Multilinearity and Actual Unilinearity

In general, development is unilinearly continuous and multilinearly open to discontinuities. The reality of life of any developing organism as it has already taken place (to the present moment) is always uniquely unilinear. Yet the moment of construction of the future (in the present) is multilinear. The set of possibilities of the next step toward the future creates the multilinearity (and uncertainty), which through the process of relating to the environment becomes a step in the unilinear actual life course (already of the past). Or it can be depicted graphically:

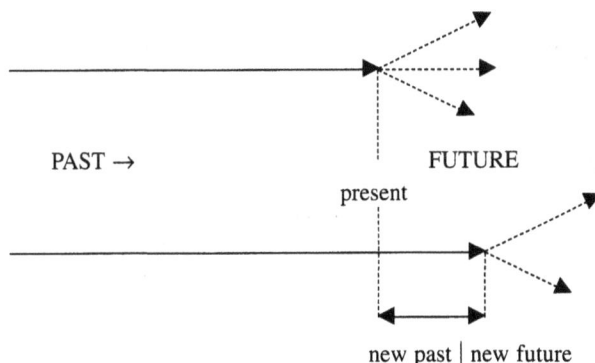

Here is hidden a very simple "theoretical headache" for any developmental scientist. Instead of trying to prove that development is either unilinear or multilinear, we can see that both unilinearity and multilinearity are parts of the processes of actual development. For reason of identity of the existing organism, its life history constitutes some kind of unilinear structure-in-time.

Here we are not talking about an obscure philosophical issue that emerges at the intersection of the reality of irreversible time and human efforts to make sense of the reality in a time-freed manner. The whole issue of how we make distinctions—and following from there, how we compare different distinguished phenomena—acquires a different slant once the unilinearity/ multilinearity issue is taken into consideration.

WAYS OF MAKING COMPARISONS

Making comparisons would be a simple issue if there were no change in the world. Then it would be basically an issue of perception (detection of differences between objects) and the evaluation of the differences. One would not worry about the sudden disappearance of the detected differences or about the change in the meanings that guide the evaluation.

The discussions of primate "cultures" and "language capacities" are a prime example for how the simple (nondevelopmental) way of making comparisons becomes incredibly complicated. Whatever the primates in language-teaching environments have "acquired" is the outcome of a process of experiencing these environments by these particular individuals. Thus, to claim that "apes *can* learn a language" is based on some of them who have indeed developed new ways of functioning under specific conditions. Three features are important here. First, there is a move from an *outcome* (ape X did demonstrate the mastery of a particular language system by some criteria) to the *potential* ("can"—implying the universal process from that to the outcome). Secondly, there is the shift from *individual examples* to the *full population* through the generic notion of the modal specimen (Valsiner, 1986). Finally, there is the adoption of an arbitrary *comparison base* and *selected normativity* of that base—that of the human species (i.e., "apes can learn our language" versus "we can learn apes' [natural] language"). Developmental science is making use of the comparative method and facing all the consequences that phenomena of development bring to making of comparisons.

Formal Exploration: Comparing Discrete Outcomes

What happens when we make comparisons? Two directions of mental construction of that act can be outlined. First, the comparison of discrete outcomes. We have sets of outcomes of unknown processes, classified into two classes (X,Y):

Class X = {a, A, a, a, a, A}

Class Y = {b, B, B, b, b}

It is obvious that the two classes have no overlap as to the quality they entail (a,b), while within each of them there exist differences in the particular form and size of the specimens. These classes are heterogeneous classes of unitary objects and free of any context dependency. No interdependencies of either temporal (historical) kind or of immediate contextual embeddedness are present.

Developmental Comparisons

The phenomena we need to compare in developmental and cultural psychologies are different—they are context-bound. Consider comparison of two sets of such phenomena (W,Q):

Class W = {a(0), $A(B)$, a(c), $a(d)$, a, $A(b)$}

Class Q = {b(0), $B(a)$, B(c), b(d), $b(a)$}

Here the entities in parentheses designate the context within which the member of the set is intricately tied. The specimens from W partly create contexts for some of the Q, and vice versa. Although the main items in W and Q are distinct from one another's class, the two classes are mutually interdependent. This can often be the case of comparisons in cross-cultural psychology, where

To characterize something, X, we do compare it with something else, Y. But when an X–Y comparison is made into the study's primary purpose . . . a selective reductionism takes place as a methodological necessity; a limited number of comparable tendencies are chosen and the rest are discarded. The final product is a set of abstractions, devoid of complexity, depth, and wholeness of each separate issue. (Lebra, 2000, p. 1148)

This issue surfacing in Lebra's expression in making sense of comparisons between U.S. and Japanese human societies is equally applicable to comparison between species in a comparative-psychological or evolutionary scheme. Furthermore, both in case of societies and species, the direct comparisons grow out of some (unobservable at the present) background history. Consider the example of classes T and U:

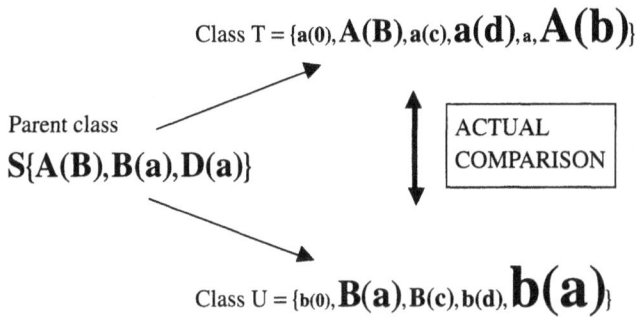

Class T = {a(0), $A(B)$, a(c), $a(d)$, a, $A(b)$}

Parent class

$S\{A(B), B(a), D(a)\}$

ACTUAL COMPARISON

Class U = {b(0), $B(a)$, B(c), b(d), $b(a)$}

Here the two classes—T, U—of context-dependent kind have grown out of an unknown (posited) common ancestor S. If one reconstructs that common ancestor from the present evidence then all one can rely on is the presence of similar parts in *different systemic configurations* [B(a) and A(B)] that allow us a hypothesis that they share common ancestry. If only manifest expressions—A, B—are considered, there is no basis for tracing any common ancestry.

But as the ancestor is not visible (and T and U are), all reconstructions of the historical kind need to find extrapolation of our contemporary synchronic evidence. It is a retrospective reconstruction based on the knowledge of the outcomes T, U and extrapolated from the synchronous comparison backward into the past. It is an example of "backward exhaustion" (see Baldwin's "second postulate," above). While actual phylogenetic development took place progressively, eliminating different options en route and ending up with the present species, our reconstructions of that are necessarily back projections that cannot chart out those phylogenetic possibilities that were there at the time but that were not actualized. Only if there is evidence of actualized "side trajectories" (which later became extinct) can we make claims about what *some* of the possibilities (then) were. This contrast between comparison of existing and existed species on the one hand (reliance on outcomes) and efforts to reconstruct progressive development is at the heart of the discourse of cladistic and adaptationist kind in biology (Delisle, 2001).

COMMUNICATION PROCESSES AND CULTURAL TOOLS

Phylogenetic development toward the use of semiotic mediation in communication and the efforts to deal with ontogenetic analogs of those in case of ape language projects and demonstrations of "primate culture" in the wild require a new way to make comparisons. Yet most of the models of comparisons seen in the discussions are of the traditional (nondevelopmental) kind.

Efforts to make sense of the use of new cultural tools in communication are hindered by the assumptions made in traditional human linguistic sciences. The "norm of language" is that of the already established, functioning system that humans use—and the accomplishments of other primates are evaluated by comparing them directly to the human language.

However, the nonhuman primates, in the wild or in humanized environments (laboratories or zoos), live in settings that differ cardinally from those in which humans use their language. Thus,

Scientists who are interested in the study of communication by other species must . . . begin with one hand tied behind their backs. They must assume that, unless they are able to prove otherwise, other animals have no words, no grammar, and no intentional system of communication. Thus, *the first course of business is not to look at animal communication from the top down, by asking what sort of information animals might wish to convey to one another.* By contrast, scientists undertake the study of another human language by trying to learn what it is that people are saying to each other or to the researchers. (Savage-Rumbaugh et al., 1996, p. 174; emphasis added)

The meta-theoretical stumbling block in this segregation of humans and nonhuman species is the acceptance (or rejection) of the *assumption of intentionality* in communication between conspecifics. Simplified reliance on the evolutionary perspective (of post-factum selection of emerged forms) has blocked the development of notions of intentionality that would be free of the voluntaristic nuances of "free will."

Intentionality may be a repressed, yet pervasive, notion in psychology. Historical roots for the treatment of intentionality exist in the philosophical heritage of the "Graz tradition" in psychology (Alexius Meinong, theory of presentations) (Meinong, 1902, 1917; for overview, Rollinger, 1993). Recognizing the role of each sign (or concept) to both *re*-present something from previous experience and *pre*sent something for anticipation of the future is a breakthrough in science that unifies the time-dependency of meaning-making and its abstractive generalization (Valsiner, 2002). In the wider scope of all animal psychology, that semiotic specificity is antedated by the extrapolative behavior animals demonstrate in their environments.

Contemporary cognitive psychology has selectively borrowed from that past focus. Current interest in processes of anticipation (Hoffmann & Stock, 2000) come from the intellectual tradition of Brentano and Meinong, via the intermediary of the "Würzburg tradition" of Oswald Külpe, Karl Bühler, and Otto Selz.

The focus on goals-oriented nonoptimized processes is present in modern economics (Selten, 1998, 2001), as well as in evolutionary theory (Baldwin, 1902, 1915).

In its minimal version, the assumption of intentionality needs to entail *change orientation from an established* (already developed) state of a system *toward some* state of affairs. The latter can include the already established state (in that case we observe intentionality of the maintenance of the existing state). Acceptance of this assumption does not contain information about causes of such change orientation. Those may be inherent to the system or to its environment, or—as in open systems—in the relation between system and its environment. The contrast between acceptance and rejection of that assumption is between viewing the object of investigation as existing in the way it is (rejection) or viewing it *as on its way toward* some new state (acceptance). Obviously, any developmental perspective needs to accept the assumption of intentionality.

Transcending a Species-Centric Assumption:
When One CAN Talk, One WILL

Research on human and primate communication systems seems to have been based on the assumption of the irresistible urge to talk. Although that orientation can be easily verified in case of some representatives of the human species, its general adequacy can be questioned. Language is a tool that makes communication possible, rather than obligatory. What determines the actual act of speaking is if it has some purpose or if there is something to speak about.

Consider a human example. We sit in a room, and one of the humans says "the window is not broken." At the manifest level, this statement reflects the true state of affairs (indeed, the window is intact). The reason the person utters the obvious has something to do with that person's communication of his or her expectations ("one would expect windows to be broken, but this one is not"), or even to call for action ("windows should be broken, but this one is not"). In both cases the expectation (or prescription) deals with the comparison between the present state of affairs with some other state—over time and place. Most of the features in any here-and-now setting are not mentionable—there is no reason to speak about them. Neither is there any possibility—full verbal coverage of *the whole* field of the person (which is simultaneously present) cannot be translated into sequentially organized flow of speaking already by reason of time limits. The immediate field is already long in the past when a very verbal person finishes narrating all of its contents. Speaking about the present is necessarily discourse about the past, yet its function is to move toward the future. Hence the centrality of goal orientations in the emergence of speaking.

It should thus not be surprising that humans—the hyper-talking highest primates—actually use speech on relatively few occasions (in relation to the totality of the fields in which they are embedded). Speaking is *selective*, and the goal-orientations provide form to that selectivity. What looks to us as hyper-talking (in case of nonstop chatter by some humans) is actually very limited referencing activity when viewed from the perspective of the multifaceted setting that talker is in.

Let us carry this view over to our contemporary higher primates—in the field or in a laboratory. Instead of wondering why they do not learn a language (even if they could, in case of sign language) or why they don't use it (except for the highest-educated apes in Atlanta or a few other places), the question is—what is there to say? What aspects of the here-and-now worlds of these apes guide them toward the goal-orientations that make communicative efforts necessary. Once these efforts are made necessary,[3] there is no doubt that some version of communicative means would be created—by some of the apes some of the time. So, when there is abundant food in the forest, all apes can reach it without any need of pointing to others where it is, without misinforming others about its location. The appearance of a predator is a different story, yet the task here is limited (to attack or to escape). Under laboratory or zoo conditions (except for the environments in "ape language labs") there is even less in the settings that are worth the efforts to develop a new system of referential communication.

That is the reality of needs—which the researchers perceive from their own vantage points. The latter create the curious "double standard" (see Gibson, this volume): it is the nonhuman behavior that becomes perceived as generated by lower-level mechanisms than is a similar behavior in humans. The narrow[4] application of "Morgan's canon" can lead to this result—reduction of complexity to elementary components.

Satisficing, Not Maximizing

Psychologists often presume that human beings (as well as other animals) operate at the level of their maximum gains (and minimum costs)—that they are some kinds of rational business machines. It has been clear even in economics, however, that this cannot be the case in complex life situations, and that instead of maximization strategies, satisficing is the case. Organisms "get by" just as they can—under the present circumstances—rather than "do their best."

When it comes to the use of communication means, even humans do not operate by using their highest semiotic capacities (or mental functions). Support to this challenge comes from the studies made on human language use—yet by researchers of a slightly unexpected kind. In their dramatic description of the life course of a post-revolutionary romantic vagabond Ostap Bender, Ilf and Petrov (1961) describe the level of sufficiency of human language use that can occur in our common-sense world. The legendary hero meets a nice young Russian "new rich" housewife (of the 1920s) whose language use is described as probably needing many fewer words than our contemporary language-learning apes have diligently mastered:

William Shakespeare's vocabulary has been estimated by the experts at twelve thousand words . . . Ellochka Shukin managed easily and fluently on thirty.

Here are the words, phrases, and interjections which she fastidiously picked from the great, rich, and expressive Russian language:

1. Don't be rude.
2. Ho-ho (expresses irony, surprise, delight, loathing, joy, contempt, and satisfaction, according to the circumstances).
3. Great!
4. Dismal (applied to everything—for example: "dismal Pete has arrived", "dismal weather", or a "dismal cat").
5. Gloom.
6. Ghastly (for example: when meeting a close female acquaintance, "a ghastly meeting").
7. Kid (applied to all male acquaintances, regardless of age or social position).
8. Don't tell me how to live!
9. Like a child ("I beat him like a child" when playing cards, or "I brought him down like a child" evidently while talking to a lease holder).
10. Ter-r-rific!
11. Fat and good-looking (used to describe both animate and inanimate objects).
12. Let's go by horse-cab (said to her husband).
13. Let's go by taxi (said to a male acquaintance).
14. You're all white on the back! (joke)
15. Just imagine!
16. Ula (added to name to denote affection—Mishula, Zinula).
17. Oho! (irony, surprise, delight, loathing, joy, contempt, and satisfaction).

(Ilf & Petrov, 1961, pp. 205–206)

It is a humano-centric perspective that emphasizes the richness of the semiotic system as it exists—rather than its *generative availability* for an organism when the tasks demand it. It is only under such demand pressures where the flexibility of the organisms is enhanced by the possibility to generate semiotic means to assist in their strategic actions—and survival and success of the individuals. This makes a difference.

Intentionality in Actions

Evidence for intentionality in the gesturing in chimpanzees (Leavens, Hopkins, & Bard, 1996; Leavens & Hopkins, 1998) and territorial marking in bonobos (Savage-Rumbaugh et al., 1996) leads to new possibilities of how phylogenetic reconstruction of proto-hominid relations with that part of their environment— locations and nature of objects—can be modeled.

Much of the discussion above may seeme out of place at the contemporary frontier of primate language research. After all, the description of the long processes of establishment of sign systems in higher primates do describe development of major novelty. Yet these novel accomplishments are ontogenetically slow and variable among different individual primates. In a similar vein, the ontogenetic establishment of complex strategic action patterns (collaborative hunting) in chimpanzees in the wild is a long-lasting and inter-individually variable process (Boesch & Boesch-Achermann, 2000, chap. 8).

As Vauclair (this volume) has pointed out, there exist different solutions for the problems that organisms face in their everyday environments—some benefit from language availability, others do not. Communication processes in a group may vary greatly when the group tries to threaten off a predator or organize a half-hour long group hunt in the forest (Boesch & Boesch-Achermann, 2000). In the latter case it is the strategic inhibition of actions, together with collective coordination of actions between group members, that is necessary for success. Such processes may be mental, yet not mediated by any language in the traditional (i.e., human) sense. Higher primates can well be ready for representational and re-representational mental functions (Whiten, 2000a, 2000b). Yet that readiness need not entail more than the emergence of those functions under pointedly supportive circumstances.

GENERAL CONCLUSION: BUFFERED NATURE OF DEVELOPMENT AT DIFFERENT LEVELS

The main conclusion here is: development is generative, historical, and conservative. It takes place through continuous facing of uncertainty at the borderlines of the "time window" between the past and the future. That "time window" is infinitesimally small.

Development in general is conservative—the immediate creative solutions to problems that are worked out by individuals under task demands (in the wilderness of the forest or in a laboratory) may become translated into the repertory of the individuals (and the species) with considerable delay and transcontextual testing. Microgenesis is *not equivalent to* ontogenesis, and neither is the latter a model for phylogenesis. Between each of these three processes there are translation possibilities—both upward (microgenesis → ontogenesis → phylogenesis) and downward (phylogenesis → ontogenesis → microgenesis). The inadequacy of Ernst Haeckel's "biogenetic law"—considering these processes repetitive of one another—does not solve the problem. By making critical claims about Haeckel's inadequate solution, we also eliminate the issue itself from consideration. Yet the problem remains: the three kinds of developmental processes are mutually linked. The question is to find out *how* that linkage is organized.

Both the "upward" and "downward" translation processes necessarily include buffering mechanisms that would not let a particular idioadaptation at one level to undermine the processes at another. It is possible that it is only under limite conditions of time/circumstances where such translations take place at all. A most likely scenario is that the innovations at one level (say those in microgenesis) become attenuated and lead to selective reconstruction at the level of ontogenesis. As an example, most of our lived-through experiences become lost in our ontogenetic life courses, but some of them are relevant for the latter. Likewise, some of the ontogenetic modifications (at the level of the species) may, under some circumstances, lead the course of phylogeny. Most of these modifications remain idioadaptations (in Severtzoff's sense), however, and do not result in further evolutionary "qualitative jumps"—*aromorphoses* in Severtzoff's terms—for the species.

All this leads to a description of development in general that unites the (seeming) two opposites of being and becoming: while the organisms constantly create novelty in their adapting environments to themselves (and themselves to environments), that novelty is largely "wasted" as ephemeral. Each next level of the developmental organization is well buffered against excessive phenomena that can occur at adjacent levels. In an other sense—development (at all levels) is excessively "wasteful"—novelty is being *produced in abundance*—and *abandoned in almost equal abundance*. It is through this overproduction, or "wastefulness," that the basis for development at each adjacent level is created—for some moments where the interlevel buffering mechanisms allow these adjacent levels to become transformed. Development in general is *simultaneously* hyperproductive and hyper-constrained.

Why do we know very little about the linkages between phylogeny, ontogeny, and microgenesis? Social factors in science may provide an answer to this question. There is a curious process going on in contemporary psychology: issues of development are discussed, their scientific study is called for, and what is done under the label of developmental research barely touches the "tip of the iceberg" of the developmental processes. Contemporary psychology has moved away from making development its center of scientific investigation. Whereas the beginning of the twentieth century can be described by multifaceted interest in development of persons, animal species, and human societies (see detailed coverage in Valsiner & van der Veer, 2000), the beginning of the twenty-first century is dominated by nondevelopmental theoretical orientations that penetrate even into developmental theories (Shanahan, Valsiner & Gottlieb, 1996). Although there are efforts to counteract that dominance of the nondevelopmental intellectual ambience (Cairns, 1979; Cairns, Elder, & Costello, 1996; Ford & Lerner, 1992; Gottlieb, 1997, 2002), the popularity of essentialist thinking in cognitive science and applied uses of modern genetics is a powerful attenuator of the focus on development. Developmental thought remains central in areas of science where it is inevitable—such as embryology, immunology, or modern protein genetics,[5] but it has remained recessive in the social sciences.

Here again the story of the comforts of "normal science" returns. Efforts to learn about primate culture and language systems have opened for us the need to think differently about our own species and about the science of comparative psychology. The challenges are theoretical first and empirical second. In some sense, scientists are facing the same problem that the Japanese macaques were in the process of inventing their new technologies for food getting. The insight that would lead us to making sense of ape mentalities is still ahead of us.

NOTES

The writing of this chapter benefited greatly from the critical feedback from Aaro Toomela. The ideas that led to the suggested synthesis here gradually developed in the course of the "kitchen seminar" at Clark University in 1997–2001, and through lunchtime interactions with Gilbert Gottlieb and Robert B. Cairns.

1. For example, see the discussion of "how novel is novel?"—Whiten, 2000b, p. 148.

2. Note that the focus on development is not a general panacea, solution to our problems in science. Many relevant questions about general knowledge can be (and are) asked entirely within the realm of ontology. It is only *the mixing* of the axiomatic frames or presenting the study of "being" *as if* it explained "becoming" that is at issue here. Science thrives on doubts about the nature of the phenomena, but not on the basis of ever-increasing conceptual confusion.

3. I would claim that the success of many of the "ape language" projects demonstrates the learning by humans about how to set up conditions that would create such goal orientations. The success of the "language learning" by the apes is actually the success of the other species teaching ours some aspects of how to promote the development of novelty.

4. See Valsiner, 1998, for an analysis of the "Morgan's canon." That "canon" was not aimed at reduction of complexity to its elementaristic constituents, but at the recognition of how to coordinate introspective and extrospective sides of scientific research.

5. In domains where issues of innovation by way of reverse transcription (RNA → DNA), regulation (different types of RNA activating and deactivating one another), or where the outcomes of new biological formations are thought through systemic understanding of the functioning of the cell. The goals of the Human Genome Project need not belong here.

REFERENCES

Baldwin, J. M. (1902). *Development and evolution.* London: McMillan.

Baldwin, J. M. (1906). *Thought and things: A study of the development and meaning of thought, or genetic logic. Vol. 1. Functional logic, or genetic theory of knowledge.* London: Swan Sonnenschein & Co.

Baldwin, J. M. (1915). *Genetic theory of reality.* New York: G. P. Putnam's sons.

Bergson, H. (1907/1945). *L'Evolution créatrice.* Genève: Éditions Albert Skira.

Boesch, C., & Boesch-Achermann, H. (2000). *The chimpanzees of the Taï forest.* New York: Oxford University Press.

Byrne, R. W. (2000). Evolution of primate cognition. *Cognitive Science, 24,* 3, 543–570.

Cairns, R. B. (1979). *Social development: The origins and plasticity of interchanges.* San Francisco: W.H. Freeman.

Cairns, R. B. (1998). The making of developmental psychology. In W. Damon & R. Lerner (Eds.), *Handbook of child psychology. 5th edition. Vol. 1. Theoretical models of human development* (pp. 25–105). New York: Wiley.

Cairns, R. B., Elder, G. H., & Costello, E. J. (Eds.) (1996). *Developmental science.* New York: Cambridge University Press.

Delisle, R. (2001). Adaptationism versus cladism in human evolution studies. In R. Corbey & W. Roebroeks (Eds.), *Studying human origins* (pp. 107–121). Amsterdam: University of Amsterdam Press.

Ford, D. H., & Lerner, R. (1992). *Developmental systems theory.* Newbury Park, Ca: Sage.

Gibson, K. R. (2002). Continuities between great ape and human behaviors. In A. Toomela (Ed.), *Cultural guidance in the development of the human mind.* Westport, Conn.: Greenwood Press.

Gottlieb, G. (1997). *Synthesizing nature/nurture.* Mahwah, N.J.: Erlbaum.

Gottlieb, G. (2002). Probabilistic epigenesis of development. In J. Valsiner & K. J. Connolly (Eds.), *Handbook of developmental psychology.* London: Sage.

Hermans, H. J. M. (2001). The dialogical self: Toward a theory of personal and cultural positioning. *Culture and Psychology, 7,* 243–281.

Hoffmann, J., & Stock, A. (2000). Intention als psychischer Prozess: Eine Suche nach Spuren in der allgemeinpsychologischen Forschung. *Zeitschrift für Psychologie, 208,* 304–321.

Ilf, I., & Petrov, E. (1961). *The complete adventures of Ostap Bender.* New York: Random House.

Kuhn, T. (1962). *The structure of scientific revolutions.* Chicago: University of Chicago Press.

Leavens, D. A., & Hopkins, W. D. (1998). Intentional communication by chimpanzees: a cross-sectional study of the use of referential gestures. *Developmental Psychology, 34, 5,* 813–822.

Leavens, D. A., Hopkins, W. D., & Bard, K. A. (1996). Indexical and referential pointing in chimpanzees *(Pan troglodytes)*. *Journal of Comparative Psychology, 110, 4,* 346–353.

Lebra, T. S. (2000). New insight and old dilemma: a cross-cultural comparison of Japan and the United States. *Child Development, 71, 5,* 1147–1149.

Magnusson, D., & Cairns, R. B. (1996). Developmental science: toward a unified framework. In R. B. Cairns, G. H. Elder, & E. J. Costello (Eds.), *Developmental science* (pp. 7–30). New York: Cambridge University Press.

Markova, I. (2002). Semiotics of culture in scientific and carnivalistic guises: Michail Bakhtin and Yuri Lotman. In A. Toomela (Ed.), *Cultural guidance in the development of the human mind.* Westport, Conn.: Greenwood Press.

McGrew, W. C. (1998). Culture in nonhuman primates? *Annual Review of Psychology, 27,* 301–328.

Meinong, A. (1902/1983). *On assumptions.* Berkeley: University of California Press.

Meinong, A. (1917/1972). *On emotional presentation.* Evanston, Ill.: Northwestern University Press.

Prigogine, I. (1973). Irreversibility as a symmetry-breaking process. *Nature, 246,* 67–71.

Rollinger, R. D. (1993). *Meinong and Husserl on abstraction and universals.* Amsterdam: Rodopi.

Sander, F. (1930). Structure, totality of experience, and Gestalt. In C. Murchison (Ed.), *Psychologies of 1930* (pp. 188–204). Worcester, Mass.: Clark University Press.

Savage-Rumbaugh, E. S., Williams, S. L., Furuichi, T., & Kano, T. (1996). Language perceived: *Paniscus* branches out. In W. C. McGrew, L. F. Marchant, & T. Nishida (Eds.), *Great ape societies* (pp. 173–184). Cambridge: Cambridge University Press.

Selten, R. (1998). Aspiration adaptation theory. *Journal of Mathematical Psychology, 42,* 191–214.

Selten, R. (2001). What is bounded rationality? In G. Gigerenzer & R. Selten (Eds.), *Bounded rationality* (pp. 13–36). Cambridge, Mass.: MIT Press.

Severtzoff, A. N. (1929). Direction of evolution. *Acta Zoologica, 10,* 59–141.

Shanahan, M., Valsiner, J., & Gottlieb, G. (1996). The conceptual structure of developmental theories. In J. Tudge, M. Shanahan, & J. Valsiner (Eds.), *Comparative approaches in developmental science.* New York: Cambridge University Press.

Smedslund, J. (1995). Psychologic: common sense and the pseudoempirical. In J. A. Smith, R. Harré, & L. van Langenhove (Eds.), *Rethinking psychology* (pp. 196–206). London: Sage.

Tomasello, M., & Call, J. (1997). *Primate cognition.* New York: Oxford University Press.

Valsiner, J. (1986). Between groups and individuals: psychologists' and laypersons' interpretations of correlational findings. In J. Valsiner (Ed.), *The individual subject and scientific psychology* (pp. 113–152). New York: Plenum.

Valsiner, J. (1994). Bidirectional cultural transmission and constructive sociogenesis. In W. de Graaf & R. Maier (Eds.), *Sociogenesis reexamined* (pp. 47–70). New York: Springer.

Valsiner, J. (1997). *Culture and the development of children's action.* 2nd ed. New York: Wiley.

Valsiner, J. (1998). The development of the concept of development: Historical and epistemological perspectives. In W. Damon & R. Lerner (Eds.), *Handbook of child psychology.* 5th edition. Vol. 1. *Theoretical models of human development* (pp. 189–232). New York: Wiley.

Valsiner, J. (2000a). Entre a "Democracia da Literatura" e a paixao pela compreensão: Entendendo a dinâmica do desenvolvimento. *Psicologia: Reflexão e critica, 13, 2,* 319–325.

Valsiner, J. (2000b). *Culture and human development.* London: Sage.

Valsiner, J. (2001a). The first six years: culture's adventures in psychology. *Culture & Psychology, 7, 1,* 5–48.

Valsiner, J. (2001b). Cultural developmental psychology of affective processes. Invited Lecture at the *15. Tagung der Fachgruppe Entwicklungspsychologie der Deutschen Gesellschaft für Psychologie,* Potsdam, September 5.

Valsiner, J. (2002). Irreversibility of time and ontopotentiality of signs. *Estudios de Psicologia* (in press).

Valsiner, J., & Allik, J. (1982). General semiotic capabilities of the higher primates: some hypotheses on communication and cognition in the evolution of human semiotic systems. In M. R. Key (Ed.), *Nonverbal communication today: Current research* (pp. 245–257). New York: Mouton.

Valsiner, J., & van der Veer, R. (2000). *The social mind: Construction of the idea.* New York: Cambridge University Press.

Vauclair, J. (2002). Would humans without language be apes? In A. Toomela (Ed.), *Cultural guidance in the development of the human mind.* Westport, Conn.: Greenwood Press.

Werner, H., & Kaplan, B. (1956). The developmental approach to cognition: its relevance to the psychological interpretation of anthropological and ethnolinguistic data. *American Anthropologist, 58,* 866–880.

Whiten, A. (2000a). Primate culture and social learning. *Cognitive Science, 24, 3,* 477–508.

Whiten, A. (2000b). Chimpanzee cognition and the question of mental re-representation. In D. Sperber (Ed.), *Metarepresentations* (pp. 139–167). New York: Oxford University Press.

Whiten, A., & Ham, R. (1992). On the nature and evolution of imitation in the animal kingdom: Reappraisal of a century of research. In P. Slater, J. Rosenblatt, C. Beer, & M. Milinski (Eds.), *Advances in the study of behavior.* Vol. 21 (pp. 239–283). San Diego, Calif.: Academic Press.

Part II: Culture in the Developing or Regressing Brain

4. Culture in Our Brains: Cross-Cultural Differences in the Brain-Behavior Relationships

Alfredo Ardila

In this chapter I will try to develop two simple ideas: (1) Our brain possesses certain basic capabilities. When I say "capabilities," I mean "ways of processing information." These basic capabilities can potentially be used for different types of cognition depending on the specific contents. And (2) culture provides the contents to these basic capabilities.

Four topics will be analyzed in this chapter. Initially, I will take the example of calculation abilities. I will propose that calculation abilities arise from finger sequencing. Numerical systems and number representation appeared in human history through a long process. Arithmetic is a relatively recent human acquisition and required the ability to permute numbers. In the second section, I will argue that some basic spatial abilities are required in many contemporary activities, such as understanding chemistry or playing chess. Further, I will refer to one of the best-studied topics in neuropsychology: reading and writing. I will emphasize that even though there are some basic principles in writing (i.e., writing implies graphically representing spoken language), different writing strategies have arisen. These strategies may require the use of different basic capabilities and are associated with different patterns of brain activation. Finally, I will try to speculate about cognitive abilities in the absence of written language. This means cognition in illiterates.

In this chapter I am attempting to integrate some ideas previously presented in several papers. The reader can find previous versions of the sections included in this chapter in various journal articles (Ardila, 1993a, 1993b, 1995, 1996; Ardila, Ostrosky-Solis, & Mendoza, 2000).

FROM FINGER SEQUENCING TO THE COMPUTER

Calculation abilities have followed a long historical process, from initial quantification of events and elements, to modern algebra, geometry, and calculus. Some rudimentary numerical concepts are observed in animals, and there is no question that prehistorical humans used some quantification. The ability to represent quantities, the development of a numerical system, and the use of arithmetical operations, however, are found only in old civilizations.

The origin of mathematical concepts can be traced to subhuman species. There is a general agreement that some rudimentary numerical concepts are observed in animals. These basic numerical skills can be considered as the real origin of the calculation abilities found in contemporary humans. For instance, pigeons can be trained to pick a specific number of times on a board, and rats can be trained to press a lever a certain number of times to obtain food (Caspaldi & Miller, 1988; Koehler, 1951; Mechner, 1958). It could be conjectured that pigeons and rats can count, at least up to a certain quantity: They can recognize how many times a motor act—to pick on a board or to press a lever—has been repeated. Whether this behavior can or cannot be interpreted as counting is nonetheless questionable. But it is observed, at least after a long and painstaking training. Interestingly, these animal responses (to pick or to press the lever) are not accurate but just approximate. In other words, when the rat is required to press the lever seven times, the rat presses it *about* seven times (i.e., 5, 6, 7, 8 times). As Dehaene (1997) emphasizes, for an animal 5 plus 5 does not make 10, but only about 10. According to him, such fuzziness in the internal representation of numbers prevents the emergence of exact numerical arithmetical knowledge in animals. Using highly controlled and sophisticated designs, it has been pointed out that chimpanzees can even use and add simple numerical fractions (e.g., $^2/_4 + ^1/_4 = ^3/_4$) (Woodruff & Premack, 1981). These observations support the assumption that some quantity concepts can be found in animals.

Counting (or rather, approximate counting) motor responses is just a motor act like walking or running. "Counting" lever pressings is not that different from estimating the effort (e.g., number of steps or general motor activity) required to go from one point to another. Counting could be linked to some propioceptive information.

Not only chimpanzees but also rats and many other animals can distinguish numerosity (i.e., global quantification): they prefer the bowl containing the larger number of nutritive elements (chocolates, pellets, or whatever) when selecting between two bowls containing different amounts (Davis & Perusse, 1988). It may be conjectured that global quantification (numerosity perception) and counting (at least the approximate counting of motor responses) represent some kind of basic calculation abilities found at the animal level. Rats prefer the bowl containing 20 pellets to the bowl containing 10 pellets; however, they do not prefer the bowl containing 21 pellets to the bowl containing 20 pellets. Obviously, numerosity perception is related to size and shape of the visual image projected to the retina. It can be assumed that 20 pellets in a bowl result in a larger and more complex retinal image than do 10 pellets. But the visual image corresponding to 20 pellets is difficult to distinguish from the visual image corresponding to 21 pellets.

Chimpanzees are capable of various forms of numerical competence, including some correspondence constructions for low quantities (Davis & Perusse,

1988; Premack, 1976). Most likely, these numerical abilities also existed in prehistorical humans. *Homo sapiens* ancestors may have been capable of using correspondence constructions in some social activities, such as food sharing. It has been proposed that *Homo habilis* (ancestor of *Homo erectus*, living about 2.5 million years ago) used correspondence constructions when butchering large animal carcasses (Parker & Gibson, 1979). Distributing pieces of a divided whole (e.g., a prey) into equal parts required the ability to construct one-to-one correspondences. Probably, Paleolithic humans were able to match the number of objects in different groups. And eventually, the number of objects in a collection could be matched with the number of items in some external cue system (e.g., fingers or pebbles, incidentally, *calculus* means pebbles).

The immediate recognition of certain small quantities is found not only in animals but also in small children. Animals and children can readily distinguish one, two, or three objects (Fuson, 1988; Wynn, 1990, 1992). Beyond this point, however, errors are observed. Oneness, twoness, and threeness seemingly are basic perceptual qualities that our brain can distinguish and process without counting. It can be conjectured that when prehistorical humans began to speak, they may have been able to name only the numbers 1, 2, and perhaps 3, corresponding to specific perceptions. To name them was probably no more difficult than naming any other sensory attribute (Dehaene, 1997). It is noteworthy that all the world's languages can count up to three, even though three may represent "many," "several," or "a lot" (Hurford, 1987). "One" is obviously the unit, the individual (the speaker may also be "one"). "*Two*" conveys the meaning of "another" (e.g., in English and also in Spanish, "second" is related with the verb "to second," and the adjective "secondary"). "Three" may be a residual form from "a lot," "beyond the others," "many" (e.g., "troppo," which in Italian means "too much," is seemingly related with the word three—*tre*-). In the original European language, spoken perhaps some 15 to 20 thousand years ago, apparently the only numbers were "one," "one and another" (two), and "a lot," "several," "many" (three) (Dehaene, 1997). In some languages, two different plurals are found: a plural for small quantities (usually two, sometimes three and four) and a second plural for large quantities.

Arithmetical abilities are clearly related to counting. Counting—not simply recording the approximate amount of motor responses required to obtain a reinforcement, but to say a series of number words that correspond to a collection of objects—is relatively recent in human history. Counting is also a relatively late skill in child development. In human history as well as in child development (Hitch, Cundock, Haughey, Pugh, & Wright, 1987), counting using number words begins with sequencing the fingers (i.e., using a correspondence construction). The name of the finger and the corresponding number can be represented using the very same word (that means, the very same word is used for naming the thumb and the number one; the very same word is used to name the index finger and the number two, etc.). The fingers (and toes; as a matter of fact, many languages, e.g., Spanish, use a single word [*dedo*] to name the fingers and toes) are usually sequenced in a particular order. This strategy represents a basic procedure found in different ancient and contemporary cultures around the world (Levy-Bruhl, 1910/1947). Interestingly, it has been demonstrated that children with low arithmetical skills also present a finger misrepresentation on the Draw-a-Person test (Pontius, 1995). This observation has been confirmed in different cultural groups.

Taking a typical example as an illustration, the Colombian Sikuani Amazonian jungle Indians count in the following way: the person (a child when learning to count or an adult when counting) places his/her *left* hand in supination; to point number 1, the right index points to the left little finger, which is then bent (Quixalos, 1989). The order followed in counting is always from the little finger to the index. To point to number 5, the hand is turned and the fingers opened; for 6, both thumbs are joined, the left fingers are closed, and the right opened; they are opened one after the other for 7, 8, 9, and 10. Between 11 and 20, the head points to the feet and the sequence is reinitiated. The lexicon used is:

1: *kae* (the unit, one)

2: *aniha-behe* (a pair, both)

3: *akueyabi*

4: *penayanatsi* (accompanied; that is, the fingers together)

5: *kae-kabe* (one hand)

Numbers from 6 to 9 are formed with "one hand and (a certain number) of fingers." Ten becomes "two hands."

6: *kae-kabe kae-kabesito-nua* (one hand one finger)

7: *kae-kabe aniha-kabesito-behe* (one hand and a pair of finger)

10: *aniha-kabe-behe* (two hands)

"Two hands" is maintained between 10 and 20. Toes (*taxawusito*) are added between 11 and 14; and "one foot" (*kae-taxu*) is used in 15. Twenty is "two hands together with two feet":

11: *aniha-kabe-behe kae-taxuwusito* (two hands one toe)

12: *aniha-kabe-behe aniha-tuxuwusito-behe* (two hands two toes)

15: *aniha-kabe-behe kae-taxu-behe* (two hands one foot)

16: *aniha-kae-behe kae-taxu-behe kae-taxuwusito* (two hands, one foot, and one toe)

20: *aniha-kabe-behe aniha-taxu-behe* (two hands two feet)

Fingers are named according to their order in counting (as mentioned above, counting begins always with the little finger of the left hand). Sikuani language possesses number words only up to three (*kae, aniha-behe, akueyabi*). Four (*penayanatsi* = accompanied, together) represents a correspondence construction. Strictly speaking, Sikuani language counts only up to three. From four to twenty, they use a correspondence construction, not really counting; and for higher quantities, they recur to a global quantification. Sometimes not only the fingers (and toes) but also other body segments may be used in counting: the wrist, the shoulders, the knees, and so forth (Cauty, 1984; Levy-Bruhl, 1910/1947). But sequencing the fingers (and toes) represents the most universal procedure in counting. Some languages (e.g., some Mayan dialects and Greenland Eskimo) use the same word to denote the number 20 (that is, "all the fingers and all the toes") and "a person."

In different Amerindian languages, for higher than 10 or 20 figures, most often "many" is used (global quantification principle) (Cauty, 1984). Or they can recur to other people's hands (correspondence construction) (e.g., thirty-five might be something like "my two hands, my two feet, my father's two hands, my father's one foot"). As mentioned, "twenty" sometimes becomes something like "one person," a sort of highers order numeral. It is interesting to note that in some contemporary languages (like English and Spanish) "one" means the unit, but it is also used as a sort of indefinite personal pronoun. In English and Spanish we can also use "one" as synonymous of "myself." Twenty is found to be the base number in the Mayas' numerical system (Cauty, 1984; Swadesh, 1967). In many contemporary languages, a ten and/or twenty base can be evident.

"Digit" (from *digitus*, Latin) in English or Spanish (*digito*) means number but also finger. The correspondence construction between numbers and fingers is evident.

From a neuropsychological perspective, the strong relationship existing between numerical knowledge, finger gnosis, and even lateral (right–left) knowledge is evident. Finger agnosia (and probably right–left discrimination disturbances) could be interpreted as a restricted form of autotopagnosia (Ardila, Rosselli, & Rosas, 1989). It is not surprising to find that a decimal (or vigecial) system has been most often developed. Simultaneously or very close in time, decimal systems appeared in different countries (Sumer, Egypt, India, and Crete). Different symbols were used to represent 1, 10, 100, and 1000 (Childe, 1936).

So, reviewing the history of numerical concepts, it is found that world languages developed a base 10 (10 fingers) or 20 (10 fingers plus 10 toes) or even five (five fingers) to group quantities. In some contemporary Indo-European languages, for example in French, a residual 20-base can be found (e.g., in French 80 is "four twenties"). In many contemporary languages, different words are used to name numbers between 1 and 10. Between 10 and 20 the numerical systems usually become irregular, unpredictable, and idiosyncratic. From 20 and higher, new numbers are formed simply with the words "twenty plus one," "twenty plus two," and so on. Some contemporary languages still use a 5-base in counting. For instance, in the Amerindian language Tanimuca in South America, they count up to five. Between five and 10, numbers are "five one," "five two," and so on.

Written numbers appeared earlier in history than written language. Some cultures (e.g., Incas) developed a numbers representing system but not a languages representing system (Swadesh, 1967). "Calculus" means pebble in Latin. Pebbles, or marks, or knots, or any other element, were used as a correspondence construction to record the number of elements (people, cows, fishes, houses, etc.). In Sumer, the first number-writing system has been found (about 3000 B.C.) (Childe, 1936): Instead of using pebbles, fingers, or knots, it was simpler just to make a mark (a stroke or a point) on the floor or on a tree branch or on a board if you wanted to keep the record. In Egypt, India, and later in Crete, a similar system was developed: units were represented by a conventional symbol (usually a stroke) repeated several times to mean a digit between one and nine; a different symbol was used for 10 and 10-multiples.

Positional digit value is clearly disclosed in Babylonians, and about 1000 B.C. the zero was introduced. Positional value and zero are also disclosed among the Mayan Indians (León-Portilla, 1986). Egyptians and Babylonians commonly used fractions. Small fractions ($^1/_2$, $^1/_3$, and $^1/_4$) are relatively simple numerical concepts, and even chimpanzees can be trained to use small fractions (Woodruff & Premack, 1981).

As mentioned above, recognition of individual marks or elements up to three is easy: It represents an immediate, readily recognizable perception. Beyond three, the number of marks (strokes or dots) has to be counted and errors can be observed. Furthermore, it is rather time-consuming and cumbersome to be all the time counting marks. Noteworthy, the different digit notational systems always represent one, two, and three with strokes (or points, or any specific mark). It means the numbers one, two, and three are written making one, two, or three strokes. But beyond that figure, digit writing may recur to other strategies. In our Arabic digit notation system, "one" is a vertical line, whereas 2 and 3 were originally horizontal lines that became tied together by being handwritten. This observation may be related to the inborn ability to perceptually recognize up to three elements. Beyond three, errors become progressively more likely. Perceptually distinguishing between 8 and 9 is not as easy as distinguishing between 2 and 3 strokes. The introduction of a different representation for quantities over 3 was a useful and practical simplification.

In neuropsychology, some common brain activity for finger knowledge and calculation abilities can be conjectured. Finger agnosia and acalculia appear as two simultaneous signs of a single clinical syndrome (Gerstmann, 1940), usually known as "Gerstmann syndrome" or "angular gyrus syndrome" (Ardila, Concha, & Rosselli, 2000). For prehistorical humans, finger agnosia and acalculia could have represented just the same defect.

Adding, subtracting, multiplying, and dividing were possible in the Egyptian system, but, of course, following procedures quite different from those we currently use. They based multiplication and division on the "duplication" and "halving" method (Childe, 1936). Interestingly, this very same procedure (duplicating and halving quantities) is also observed in illiterate people when performing arithmetical operations. So, in the Egyptian system, to multiply 12×18, the following procedure was followed:

1	18
2	36
*4	72
*8	144
Total	216

The number 18 is duplicated one or several times, and the amounts corresponding to 12 (4 + 8 in this example) are selected and summed up: 72 + 144 = 216. For dividing, the inverse procedure was used. So, to divide 19 by 8 would be:

1	8
*2	16
2	4
*4	2
*8	1

That is, $2 + 4 + 8(2 + 1/4 + 1/8)$, that is, 2.375.

In brief, arithmetical abilities and number representation have been used for only some five to six thousand years. Most likely, during the Stone Age only simple counting up to three was present and, of course, "bigger" and "smaller" (magnitude judgment) concepts. Global quantification already existed at prehuman levels. Correspondence constructions allowed increasing the amount of numbers. The most immediate correspondence construction is done with the fingers. Finger knowledge and counting represent to a certain extent the same cognitive ability, as is still evident in some contemporary languages such as the Sikuani language.

Counting, finger gnosis, and even lateral spatial knowledge may have a common historical origin. Calculation abilities were evidently derived from finger sequencing. Number representation and arithmetical operations were developed only some five to six thousand years ago. Currently, calculation abilities are evolving rapidly because of the introduction of modern technology. After a long cultural evolution, contemporary humans have replaced the ability to name and sequence fingers with the ability to use computers. Although the basic capabilities may be the same in both cases, cultural evolution has provided new contents.

WHAT HAPPENED WITH SPATIAL ABILITIES?

Contemporary city life, in which direct orientation in space has been replaced by the logical application of mathematical coordinates, represents a relatively recent cultural acquisition. For a very long time, education consisted of learning to get oriented in space, to recognize the pertinent signals to follow a prey, and to move in the surrounding spatial environment. This, of course, is still valid for contemporary people living in the Amazonian jungle, for Eskimos, for desert inhabitants, and many other world inhabitants. For thousands (and even millions) of years, human survival depended on the correct interpretation of spatial signals, memory of places, calculation of distances, and so forth, and the human brain must have become adapted precisely to handle this type of spatial information (Ardila & Ostrosky, 1984).

The Paleolithic Era extended for about 2,300,000 years (first hominids using stone tools), until some 10,000 years ago (Childe, 1936; Hours, 1982). At about this time, agriculture appeared, and humans began to domesticate and raise some animals. This produced a tremendous change in their way of life (the *Neolithic Revolution*). The Paleolithic, however, represents the vast majority of human history (about 98%).

It could be supposed that the biological adaptation of humans was accomplished to survive under those conditions existing during the Paleolithic time. Recent human evolution corresponds more exactly to a cultural type of evolution, not necessarily requiring further biological changes, but the development and use of the basic cognitive capabilities of humans already existed during the Paleolithic. Agriculture replaced fruit collection; domestication of animals replaced hunting; written language extended oral language; arithmetic extended finger counting; and the use of maps and logical spatial coordinates extended the direct orientation in space (Vygotsky, 1962).

There is evidence that *Australopitecus africanus* (probably the direct ancestor of *Homo*) lived on open savannas. Although their ancestors lived in forests, they moved to live in open fields (Lee & DeVore, 1968; Wilson, 1975). They strongly depended on animal food, especially small preys (tortoises, lizards, snakes, rabbits) and on collecting fruits. *Homo sapiens* appeared in Europe about 50,000 years ago (middle Paleolithic), and it is supposed that they hunted, usually small but also big preys, used rudimentary stone tools (knives, axes), and lived in caverns or rudimentary shelters built with tree branches. They were nomad and they constantly had to move from one place to another looking for preys, fruits, and shelter. They created some hunting weapons, such as the arrow and the spear, and used fire (Washburn, 1978; Hours, 1982).

It could be supposed that spatial abilities were even more crucial for survival in prehistorical humans than in contemporary times. Survival under current urban living conditions requires different cognitive abilities. We go around in our cities using logical-mathematical coordinates, reading a printed-on-paper map, without taking into consideration the position of the sun in the sky or the need to avoid potential predators. Adaptation to contemporary world conditions requires more verbally based abilities. If the question "What moon phase is today?" (instead of "What date is today?") were included in a mental state examination, the majority of city people probably would fail. By the same token, city people usually ignore the exact points of sunrise and sunset (they usually respond "east and west"), but the points of sunrise and sunset change a little everyday, and they could have been as important a piece of information for prehistorical human survival as it is for contemporary humans to know that "Today is May 7th, 2002." Furthermore, our current educational system strongly emphasizes verbal, logical, and mathematical abilities, not spatial orientation abilities. Of course, these are currently the most useful abilities with which to survive in our contemporary world. Generally speaking, city people have limited opportunities to develop and use spatial orientation abilities.

Cross-cultural differences in spatial orientation strategies under normal and pathological conditions could be illustrative to understand how prehistorical humans could have used spatial information. Furthermore, it could shed some light about the potential spatial abilities that contemporary humans possess. Brain organization of spatial abilities under pathological conditions has been extensively studied in contemporary schooled Western (particularly European and North American) people. To my best knowledge, however, no clinical observation about disturbances in spatial abilities associated with brain pathology have ever been reported in other (non-Western) cultures.

Perceptual constancy (stability of perception despite changes in the actual characteristics of the stimuli) represents the most fundamental ability in the interpretation of the surrounding spatial environment (Ardila, 1980). Cross-cultural comparisons have in general demonstrated that perceptual constancy (size and shape constancy) is more accurate in low-schooled and non-Western people than in literate and Westernized subjects (Pick & Pick, 1978). Beveridge (1940) demonstrated a greater constancy of shape and size among West African adults than among British adults. Myambo (1972) observed almost perfect shape constancy in uneducated Malawi adults, whereas the educated Africans and Europeans did not perform so accurately. Perceptual constancy may be expected to have been high (and crucial for survival) not only in prehistorical humans, but also in people currently requiring a complex interpretation of the surrounding spatial environment.

People living in different environments develop different systems of spatial reference (rivers, mountains, sun position, streets, buildings, etc.). Geographic features affect the terms of local reference systems, and differences in reference systems may, in turn, be related to differences in perception of spatial orientation (Pick & Pick, 1978). The analysis of different reference systems can be illustrative. Gladwin (1970) analyzed the system used by Puluwat sailors to navigate among clusters of islands in the Western Pacific. He disclosed that many different features of the sea and sky comprise the information on which the system is based. Knowledge of the habits of local sea birds provides cues for one's location. The sailors learn to detect the coral reef's formation changes, which, of course, differ depending on the conditions of the weather, sea, and sky. Ability to detect change in the "feel" of the boat moving through the waves on a particular course is a skill used to maintain a course. There is a complex reference system based on the position and patterns of stars in the night sky, and the rules for navigating between specific islands are described in terms of the star patterns and islands. Parallax information is also explicitly included in the system as descriptions of the way in which the islands "move" as the boat passes on one or the other side of them.

Evidently, members of different cultures and dwelling in different spatial environments operate in terms of complex spatial reference systems, depending on their particular demands and geographic environments. Demands and geographic environment were quite different in Paleolithic times than they currently are.

Cross-cultural differences in perceptual abilities have been extensively studied and can be particularly illustrative to understand perceptual skills in prehistorical humans (Brislin, 1983; Laboratory of Comparative Human Cognition, 1983; Segall, 1986). Hudson (1960, 1962) studied depth perception using pictures that contained figures of an elephant, an antelope, and a man with a spear; the basic question referred to what the man was doing with the spear. There were four pictures differing with respect to the cues available for the interpretation of the picture. This set of pictures was used with different groups of people from Africa and Europe. It was observed that European children around 7 to 8 years of age have a great difficulty perceiving the picture as three-dimentional. However, around 12 years of age, virtually all of the European children perceived the picture as three-dimensional. Not so with Bantu or Guinean children. Nonliterate Bantu and European laborers responded to the picture as flat, not three-dimensional. They cannot interpret represented-on-a-paper three-dimensional figures; this also holds true in general for illiterate people (Ardila, Rosselli, & Rosas, 1989). As mentioned above, however, illiterate African people do better than Western literate subjects in perceptual constancy tasks with real objects. But they do worse when the external space is represented on a paper.

Berry (1971, 1979) proposed that hunting people with specific ecological demands usually present good visual discrimination and excellent spatial skills. For instance, the embedded figures tests are better performed by cultural groups for whom hunting is important for survival. Berry emphasizes that ecological demands and cultural practices are significantly related to the development of perceptual, spatial, and cognitive skills. A good example of a specific culture-dependent cognitive skill was that reported by Gay and Cole (1967); when Kpelle farmers are contrasted with working-class Americans, the former were considerably more accurate in estimating the amount of rice in several bowls of different sizes containing different amounts of rice. By the same token, any cattle farmer is able to calculate accurately the weight of a cow; or any dactilographist can easily and quickly distinguish two different fingerprints; and any neurologist can distinguish a Parkinsonian patient at one glance. Demands and training history are strongly associated with visuoperceptual abilities.

Visuospatial impairments resulting from brain damage have been extensively analyzed in neuropsychology (e.g., De Renzi, 1982, 1985; Hécaen, 1962; Morrow & Ratcliff, 1988; Newcombe & Ratcliff, 1989; Rosselli, 1986). Different brain syndromes have been distinguished. Spatial agnosia represents an impairment in the perception and use of spatial-dependent information resulting from brain pathology. It refers to an acquired inability to recognize and integrate spatial information, without a primary sensory defect capable to explain it (Ardila & Rosselli, 1992). Spatial agnosia includes impairments in the recognition of line orientation, defects in depth perception, impairments in handling spatial information, and deficits in spatial memory (De Renzi, 1982; Hécaen & Albert, 1978).

Different types of spatial agnosia have been distinguished. Holmes (1918) separates different categories of spatial agnosia: defects in localization of objects, topographic amnesia, inability to count objects, inability to perceive movement, loss of stereoscopic vision, and deficits in eye movements. Critchley (1968) includes the following groups: (1) disorders in spatial perception with regard to the three-dimensional perception, (2) disorders in spatial concepts, and (3) disorders in spatial manipulation, which include disorders in topographical memory, defects in orientation, and unilateral spatial agnosia. Hécaen (1962) proposed separating: (1) disorders in spatial perception; (2) defects in spatial manipulation, including the loss of topographical concepts and unilateral spatial agnosia; (3) loss of topographical memory; and (4) Balint's syndrome. De Renzi (1982, 1985) presents some modifications to Hécaen's classification. Balint's syndrome is included within visual exploration disorders and, instead of disorders in manipulation of spatial information, introduces the group of disorders in spatial thought.

It is interesting to emphasize that all these disorders appear (mainly or exclusively) in cases of right hemisphere pathology. The right hemisphere seems to be specialized in spatial cognition. Seemingly, language and ideomotor praxis abilities developed in an area of the left brain that in the right brain is involved in spatial cognition (LeDoux, 1984).

Similar fundamental spatial cognition disturbances are supposedly found in a similar way in every species member, regardless of the cultural background and the ecological demands. Not only commonality, however, but also differences are expected. If the *degree* (not the *direction*) of brain lateralization of language depends on literacy, and in general on the verbal training history (Lecours et al., 1987a, 1987b, 1988; Matute, 1988), it is reasonable to suppose that the degree of lateralization of spatial cognition would also depend on the spatial abilities training history. At least some spatial disturbances (e.g., hemispatial neglect) have been reported to be more frequently observed associated with left-hemisphere pathology, in individuals with a history of low verbal training (but normal or even superior training in spatial abilities) (Rosselli et al., 1985).

Nonetheless, contemporary city human spatial abilities are not necessarily inferior to those of prehistorical humans or Amazonian Indians. Spatial abilities may have evolved with the new living and cultural conditions (in a similar way as spoken language evolved and extended with the development of new cultural conditions, e.g., through written language). Spatial abilities can be required in many contemporary conceptual and historically recent skills. I had the opportunity to study a chemistry university professor who suffered a small right-parietal infarction. Although she did not have any evident spatial difficulty in her everyday activities or in standard neuropsychological testing, she could not continue teaching chemistry because she was "unable to have a spatial representation of molecules and all the time got confused." Mathematics (Ardila & Rosselli,

1990; Luria, 1977), painting, playing chess (Chabris & Hamilton, 1992), reading and writing (Ardila, 1996; Rosselli, 1993; Benson & Ardila, 1996), mechanics (Benton, 1989), and even music (Henson, 1985) all represent—at least partially—spatially based skills. In urban humans, mathematics, painting, playing chess, reading and writing, mechanics, and music abilities can be impaired in cases of damage to those same areas of the right hemisphere that in a Eskimo or Amazonian Indian would simply result in an impossibility to move around the snow or the jungle.

In summary, it can be proposed that: (1) *Homo sapiens* presented a nomadic way of life during the majority of their history. A more sedentary way of life appeared only with the domestication of animals and the development of agriculture, that is, some ten thousand years ago. A nomadic way of life is strongly associated with high spatial ability demands. (2) Disorders in spatial cognition represent a particularly complex and insufficiently understood array of impairments. Spatial knowledge has been strongly associated with right hemisphere activity. Virtually all the defects in spatial perception and orientation are found exclusively or predominantly in cases of right hemisphere damage. (3) It might be supposed that right hemisphere specialization for spatial abilities could be correlated with language acquisition and evolution. Spoken language evolved with the appearance of new cultural conditions, and it might be supposed that spatial abilities also evolved with the appearance of new cultural and ecological conditions. (4) It might be proposed that early hominids and prehistorical humans presented a more bilateral representation of spatial abilities. Visuospatial disorders might have been expected in cases of right and left hemisphere pathology. Not only language development and language complexization, but also the development of new spatially based abilities may have increased the right hemisphere specialization for handling information with a spatial content, as well as the left specialization for linguistic abilities.

HOW THE BRAIN READS

Different strategies to represent spoken language have been developed during the course of human history. A major division has been established between logographic and phonographic writing systems (Sampson, 1985). Logographic systems are those based on meaningful units (morphemes, words), whereas phonographic systems are those based on phonological (sound) units.

It seems reasonable to expect that alexia characteristics may correlate with the idiosyncrasies of writing systems (Ardila, 1998; Coltheart, 1982). Unfortunately, alexias and agraphias have been studied particularly in Indo-European language writing systems, and cross-linguistic analyses are scarce. With the exception of some studies on the Japanese Kana and Kanji (e.g., Sasanuma & Fujimura, 1971; Sugishita, Otomo, Kabe, & Yunoki, 1992; Yamadori, 1975, 1988), and a case study of alexia without agraphia in Arab language (El Alaoui-Faris, Benbeland,

Alaoui, Tahiri, Jiddane, Amarti, & Chikili, 1994), comparative research on alexias and agraphias in different languages has been limited.

It is interesting to note that in brain-damaged bilingual individuals, the ability to read in the two writing systems can become dissociated. That is, alexia can affect only (or mainly) one of the two reading systems. This holds true not only for overtly and evidently different writing systems, such as syllabic Kana and logographic Kanji (Iwata, 1984; Sasanuma & Fujimura, 1971; Yamadori, 1975), but even for closer alphabetic writing systems, such as Russian and French (Luria, 1966) and even Spanish and English (personal observation). Reading in different writing systems may represent different cognitive tasks, and therefore brain organization of written language may be somewhat different.

Some studies have approached the question of interlinguistic differences in written word recognition (lexical decision) tasks. Haata (1978, 1992) observed in Japanese Kanji a left-visual field advantage for single-character words and the reverse for two-character words. Similar results have been reported in the Chinese language (Rastatter, Scukanec, & Grilliot, 1989). Rastatter and Scukanec (1990) suggested that, when comparing English-proficient Chinese-Mandarin speakers and a group of monolingual English speakers in a lexical decision task, English-speakers had a dissociation between the left and right hemispheres for linguistic processing, whereas in Chinese subjects, the left hemisphere was responsible for the final phonological stages in linguistic analysis.

Lukatela and Turvey (1990) proposed a model of written language recognition for the Serbo-Croatian languages in which word processing was mediated by phoneme-processing units. Yamada and associates (1990) proposed a dual-route hypothesis for reading syllabic Japanese Katakana: lexical access may be achieved by both a process of assembled segmental phonology and the use of a visual orthographic lexicon. These studies as a whole indicate that lexical access and lexical decision can be under the influence of the idiosyncrasies of the individual reading systems.

Ardila (1998) has challenged applicability of current double-route psycholinguistic models of alexias (acquired dyslexias) to Spanish language. He argues that Spanish language uses a graphophonemic reading strategy and that under *normal* circumstances logographic reading is not required. Examining the cases of semantic paralexias published both in Spanish and English, Ardila concluded that, although Spanish reading proceeds using a graphophonemic strategy, additional strategies can also be introduced under special circumstances. Semantic paralexias represent a rather frequent phenomenon in English-speaking aphasics (Landis, Regard, Graves, & Goodglass, 1983). This phenomenon is quite unusual in Spanish-speaking aphasics and is restricted to a very specific aphasic subsample. Lastly, Ardila proposes that the characteristics of alexic disturbances will positively correlate with the idiosyncrasies of the respective writing systems.

Paulesu and coworkers (2000) observed differences in the pattern of brain activation when reading Italian and English. Italian orthography is consistent, enabling reliable conversion of graphemes to phonemes to yield correct pronunciation of the word. English orthography is inconsistent. Italians showed faster word and non-word reading than do English speakers. Using position emission tomography scans, Italian speakers showed greater activation of the left superior temporal region associated with phoneme processing. In contrast, English readers showed greater activation, particularly for non-words, in the left posterior inferior temporal gyrus and the anterior inferior frontal gyrus, areas associated with word retrieval during both reading and naming tasks. It can be concluded that the brain activity supporting reading in Italian and English is only partially coincidental.

Nakamura and colleagues (2000) observed activation of the left posterior inferior temporal cortex in writing and mentally recalling Kanji characters (ideographic reading). Different brain pathways for reading Japanese Kana and Kanji have been proposed (Iwata, 1984): whereas the left occipitoparietal areas are especially important in reading and writing Kanji, more dorsal or occipitoparietal connections play a role in reading Kana.

Castro-Caldas and associates (1988) claim that learning a specific skill during childhood may partly determine the functional organization of the adult brain. These authors studied language processing in illiterate subjects who, for social reasons, had never entered school and had no knowledge of reading or writing. In a brain-activation study using PET and statistical parametric mapping, word repetition and pseudoword repetition in literate and illiterate subjects were compared. Results confirmed behavioral evidence of different phonological processing in illiterate subjects. During repetition of real words, the two groups performed similarly and activated similar areas of the brain. Illiterate subjects had more difficulty repeating pseudowords correctly, however, and did not activate the same neural structures as did literates. These results are consistent with the hypothesis that learning the written form of language (orthography) interacts with the function of oral language. Current results indicate that learning to read and write during childhood influences the functional organization of the adult human brain.

In conclusion, different, partially but not totally coincidental writing systems have been developed. They may require the use of somehow different fundamental cognitive abilities and are associated with specific patterns of brain activation. Even though the fundamental capabilities are the same, the culture provides the specific content.

HOW ILLITERATES THINK

A significantly decreased neuropsychological test performance has been documented in illiterate individuals (Ardila, Rosselli, & Rosas, 1989; Goldblum & Matute, 1986; Lecours, Mehler, Parente, et al., 1987a, 1987b, 1988; Manly, Jacobs, Sano, et al., 1999; Ostrosky, Ardila, Rosselli, et al., 1998; Reis & Castro-Caldas, 1997; Rosselli, Ardila, & Rosas, 1990). Lowered scores are observed in most cognitive domains, including naming, verbal fluency, verbal memory, visuoperceptual abilities, conceptual functions, and numerical abilities. Language repetition can be normal for meaningful words but abnormal for pseudowords (Reis & Castro-Caldas, 1997; Rosselli, Ardila, & Rosas, 1990). Similarly, copying meaningful figures can be easier than copying nonsense figures (Ostrosky, Ardila, Rosselli, et al., 1998). Furthermore, it can be notoriously easier for illiterate people to use concrete situations than non-real and abstract elements. When the information is related to real life, it can be significantly easier to understand. Thus, for the illiterate person, it is easier to solve the arithmetical operation, "If you go to the market and initially buy 12 tomatoes and place them in a bag, and later on you decide to buy 15 additional tomatoes, how many tomatoes will you have in your bag?" than to solve: "How much is 12 plus 15?" Semantic verbal fluency is easier than phonological verbal fluency (Reis & Castro-Caldas, 1997; Rosselli, Ardila, & Rosas, 1990), seemingly because phonological abstraction is extremely difficult for the illiterate person. Semantic verbal fluency requires the use of concrete elements (e.g., animals, fruits), whereas phonological fluency is tapping a metalinguistic ability.

It could be conjectured that learning to read stimulates the development of certain cognitive abilities: verbal memory, visuoperceptual abilities, phonological abstraction, verbal knowledge, and so forth. As a matter of fact, very important cognitive consequences of learning to read and to write have been suggested: changes in visual perception, logical reasoning, and remembering strategies (Laboratory of Comparative Human Cognition, 1983). Even the influence of schooling on formal operational thinking (Laurendeau-Bendavid, 1977) and functional brain organization (Castro-Caldas et al., 1998) have been pointed out. Conversely, training these abilities may make it easier to learn to read and to write.

It may be conjectured that learning to read reinforces certain fundamental abilities, such as verbal memory, phonological awareness, and certain type of visuospatial discrimination. It is not surprising that illiterate people score low on cognitive tests that tap these abilities. Furthermore, attending school also reinforces certain attitudes and values that may speed the learning process, such as, for example, the attitude that memorizing information is important, knowledge is highly valuable, and learning is a stepwise process moving from the simpler to complex. It has been emphasized that schooling improves an individual's ability to explain the basis of performance on cognitive tasks (Laboratory of Comparative Human Cognition, 1983). The fundamental aims of schools are equivalent for all schools and school reinforces certain specific values regardless of where they are located. Hence, school could be seen as a culture onto itself, a transnational culture, the culture of school. School not only teaches but also helps in developing certain attitudes that will be useful for future new learning. Ciborowski (1979) observed that schooled and nonschooled children can learn a new rule equally well, but once a rule is acquired, schooled children tend to apply it more frequently in subsequent similar cases.

Ardila, Ostrosky, and Mendoza (2000) developed a method for learning to read, called NEUROALFA, that is based on the observation that illiterate subjects significantly score low in some neuropsychological tests. NEUROALFA is directed to reinforce these underscored abilities during the learning-to-read process. This method was tested in a sample of 21 adult illiterates in Mexico. Results were compared with two control groups, which used more traditional procedures for learning. The NEUROPSI (Ostrosky, Ardila, & Rosselli, 1997, 1999) neuropsychological test battery was administered to all the participants before and after completing the learning-to-read training program. All three groups presented some improvement in the NEUROPSI test scores. Gains, however, were significantly higher in the experimental group in Orientation in Time, Digits Backward, Visual Detection, Verbal Memory, Copy of a Semi-Complex Figure, Language Comprehension, Phonological Verbal Fluency, Similarities, Calculation Abilities, Sequences, and all the recall subtests, excluding Recognition. Performance on standard reading tests was also significantly higher in the experimental group. Correlations between pre-test NEUROPSI scores and reading ability were low. However, correlations between post-test NEUROPSI scores and reading scores were higher and significant for several subtests. Results were interpreted as supporting the assumption that the reinforcement of those abilities in which illiterates significantly underscore results in a significant improvement in neuropsychological test scores and notoriously facilitates the learning-to-read process.

To separate the effects of literacy from the effects of school is not easy. School not only teaches but also reinforces some attitudes and values. Scribner and Cole (1981) attempted to separate the effects of literacy from the school effect. Among the Vai people in Liberia they found some individuals who were literate in the Vai script but who had not attended formal schools. Using a battery of cognitive tests they found that there were no general cognitive effects of literacy, but there were some specific test performances that were related to the particular features of the Vai script. They concluded that literacy makes some differences to some skills in some contexts. Berry and Bennett (1989) carried out a partial replication of this study among the Cree of Northern Ontario.

It should be emphasized that in both the Scribner and Cole and the Berry and Bennett studies the emphasis is placed on reading, not on writing. This was a major difference from the above-mentioned Mexican study that potentially may account for some of the differences observed in test performance. Learning to write requires the use of significant graphomotor and visuospatial abilities that are not crucial for reading and are not reinforced when just learning to read.

It is important to emphasize that in Ardila, Ostrosky-Jolis, and Mendoza's study, correlations between pre-test scores and reading ability scores were in general low and nonsignificant. However, correlations between post-test NEUROPSI scores and reading ability scores were significant in several subtests. This observation supports the assumption that neuropsychological test scores do not exactly predict learning to read scores, but learning to read reinforces those abilities required to obtaining a high performance in neuropsychological tests. This observation may be most important in the cognitive testing domain and in the analysis of the relationship between education and cognitive test performance.

Despite the well-established fact that there is a significant correlation between cognitive test scores (e.g., IQ) and school attendance (e.g., Matarazzo, 1972), interpreting this correlation has been polemic (Brody, 1992; Neisser, Boodoo, Bouchard, et al., 1996). The really crucial question is: Do cognitive (intelligence) tests indeed predict school performance? Or rather, does school train those abilities appraised in intelligence tests? To answer these questions is not easy, even though frequently the interpretation has been that IQ predicts school performance (e.g., Hunter, 1986). Other researchers, however, consider that IQ scores are to a significant extent a measure of direct and indirect school learning (e.g., Ardila, 1999; Ceci, 1990).

Ceci (1991) presented an extensive and detailed review of available data in this area. The general conclusion is that school attendance accounts not only for a substantial portion of variance in children's IQs but also apparently some, although not all, of the cognitive processes that underpin successful performance on IQ tests. The magnitude of this influence ranges between 0.25 to 6 IQ points per year of school. In consequence, the association between IQ and education cannot be interpreted as just assuming that IQ predicts school success. Intelligence and schooling have complex bidirectional relationships, each influencing variations in the other (Ceci & Williams, 1997). According to our results, even though bidirectional relationships may exist, the really significant relationship is between schooling (in our case, learning to read) and cognitive test performance. That is, learning to read significantly impacts cognitive test performance. But, most important to emphasize, despite being significantly associated with cognitive test performance, learning to read is not necessarily related with the ability to solve everyday problems (Cornelious & Caspi, 1987).

Learning to read, as a cultural extension of oral language, provides new strategies to organize and conceptualize the incoming information. It further reinforces certain abilities (verbal memory, lexical knowledge, etc.) frequently included in standard cognitive testing.

IS THERE ANYTHING SPECIAL IN THE HUMAN BRAIN?

Telencephalization represents a major trend in human brain evaluation. Telencephalization may be associated with two significant changes in human cognition: (1) an increased ability to retain and process information (i.e., to learning and complex perception); and (2) an increased ability to make use of this information (i.e., executive functioning). As a matter of fact, *Homo sapiens* represents the last step in a long evolution process, and many hominids, precursors of the contemporary *Homo sapiens*, have been found. Most likely, these abilities were present in prehistorical hominids with relatively simpler brains, but to a lesser degree.

The increased ability to learn by modeling, and even more important, by teaching (i.e., to share learning and transmit knowledge to others), resulted in culture development. Some rudimentary cultural processes (or, rather, precultural processes, considering that culture is usually defined with regard to humans; culture is usually understood as the specific way of living of a human group), however, can be found in nonhuman primates. The best known example is the ability to chase ants and termites using small sticks observed in chimpanzees. This ability is transmitted from parents to offsprings.

Cultural evolution represented a new, qualitatively different type of evolution. Arithmetical abilities extended finger sequencing; written language extended oral language; drawing extended visuoperceptual recognition, and so on. This type of evolution does not require further biological changes (Vygotsky, 1989). Most likely, the human brain has remained virtually unchanged over the past 10 to 20 thousand years, despite the tremendous cultural changes observed during this time.

To compare contemporary cultures is not easy. Even though some general culture evolution trends can be pointed out, each culture may emphasize certain elements, depending on their specific environmental conditions, history, and contact with other cultures. To attempt to compare cultures is so complex, and potentially so biased, as comparing languages and major cultural elements. The final result, according to Harris (1989) is that "All of the three thousand or so different languages spoken in the world today possess a common fundamental structure and need only minor changes in vocabulary to be equally efficient in storing, retrieving, and transmitting information. So the conclusion of the great anthropological linguistic Edward Sapir stands unchallenged: 'When it comes to linguistic form, Plato walks with the Macedonian swineherd, Confucius with the head-hunting savages of Assam'" (p. 73).

CONCLUSION

This chapter has tried to illustrate that even though there are some basic cognitive abilities found in every person regardless of the culture and environmental conditions, culture provides the specific contents to these basic capabilities. Human basic cognitive abilities are universal and represent the result of millions of years of brain evolution. Cultural evolution has allowed an extension and sophistication of these basic cognitive abilities. Each cultural context provides a specific way to develop and express these basic cognitive capabilities.

REFERENCES

Al Alaoui-Faris, M., Benbeland, F., Alaoui, C., Tahiri, L., Jiddane, M., Amarti, A., & Chkili, T. (1994). Alexia sans agraphie en langue Arabe: tude neurolinguistique et IRM. *Revue Neurologique, 150*, 771–775.

Ardila, A. (1980). *Psicologia de la percepción* [Psychology of perception]. Mexico: Editorial Trillas.

Ardila, A. (1993a). Historical evolution of spatial abilities. *Behavioral Neurology, 6,* 83–88.

Ardila, A. (1993b). On the origins of calculation abilities. *Behavioral Neurology, 6,* 89–98.

Ardila, A. (1995). Directions of research in cross-cultural neuropsychology. *Journal of Clinical and Experimental Neuropsychology, 17,* 143–150.

Ardila, A. (1996). Towards a cross-cultural neuropsychology. *Journal of Social and Evolutionary Systems, 19,* 237–248.

Ardila, A. (1998). Semantic paralexias in Spanish language. *Aphasiology, 12,* 885–900.

Ardila, A. (1999). A neuropsychological approach to intelligence. *Neuropsychology Review, 9,* 117–136.

Ardila, A., Concha, M., & Rosselli, M. (2000). Angular gyrus (Gertsmann's) syndrome revisited: acalculia, finger agnosia, right-left disorientation, and semantic aphasia. *Aphasiology, 14,* 743–754.

Ardila, A., Galeano, L. M., & Rosselli, M. (1998). Toward a model of neuropsychological activity. *Neuropsychology Review, 8,* 177–189.

Ardila, A., Lopez, M. V., & Solano, E. (1989). Semantic aphasia reconsidered. In A. Ardila & F. Ostrosky-Solis (Eds.), *Brain organization of language and cognitive processes.* New York: Plenum Publishing Company.

Ardila, A., & Ostrosky, F. (1984). Some final remarks. In A. Ardila & F. Ostrosky-Solis (Eds.), *The right hemisphere: neurology and neuropsychology* (pp. 265–273). London: Gordon and Breach Science Publishers.

Ardila, A., Ostrosky-solis, F., & Mendoza, V. (2000). Learning to read is much more than learning to read: a neuropsychologically-based learning to read method. *Journal of the International Neuropsychological Society, 6,* 789–801.

Ardila, A., & Rosselli, M. (1990). Acalculias. *Behavioral Neurology 3,* 39–48.

Ardila, A., & Rosselli, M. (1992). *Neuropsicologia clinica* [Clinical neuropsychology]. Medellin, Colombia: Prensa Creativa.

Ardila, A., & Rosselli, M. (in press). Acalculia and dyscalculia. *Neuropsychology Review.*

Ardila, A., Rosselli, M., & Rosas, P. (1989). Neuropsychological assessment in illiterates: visuospatial and memory abilities. *Brain and Cognition, 11,* 147–166.

Benson, D. F., & Ardila, A. (1996). *Aphasia: a clinical perspective.* New York: Oxford University Press.

Benton, A. (1989). Constructional apraxia. In H. Goodglass & A. R. Damasio (Eds.), *Handbook of clinical neuropsychology,* vol 2 (pp. 287–294). Amdsterdam: Elsevier.

Berry, J. W. (1971). Ecological and cultural factors in spatial perceptual development. *Canadian Journal of Behavioral Sciences, 3,* 324–336.

Berry, J. W. (1979). Culture and cognition style. In A. J. Marsella, R. G. Tharp, & T. J. Ciborowski (Eds.), *Perspectives in cross-cultural psychology* (pp. 117–135). New York: Academic Press.

Berry, J. W., & Bennett, J. A. (1989). Syllabic literacy and cognitive performance among the Cree. *International Journal of Psychology 24,* 429–450.

Beveridge, W. M. (1940). Some racial differences in perception. *British Journal of Psychology, 30,* 57–64.

Brislin, R. W. (1983). Cross-cultural research in psychology. *Annual Review of Psychology, 34,* 363–400.

Brody, N. (1992). *Intelligence,* 2nd Edn. New York: Academic Press.

Capaldi, E. J., & Miller, D. J. (1988). Counting in rats: its functional significance and the independent cognitive processes that constitute it. *Journal of Experimental Psychology: Animal Behavior Processes, 14,* 3–17.

Castro-Caldas, A., Peterson, K. M., Reis, A., Stone-Elander, S., & Ingvar, M. (1988). The illiterate brain. Learning to read and write during childhood influences the functional organization of the adult brain. *Brain, 121,* 1053–1064.

Cauty, A. (1984). Taxonomie, syntaxe et economie des numerations parlées. *Amerindia, 9,* 111–146.

Ceci, S. J. (1990). *On intelligence more or less: a bioecological treatise on intellectual development.* Englewood, N.J.: Prentice Hall.

Ceci, S. J. (1991). How much does schooling influence general intelligence and its cognitive components? A reassessment of evidence. *Developmental Psychology, 27,* 703–722.

Ceci, S. J., & Williams, W. M. (1997). Schooling, intelligence and income. *American Psychologist, 52,* 1051–1058.

Chabris, C. F., & Hamilton, S. E. (1992). Hemispheric specialization for skilled perceptual organization by chessmasters. *Neuropsychologia, 30,* 47–57.

Childe, V. G. (1936). *Man makes himself.* London: Watts.

Ciborowski, I. J. (1979). Cross-cultural aspects of cognitive functioning: culture and knowledge. In A. J. Marsella, R. G. Tharp, & T. J. Ciborowski (Eds.), *Perspectives in cross-cultural psychology* (pp. 101–116). New York: Academic Press.

Coltheart, M. (1982). The psycholinguistic analysis of acquired dyslexia: some illustrations. *Philosophical Transactions of the Royal Society of London, Series B, 298,* 151–164.

Cornelious, S. W., & Caspi, A. (1987). Everyday problem solving in adulthood and old age. *Psychology of Aging, 2,* 144–153.

Critchley, M. (1968). Clinical considerations on parietal lobe. In M. Velasco & F. Escobedo (Eds.), *Parietal lobe.* Mexico: Instituto Mexicano de Neurologia,

Dawis, H., & Perusse, R. (1988). Numerical competence in animals: Definitional issues, convent evidence, and a new research agenda. *Behavioral and Brain Sciences, 11,* 561–615.

Dehaene, S. (1997). *The number sense. How the mind creates mathematics.* New York: Oxford University Press.

De Renzi, E. (1982). *Disorders of space exploration and cognition.* New York: Wiley.

De Renzi, E. (1985). Disorder of space exploration. In J. A. M. Frederiks (Ed.), *Handbook of clinical neurology: clinical neuropsychology, vol 45* (pp. 405–422). Amsterdam: Elsevier.

Fuson, K. C. (1988). *Children's counting and the concepts of number.* New York: Springer-Verlag.

Gay, J., & Cole, M. (1967). *The new mathematics and an old culture.* New York: Holt, Rinehart & Winston.

Gerstmann, J. (1940). The syndrome of finger agnosia, disorientation for right and left, agraphia and acalculia. *Archives of Neurology, Neurosurgery and Psychiatry, 44,* 398–408.

Gladwin, T. (1970). *East is a big bird: navigation and logic in Puluwatatoll.* Cambridge, Mass.: Harvard University Press.

Goldblum, M. C., & Matute, E. (1986). Are illiterate people deep dyslexics? *Journal of Neurolinguistics, 2,* 103–114.

Haata, T. (1978). Recognition of Japonese Kanji and Hiragana in the left and right visual fields. *Japonese Psychological Research, 20,* 51–59.

Haata, T. (1992). The effects of Kanji attributes on visual field differences: examination with lexical decision, naming and semantic classification tasks. *Neuropsychologia, 30,* 361–371.

Harris, M. (1989). *Our kind.* New York: Harper & Row.

Hécaen, H. (1962). Clinical symptomatology in right and left hemisphere lesions. In V. B. Mountcastle (Ed.), *Interhemispheric relations and cerebral dominance* (pp. 215–243). Baltimore: Johns Hopkins.

Hécaen, H., & Albert, M. L. (1978). *Human neuropsychology.* New York: Wiley.

Henson, R. A. (1985). Amusia. In J. A. M. Frederiks (Ed.), *Handbook of clinical neurology: clinical neuropsychology, vol 45* (pp. 483–490). Amstrerdam: Elsevier.

Hitch, G., Cundick, J., Haughey, M., Pugh, R., & Wright, H. (1987). Aspects of counting in children's arithmetics. In J. A. Sloboda & D. Rogers (Eds.), *Cognitive processes in mathematics* (pp. 26–41). Oxford: Clearendon Press.

Holmes, G. (1918). Disturbances of visual orientation. *British Journal of Ophthalmology, 2,* 449–486.

Hours, F. (1982). *Les civilisations du Paléolithique.* Paris: Presses Universitaires de la France.

Hudson, W. (1960). Pictorial depth perception in subcultural groups in Africa. *Journal of Social Psychology, 52,* 193–208.

Hudson, W. (1962). Cultural problems in pictorial perception. *South African Journal of Sciences, 58,* 189–195.

Hurford, R. (1987). *Language and number.* Oxford: Basil Blackwell.

Hunter, J. (1986). Cognitive ability, cognitive aptitudes, job knowledge, and job performance. *Journal of Vocational Behavior, 29,* 340–363.

Iwata, M. (1984). Kanji versus Kana: neuropsychological correlates of the Japanese writing system. *Trends in Neurociences, 7,* 290–293.

Koehler, O. (1951). The ability of birds to count. *Bulletin of Animal Behavior, 9,* 41–45.

Laboratory of Comparative Human Cognition. (1983). Culture and cognitive development. In P. Musssen (Ed.), *Handbook of Child Psychology: History, Theory and Methods, Vol 1.* New York: Wiley.

Landis, T., Regard, M., Graves, R., & Goodglass, H. (1983). Semantic paralexia: a release of right hemispheric function from left control. *Neuropsychologia, 21,* 359–364.

Laurendeau-Bendavid, M. (1977). Culture, Schooling and cognitive development: a comparative study of children in French Canada and Rwanda. In P. R. Dasen (Ed.), *Piagetian psychology: cross cultural contributions.* New York: Gardner.

Lecours, A. R., Mehler, J., Parente, M. A., Caldeira, A., Cary, L., Castro, M. J., Dehaout, F., Delgado, R., Gurd, J., Karmann, D., Jakubovitz, R., Osorio, Z., Cabral, L. S., & Junqueira, M. (1987a). Illiteracy and brain damage I: aphasia testing in culturally contrasted populations (control subjects). *Neuropsychologia, 25,* 231–245.

Lecours, A. R., Mehler, J., Parente, M. A., Caldeira, A., Cary, L., Castro, M. J., Dehaout, F., Delgado, R., Gurd, J., Karmann, D., Jakubovitz, R., Osorio, Z., Cabral, L. S., & Junqueira, M. (1987b). Illiteracy and brain damage II: Manifestations of unilateral neglect in testing "auditory comprehension" with iconographic material. *Brain and Cognition, 6,* 243–265.

Lecours, A. R., Mehler, J., Parente, M. A., Beltrami, M. C., Canossa de Tolipan, L., Castro, M. J., Carrono, V., Chagastelles, L., Dehaut, F., Delgado, R., Evangelista, A.,

Fajgenbaum, S., Fontoura, C., de Fraga Karmann, D., Gurd, J., Hierro Torne, C., Jakubovicz, R., Kac, R., Lefevre, B., Lima, C., Maciel, J., Mansur, L., Martinez, R., Nobrega, M. C., Osorio, Z., Paciornik, J., Papaterra, F., Jourdan Penedo, M. A., Saboya, B., Scheuer, C., Batista da Silva, A., Spinardi, M., & Texeira, M. (1988). Illiteracy and brain damage III: A contribution to the study of speech and language disorders in illiterates with unilateral brain damage (initial testing). *Neuropsychologia, 26,* 575–589.

LeDoux, J. E. (1984). Cognitive evolution: clues from brain asymmetry. In A. Ardila & F. Ostrosky (Eds.), *The right hemisphere: neurology and neuropsychology* (pp. 51–60). London: Gordon and Breach Science Publishers.

Lee, R. B., & DeVore, I. (1968). *Man the hunter.* Chicago: Aldine Publishing Company.

León-Portilla, M. (1986). Tiempo y realidad en el pensamiento Maya [Time and reality in Maya thinking]. Mexico: Universidad Nacional Autonoma de Mexico.

Levy-Bruhl, L. (1910/1947). *Las funciones mentales en las sociedades inferiores* [Mental functions in lower societies]. Buenos Aires: Lautaro.

Lukatela, G., & Turvey, M. T. (1990). Phonemic similarity effects and prelexical phonology. *Memory and Cognition, 18,* 128–152.

Luria, A. R. (1966). Differences between disturbances of speech and writing in Russian and in French. *International Journal of Slavic Linguistic Poetics, 3,* 13–22.

Luria, A. R. (1977). *Higher cortical functions in man.* New York: Basic Books.

Manly, J. J., Jacobs, D. M., Sano, M., Bell, K., Merchant, C. A., Small, S. A., & Stern, Y. (1999). Effect of literacy on neuropsychological test performance in non-demented, education-matched elders. *Journal of the International Neuropsychological Society, 5,* 191–202.

Matarazzo, J. D. (1972). *Wechsler's measurement and appraisal of adult intelligence.* New York: Oxford University Press.

Matute, E. (1988). El aprendizaje de la lectoescritura y la especialización hemisférica para el lenguaje [Reading and writing learning, and hemispheric specialization for language]. In A. Ardila & F. Ostrosky-Solis (Eds.), *Lenguaje oral y escrito* [Oral and written language] (pp. 310–358). Mexico: Editorial Trillas.

Mechner, F. (1958). Probability relations within response sequences under ratio reinforcement. *Journal of Experimental Analysis of Behavior, 1,* 109–121.

Morrow, L., & Ratcliff, G. (1988). The neuropsychology of spatial cognition. In J. Stiles-Davis, M. Kritchevsky, & U. Bellugi (Eds.), *Spatial cognition: brain bases and development* (pp. 5–32). Hillsdale, N.J.: Lawrence Erlbaum Associates.

Myambo, K. (1972). Shape constancy as influenced by culture, Western education, and age. *Journal of Cross-Cultural Psychology, 3,* 221–232.

Nakamura, K., Honda, M., Okada, T., Hanakawa, T., Toma, K., Fukuyama, H., Konishi, J., & Shibasaki, H. (2000). Participation of the left posterior inferior temporal cortex in writing and mental recall of Kanji orthography: a functional MRI study. *Brain, 123,* 954–967.

Neisser, U., Boodoo, G., Bouchard, T. J., Boykin, A. W., Brody, N., Ceci, S. J., Halpern, D. F., Loehlin, J. C., Perloff, R., Stenberg, R. J., & Urbina, S. (1996). Intelligence: knowns and unknowns. *American Psychologist, 51,* 77–101.

Newcombe, F., & Ratcliff, G. (1989). Disorders of visuospatial analysis. In H. Goodglass & A. R. Damasio (Eds.), *Handbook of clinical neuropsychology,* vol 2 (pp. 333–356). Amsterdam: Elsevier.

Ostrosky, F., Ardila, A., & Rosselli, M. (1997). *NEUROPSI: Una bateri a neuropsicológica breve* [NEUROPSI; a brief neuropsychological test battery]. Mexico, D.F: Laboratorios Bayer.

Ostrosky, F., Ardila, A., Rosselli, M., López-Arango, G., & Uriel-Mendoza, V. (1998). Neuropsychological test performance in illiterates. *Archives of Clinical Neuropsychology, 13*, 645–660.

Ostrosky, F., Ardila, A., & Rosselli, M. (1999). NEUROPSI: A brief neuropsychological test battery in Spanish. *Journal of the International Neuropsychological Society, 5*, 413–433.

Parker, S. T., & Gibson, K. R. (1979). A developmental model for the evolution of language and intelligence in early hominids. *Behavioral and Brain Sciences, 2*, 367–407.

Paulesu, E., McCrory, E., Fazio, F., Lenocello, L., Brunswich, N., Cappa, S. F., Cotelli, M., Cossu, G., Corte, F., Lorusso, M., Pesenti, S., Gallagher, A., Perani, D., Price, C., Frith, C. D., & Frith, U. (2000). A culture effect on brain function. *Nature Neuroscience, 3*, 91–96.

Pick, A. D., & Pick, H. L. (1978). Culture and perception. In E. C. Carterette & M. P. Friedman (Eds.), *Handbook of perception, vol 10: Perceptual ecology*. New York: Academic Press.

Pontius, A. A. (1995). In similarity judgements hunter-gatherers prefer shapes over spatial relations in contrast to literate groups. *Perceptual and Motor Skills, 81*, 1027–1041.

Premack, D. (1976). *Intelligence in ape and man*. Hillsdale, N.J.: Erlbaum.

Queixalos, F. (1985). L'orientation spatiale dans la grammaire Sikuani. *Journal de la Sociéte des Américanistes, 71*, 115–128.

Queixalos, F. (1989). Numeración tradicional Sikuani [Traditional Sikuani numbering]. *Glotta, 3*, 28–31.

Rastatter, M. P., & Scukanec, G. (1990). Evidence for hemispheric specialization of lexical distinctions in bilingual Chinese-Mandarin speakers. *Cortex, 26*, 423–432.

Rastatter, M. P., Scukanec, G., & Grilliot, J. (1989). Hemispheric specialization for processing Chinese characters: some evidence from lexical decision vocal reaction time. *Perceptual and Motor Skills, 69*, 1083–1089.

Reis, A., & Castro-Caldas, A. (1997). Illiteracy: a cause for biased cognitive development. *Journal of the International Neuropsychological Society, 5*, 444–450.

Rosselli, M. (1986). Conocimiento espacial y sus alteraciones. *Acta Neurológica Colombiana, 2*, 5–10.

Rosselli, M. (1993). Neuropsychology of illiteracy. *Behavioral Neurology, 6*, 107–112.

Rosselli, M., Ardila, A., & Rosas, P. (1990). Neuropsychological assessment in illiterates II: language and praxic abilities. *Brain and Cognition, 12*, 281–296.

Rosselli, M., Rosselli, A., Vergara, I., & Ardila, A. (1985). The topography of the hemi-inattention syndrome. *International Journal of Neuroscience, 20*, 153–160.

Sampson, G. (1985). *Writing systems*. Stanford, Calif.: Stanford University Press.

Sasanuma, S., & Fujimura, O. (1971). Kanji versus Kana processing in alexia with transient agraphia. *Cortex, 7*, 1–18.

Scribner, S., & Cole, M. (1981). *The psychology of literacy*. Cambridge, Mass.: Harvard University Press.

Segall, M. H. (1986). Culture and behavior: psychology in global perspective. *Annual Review of Psychology, 37*, 523–564.

Sugishita, M., Otomo, K., Kabe, S., & Yunoki, K. (1992). A critical appraisal of neu-ropsychological correlates of Japonese ideogram (Kanji) and phonogram reading. *Brain, 115,* 1563–1586.

Swadesh, M. (1967). *El lenguage y la vida humana* [Language and human life]. Mexico city: Fondo de Cultura Económica.

Vygotsky, L. S. (1962). *Thought and language.* Cambridge, Mass.: MIT Press.

Vygotsky, L. S. (1989). Historia del desarrollo de las funciones psíquicas superiores [History of the development of higher psychological processes]. In A. L. Vygotsky, A. Leontiev, & A. R. Luria (Eds.) *El proceso de formación de la psicología marxista* [Process of formation of Marxist psychology] (pp. 156–163). Moscow: Progress.

Washburn, S. L. (1978). The evolution of man. *Scientific American, 239*(3), 194–207.

Wilson, A. O. (1975). *Sociobiology.* Cambridge, Mass.: The Belknap Press of the Harvard University Press.

Woodruff, G., & Premack, D. (1981). Primitive mathematical concepts in the chimpanzee: proportionality and numerosity. *Nature, 293,* 568–570.

Wynn, K. (1990). Children's understanding of counting. *Cognition, 36,* 155–193.

Wynn, K. (1992). Children's acquisition of the number words and counting system. *Cognitive Psychology, 24,* 220–251.

Yamada, J., Imai, H., & Okebe, Y. (1990). The use of the orthographic lexicon in reading kana words. *Journal of General Psychology, 117,* 311–323,

Yamadori, A. (1975). Ideogram reading in alexia. *Brain, 98,* 231–238.

Yamadori, A. (1988). Writing and hemispheric coordination. *Aphasiology, 2,* 427–432.

Yu-Huan, H., Ying-Guan, Q., & Gui-Qing, Z. (1990). Crossed aphasia in Chinese: a clinical survey. *Brain and Language, 39,* 347–356.

5. Art and Brain Evolution

Tabassum Ahmed
Bruce L. Miller

THE DEFINITION OF VISUAL ART

Art is a difficult concept to define and has varied definitions. The word is derived from the Latin *ars*, meaning "skill." A prerequisite of what constitutes "art" is that it is a disciplined activity that leads to a product which should provide in the person who produces it, or in the community who observes it, an experience that is aesthetic, emotional, intellectual, or, often, a combination of the three. Art involves both skill and creative imagination. Although the ancestors of humans produced tools that were valuable in the hunting of animals and in protection from the cold, these items were not produced for aesthetic reasons and thereby do not achieve a modern definition of art.

Human culture plays a key role in the types of art that are produced within a society, and the cultural milieu that surrounds the artist will profoundly influence whether he or she produces realistic or abstract work. This chapter focuses less on the cultural aspects of art and emphasizes its biological underpinnings. We argue that the human brain structure not only allows but, in some individuals, demands the production of art.

THE HISTORICAL ORIGINS OF ART

Visual art emerged on earth approximately 40,000 years ago, as evidenced by the relatively sudden appearance of sculptures, beads, and cave paintings in Europe, Africa, Australia, and the Americas at the campsites of *Homo sapiens* (Grand, 1967). Soon after the appearance of art, early humans began to write. There is little evidence to suggest that any of the previous hominid species had the cognitive capacity or the interest to produce art or writing, two major underpinnings of modern society. This change in the visual and linguistic creativity of modern humans cannot be attributed to an increase in brain volume alone, as the brain size of our evolutionary cousin *Homo neanderthalensis* was slightly larger than the brain volume of the modern human brain. Yet, despite the fact that they produced sophisticated tools (Mithen, 1998), *Homo neanderthalensis* never created art. The emergence of art and writing represented an evolutionary change in the brain of *Homo sapiens*, either the development of new brain regions or altered connectivity between regions of the brain that were already anatomically present (Miller, 1999; LeMay & Geschwind, 1975). The fact that the two emerged so closely together suggests that a similar change may be responsible for both art and writing. There are many reasons to believe that this expansion involved the posterior parietal lobes, the left side for writing and the right side for art.

To understand why art evolved, it is helpful to think about the brain regions required for the production of art in modern humans. To date, most of our understanding of brain and art has been shaped through the study of various patient populations with brain dysfunction or structural lesions in whom artist skills dissipate.

The exact location of a focal brain injury influences both the non-artist's and the artist's ability to create. In recent years, case studies of individuals with Alzheimer's disease who have lost their ability to create art have painted a vivid picture of the role of the parietal lobe in visual art and creativity (Cummings & Zarit, 1987). Conversely, the emergence of artistic ability in the degenerative disorder frontotemporal dementia has provided interesting information about the necessity of the frontal lobes for production of visual art (Miller, Cummings, Boone, Prince, Ponton, & Cotman, 1998; Miller, Boone, Cummings, Read, & Mishkin, 2000). As we describe, recent work from individuals who suffer from focal degenerative brain disorders and paintings from artistic savants offer novel information regarding the anatomical origins of art and creativity.

LOCALIZATION OF ARTISTIC FUNCTION IN THE BRAIN

Art is a complex behavior requiring the integration of multiple brain regions. The left and right hemispheres are responsible for distinctive functions. Most work suggests that the left hemisphere is more important for language-related functions including language output, comprehension, reading, writing, and calculation (Geschwind, 1970), while the right hemisphere is dominant for art (Edwards, 1989), emotion (Davidson, 1992), and visuospatial skills (Heilman & Valenstein, 1972). As will be discussed, the study of individuals with focal brain injury suggests that the process of producing visual art is more lateralized to the right hemisphere, whereas the symbolic component present in many pieces of visual art requires the left hemisphere.

The four different lobes of the brain also carry out different functions in the production of a painting or a sculpture. The frontal lobe is responsible for organization, planning, and motivation; the parietal lobe is responsible for visual construction; the temporal lobe is responsible for visual memory and visual perception; and the occipital lobe is responsible for vision. We emphasize the differing roles that these brain regions play in the artistic process and hypotheses regarding the types of deficits that would be seen with a focal injury. We suggest that painting, drawing, and sculpture will be possible with injury to every brain area except injury to the nondominant parietal lobe. Similarly, a small lesion to the dominant hemisphere angular gyrus will eliminate both reading and writing but will spare spatial abilities (Galaburda, 1993; Benson, 1979).

HOW IS ART AFFECTED WITH FOCAL BRAIN INJURY?

Patients with injury to the nondominant hemisphere, particularly nondominant parietal lobe injury, experience visual neglect, loss of visuospatial skills, and a marked deterioration in the ability to produce realistic visual art (Critchley, 1953; Heilman, Pandya, & Geschwind, 1970). In contrast, patients with dominant frontal and parietal injury experience a loss of attention to visual detail and a loss of conceptual/symbolic art but have a relative sparing of realistic art (Kaczmarek, 1991).

NONDOMINANT HEMISPHERE CONTRIBUTIONS TO ART

The ability to copy internal images into drawings is profoundly altered by injury to the nondominant parietal lobe. Realistic reproduction is lost even in previously accomplished artists (Alajouanine, 1948; Schnider, Regard, Benson, & Landis, 1993). Although these artists may still attempt to produce paintings, the precision, spatial coherence, and realism present in previous paintings are lost. This loss is due to a variety of factors relating to spatial cognition. Neglect of the contralateral visual space leads to drawings where the left half of the space is unused or only sketchily drawn (Heilman & Valenstein, 1972). The nondominant parietal lobe is essential for the representation of the contralateral visual space, and when it is injured subjects have difficulty conjuring up an image of the left side of the world. Furthermore, new research suggests that the right parietal lobe is essential for encoding remote spatial memories (Teng Stefanacci, Squime, Zola, 2000), memories that are often reproduced in a painting. Finally, with injury to the right parietal lobe, the simple process of copying or putting together two- or three-dimensional structures is impaired. The nondominant hemisphere, in particular the nondominant posterior parietal lobe, is necessary for the realistic art that was produced for the first time 40,000 years ago.

LEFT HEMISPHERE CONTRIBUTION TO ART

Less is known regarding the role of the dominant (left) hemisphere in the production of art, and it is possible to suffer a left hemisphere infarct and continue to produce precise copies of objects or paintings. In 1948, Alajouanine offered one of the first accounts on the effects of left hemisphere damage in previously productive artists. He described how aphasia-producing lesions in the brains of a writer, a musician, and a painter affected their creative output (Alajouanine, 1948). Alajouanine observed that in contrast to the musician and writer, the painter maintains his artistic ability despite the onset of Wernicke's aphasia, aphasia associated with left posterior temporal and often parietal injury

(Alajouanine, 1948). Surprisingly, he suggested that the visual artist experienced an even greater ability to create after the lesion (Alajouanine, 1948).

There does appear to be an important dominant hemisphere contribution to art, however, and in several reports, artists who suffered a left hemisphere stroke lost the ability to produce symbolic paintings. Kaczmarek (1991) reported a painter who after sustaining a left hemisphere stroke resulting in aphasia and hemiparesis preserved his ability to produce realistic art but lost the ability to represent symbolism in paintings. Similarly, Gardner (1982) observed that artists who sustained left hemisphere damage often changed their artistic style but maintained their abilities to reproduce realistic paintings. These findings are congruent with research conducted by Zaidel and Kasher (1989), whose experiments tested the difference between hemispheric processing of surrealistic versus realistic paintings in normal individuals. They showed that the left hemisphere was better at recognizing surrealistic paintings than the right hemisphere, suggesting that different regions of the brain are responsible for processing different styles of art. They suggested that symbolic painting may be related to language, reflecting similar storage and retrieval strategies utilized by the left hemisphere (Zaidel & Kasher, 1989). The left hemisphere remains important for the conceptual and verbal aspects of visual art.

A talented artist uses both hemispheres in the creation of a successful artistic product. Even a realistic artist like Norman Rockwell uses symbolism, linguistic concepts, and abstract ideas in the final product. As will be described, however, in patients who suffer from left hemisphere brain degeneration, the unleashing of an interest in art that was not present prior to the injury is possible.

DEGENERATIVE DISEASE AND ART

Two degenerative dementias, Alzheimer's disease and frontotemporal dementia, reveal contrasting ways through which focal brain injury can influence artistic expression. With Alzheimer's disease, there is a relentless loss of visuoconstructive ability (Cummings & Zarit, 1987). Drawings become distorted, with diminished accuracy and spatial perspective. These losses coincide with dysfunction in small regions of the right parietal lobe. In contrast, with frontotemporal dementia the ability to copy is relatively preserved (Miller et al., 1998). This suggests that injury to small regions in the right posterior parietal lobe eliminate drawing, whereas huge expanses of the frontal lobes can be lost without impairing visual reproduction of art.

Even though creativity disappears in most patients with frontotemporal dementia, the ability to draw is preserved late into the course of the illness. This suggests that evolution of the frontal lobes by itself does not explain the emergence of art in prehistoric times. Furthermore, in one anatomical subtype of frontotemporal dementia, patients with left anterior temporal degeneration, visual creativity often develops *de novo* (Miller et al., 1998; Miller et al., 2000). We have described individuals without previous artistic ability who suddenly began painting in the setting of anterior temporal lobe degeneration. The art in these individuals is realistic and nonsymbolic, with paintings of scenes or animals common. Yet, despite the absence of symbolism, the work can be visually appealing and successful. We have hypothesized that both visual perception and visual interest are enhanced by injury to the left anterior temporal lobe, the brain region responsible for access to semantic information.

In summary, studies of patients with structural and functional brain injury suggest that the right parietal lobe is necessary for accessing and producing the visual images required for visuoconstructive skills employed during multiple artistic tasks. An intact left hemisphere, on the other hand, is required for the conceptual symbolic component of visual art. Is there a visual art region in the brain that is chronically inhibited by the dominant hemisphere that can be released in certain conditions? As we describe, young children with no artistic training can produce art without any previous training.

ARTISTIC SAVANTS

There have been a handful of individuals from different times, cultures, continents, and languages who have produced superb art in the setting of autism. These children, called savants, isolated from the rest of the world by profound social and linguistic impairment, seem to turn on an art production system in the brain that lies dormant in the rest of us. The remarkable stories of these children have been reviewed (Selfe, 1978; Sacks, 1995; Treffert 1989; Hou, Miller, Cummings, Goldberg, Benson, & Bottino, 2000). Often in a spontaneous fashion at an age as early as 18 months, these children begin to produce realistic pictures of animals, horses, insects, or buildings in an obsessive fashion. Typically, the artistic process is sustained for hours every day, and interruption of the child's drawing leads to violent protestation. The North American savants Nadia and Dane both produced images of horses in motion. Dane started drawing horses with crayons prior to two years of age. Obsessed with the topic, he spent many hours drawing horses on anything visible in his environment, even books, walls, and floors. Dane and Nadia's paintings show startling similarities with each other and with prehistoric cave drawings. Even though neither child spent much time with horses, both chose to draw this animal. Their work emerged independently, with neither receiving any formal training. Both produced realistic and nonsymbolic art by pulling images of horses from the brain and placing them on the canvas.

What these savants tell us about art is that the ability to draw beautiful paintings of animals is independent of culture and can be accomplished at an early age by children isolated from the world both linguistically and socially through autism. The wiring for art has been set in the human brain and lies dormant ready for expression. The prolific expression that is evident in the savants and patients with left anterior temporal lobe degeneration suggests that we may have artistic brain regions that are suppressed by language areas. Perhaps language areas present in the left anterior temporal lobe suppress right hemisphere approaches to the world including drawing and painting.

WHY CAVE PAINTINGS?

We believe that *Homo sapiens* increased the connectivity and volume of the posterior parietal lobe as a precursor to the emergence of art and writing. The findings from artists with brain damage, in addition to the information from patients with frontotemporal dementia and Alzheimer's disease, and artistic savants provide us with a window to understand how the brain processes and produces art. The information from modern patient populations sheds light on the probable regions that emerged in the brains of the anatomically modern humans that facilitated their artistic creativity.

REFERENCES

Alajouanine, T. (1948). Aphasia and Artistic Realization. *Brain, 71*, 229–241.

Benson, D. F. (1979). *Aphasia, alexia and agraphia.* New York: Churchill Livingstone.

Broca, P. (1865). Sur la faculte du langage articule. *Paris Bull Soc Anthr, 6*, 337–393.

Critchley, M. (1953). *The parietal lobes.* London: E. Arnold.

Cummings, J. L., & Zarit, J. M. (1987). Probable Alzheimer's disease in an artist. *JAMA, 258*, 2731–2734.

Davidson, R. J. (1992). Anterior cerebral asymmetry and the dominance of emotion. *Brain and Cogniton, 20*, 125–151.

Edwards, B. (1989). *Drawing on the right side of the brain.* New York: G. E. Putnam.

Galaburda, A. (1993). Neurology of development dyslexia. *Vision and Optometry Science, 70*, 343–347.

Gardner, H. (1982). *Art, Mind and Brain.* New York: Basic Books.

Geschwind, N. (1970). The organization of language in the brain. *Science, 170*, 940–944.

Grand, P. M. (1967). *Prehistoric art. Paleolithic painting and sculpture.* Greenwich, Conn: New York Graphic Society.

Heilman, K. M., Pandya, D. N., & Geschwind, N. (1970). Trimodal inattention following parietal lobe ablations. *Transactions of the American Neurological Association, 95*, 259–261.

Heilman, K. M., & Valenstein, E. (1972). Frontal lobe neglect in man. *Neurology, 22*, 660–664.

Hou, C., Miller, B. L., Cummings, J. L., Goldberg, M., Benson, D. F., & Bottino, V. (2000). Artistic savants. *Neuropsychiatry, Neuropsychology & Behavioral Neurology, 13* (1), 29–38.

Kaczmarek, B. L. J. (1991). Aphasia in an artist: a disorder of symbolic processing. *Aphasiology, 5*, 361–371.

LeMay, M., & Geschwind, N. (1975). Hemispheric differences in the brains of great apes. *Brain Behavior and Evolution, 11*(1), 48–52.

Miller, D. (1999). Cave art an early example of information processing. *MD Computing,* January/February, 56–59.

Miller, B. L., Cummings, J. L. Mishkin, F., Boone, K., Prince, F., Ponton, M., & Cotman, C. (1998). Emergence of artistic talent in frontotemporal dementia. *Neurology, 51,* 978–981.

Miller, B. L., Boone, K., Cummings, J., Read, S. L., & Mishkin, F. (2000). Functional correlates of musical and visual talent in frontotemporal dementia. *British Journal of Psychiatry, 176,* 458–463.

Mithen, S. (Ed.) (1998). *Creativity in human evolution and prehistory.* London and New York: Routledge.

Sacks, O. (1995). *An anthropologist on Mars.* New York: Vintage Books.

Schnider, A., Regard, M., Benson, D. F., & Landis, T. (1993). Effects of a right-hemisphere stroke on an artist's performance. *Neuropsychiatry, Neuropsychology & Behavioral Neurology, 6,* 249–255.

Snyder, A. W., & Mitchell, D. J. (1999). Is integer arithmetic fundamental to mental processing? The mind's secret arithmetic. *Proceedings of the Royal Society of London Series B: Biological Sciences, 266*(1419), 587–592.

Selfe, L. (1978). *Nadia: a case of extraordinary drawing ability in an autistic child.* New York: Academic Press.

Teng, E., & Squire, L. R. (1999). Memory for places learned long ago is intact after hippocampal damage. *Nature, 400*(6745):675–677.

Teng, E., Stefanacci, L., Squire, L. R., & Zola, S. M. (2000). Contrasting effects on discrimination learming after hippocampal lesions and conjoint hippocampal candele lesions in monkeys. *Neuroscience, 20,* 3853–3863.

Treffert, D. (1989). *Extraordinary people.* New York: Harper & Row.

Zaidel, D. W., & Kasher, A. (1989). Hemispheric memory for surrealistic versus realistic paintings. *Cortex, 25*(4), 617–641.

Part III: Cultural Perspective of Human Development

6. Origins of Cross-Cultural Similarities and Differences in Human Behavior: An Ecocultural Perspective

John W. Berry

An ecocultural perspective on human diversity has been advocated by me for thirty-five years (Berry, 1966). It has evolved through a series of research studies devoted to understanding similarities and differences in cognition and social behavior (Berry, 1976; Berry, van de Koppell, Sénéchal, et al., 1986; Berry, Bennett, & Denny, 2000; Mishra, Sinha, & Berry, 1996). The core ideas have a long history (Jahoda, 1995) and have become assembled into conceptual frameworks (Berry, 1975, 1995) used in empirical research and in coordinating textbooks in cross-cultural psychology (Berry, Poortinga, Segall, & Dasen, 1992/2002; Segall, Dasen, Berry, & Poortinga, 1990/1999). Similar ideas and frameworks have been advanced both by anthropologists (e.g., Whiting, 1974) and psychologists (e.g., Bronfenbrenner, 1979) who share the view that human activity can be understood only within the context in which it develops and takes place.

The ecocultural perspective is rooted in two basic assumptions, both deriving from Darwinian thought. The first (the "universalist" assumption) is that all human societies exhibit commonalities ("cultural universals") and that basic psychological *processes* are shared, species-common characteristics of all human beings on which culture plays infinite variations during the course of development and daily activity. The second (the "adaptation" assumption) is that *behavior* is differentially developed and expressed in response to ecological and cultural contexts. This view allows for comparisons across cultures (on the basis of the common underlying process) but makes comparison worthwhile (using the surface variation as basic evidence). Whether derived from anthropology (e.g., Murdock, 1975) or sociology (e.g., Aberle et al., 1950), there is substantial evidence that groups everywhere possess shared sociocultural attributes. For example, all peoples have language, tools, social structures (e.g., norms, roles), and social institutions (e.g., marriage, justice). It is also evident that such underlying commonalities are expressed by groups in vastly different ways from one time and place to another. Similarly, there is parallel evidence, at the psychological level, for both underlying similarity and surface variation (Berry, Dasen, &

Saraswathi, 1997). For example, all individuals have the competence to develop, learn, and perform speech, technology, role playing, and norm observance. At the same time, there are obviously vast group and individual differences in the extent and style of expression of these shared underlying processes. This combination of underlying similarity with surface expressive variation has been given the name "universal" by Berry and associates (1992) to distinguish it from two other theoretical views: "absolutism" denies cultural influence on behavioral development and expression, whereas "relativism" denies the existence of common underlying psychological process. Of course, although variations in behavioral expression can be directly observed, underlying commonalities are a theoretical construction and cannot be observed directly (Troadec, 2001). Paradoxically, this search for our common humanity can be pursued only by observing our diversity. And this dual task is the essence of cross-cultural psychology (Berry, 1969, 2000; Bril, 1995).

Following is an outline of our current thinking about how people adapt culturally (as a group) to their longstanding ecological settings and a proposal about how people develop and perform (as individuals) in adaptation to their ecocultural situation.

ECOLOGICAL AND CULTURAL ADAPTATION

One continuing theme in cultural anthropology is that cultural variations may be understood as adaptations to differing ecological settings or contexts (Boyd & Richerson, 1983). This line of thinking, usually known as *cultural ecology* (Vayda & Rappoport, 1968), *ecological anthropology* (Moran, 1982; Vayda & McKay, 1975), or *the ecosystem* approach (Moran, 1990) to anthropology, has a long history in the discipline (see Feldman, 1975). Its roots go back to Forde's (1934) classic analysis of relationships between physical habitat and societal features in Africa, and Kroeber's (1939) early demonstration that cultural areas and natural areas co-vary in Aboriginal North America. Unlike earlier simplistic assertions by the school of "environmental determinism" (e.g., Huntington, 1945), the ecological school of thought has ranged from "possiblism" (where the environment provides opportunities and sets some constraints or limits on the range of possible cultural forms that may emerge) to an emphasis on "resource utilization" (where active and interactive relationships between human populations and their habitat are analyzed).

Of particular interest to psychologists was Steward's (1955) use of what was later called the *cognized environment*; this concept refers to the "selected features of the environment of greatest relevance to a population's subsistence." With this notion, ecological thinking moved simultaneously away from any links to earlier deterministic views and toward the psychological idea of individuals actively perceiving, appraising, and changing their environments.

The earlier ecological approaches have tended to view cultural systems as relatively stable (even permanent) *adaptations* (as a state), ignoring *adaptation* (as a process) or *adaptability* (as a system characteristic) of cultural populations (Bennett, 1976). It is clear, however, that cultures evolve over time, sometimes in response to changing ecological circumstances and sometimes as a result of contact with other cultures. This fact has required the addition of a more dynamic conception of ecological adaptation as a continuous, as well as an interactive process (between ecological, cultural, and psychological variables). It is from the most recent position that we approach the topic. It is a view that is consistent with more recent general changes in anthropology, away from a "museum" orientation to culture (collecting and organizing static artifacts) to one that emphasizes cultures as constantly changing, and being concerned with creation, metamorphosis, and recreation.

Over the years, ecological thinking has influenced not only anthropology, but also psychology. The fields of ecological and environmental psychology have become fully elaborated (see Werner, Brown, & Altman, 1997), with substantial theoretical and empirical foundations. In essence, individual human behavior has come to be seen in its natural setting or habitat, both in terms of its development and its contemporary display. The parallel development of cross-cultural psychology (see Berry et al., 1997) has also "naturalized" the study of human behavior and its development. In this field, individual behavior is accounted for to a large extent by considering the role of cultural influences on it. In my own approach, ecological as well as cultural influences are considered as operating in tandem, hence the term *ecocultural* approach.

AN ECOCULTURAL APPROACH

The current version of the ecocultural framework (see Figure 6.1) proposes to account for human psychological diversity (both individual and group similarities and differences) by taking into account two fundamental sources of influence (ecological and sociopolitical) and two features of human populations that are adapted to them: cultural and biological characteristics. These population variables are transmitted to individuals by various "transmission variables," such as enculturation, socialization, genetics, and acculturation. Both cultural and genetic transmission have been strongly advanced by recent work on culture learning (e.g., Tomasello, Kruger, & Ratner, 1993) and on the human genome project (e.g., Paabo, 2001). The essence of both these domains is the fundamental similarity of all human beings, combined with variaton in the expression of these shared attributes. Work on acculturation has also been advancing (e.g., Marin, Balls-Organista, & Chung, 2001) due to the dramatic increases in intercultural contact and change.

Overall, the ecocultural framework considers human diversity (both cultural and psychological) to be set of collective and individual adaptations to context. Within this general perspective, it views cultures as evolving adaptations to ecological and sociopolitical influences, and it views individual psychological characteristics in a population as adaptive to their cultural context as well as to

the broader ecological and sociopolitical influences. It also views (group) culture
and (individual) behavior as distinct phenomena that need to be examined independently (see discussion below).

Within psychology, the early ecological work of Barker and Brunswik and the
findings of the burgeoning field of environmental psychology have attempted to
specify the links between ecological context and individual human development
and behavior. Cross-cultural psychology has tended to view cultures (both one's
own and others one is in contact with) as *differential contexts* for development,
and to view behavior as adaptive to these different contexts.

The ecocultural approach offers a "value neutral" framework for describing
and interpreting similarities and differences in human behavior across cultures
(Berry, 1994). As adaptive to context, psychological phenomena can be understood "in their own terms" (as Malinowski insisted), and external evaluations can
usually be avoided. This is a critical point, since it allows for the conceptualization, assessment, and interpretation of culture and behavior in non-ethnocentric
ways (Dasen, 1993). It explicity rejects the idea that some cultures or behaviors
are more advanced or more developed than others (Berry, Dasen, & Witkin, 1983;
Dasen, Berry, & Witkin, 1979). Any argument about cultural or behavioral
differences being ordered hierarchically requires the adoption of some absolute

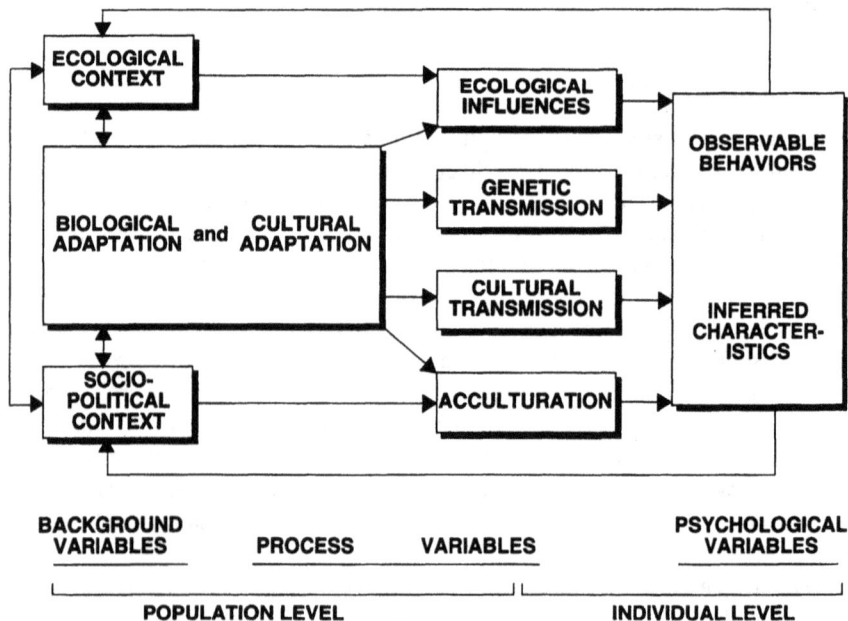

Figure 6.1
An ecocultural framework linking ecology, cultural adaptation,
and individual behavior

(usually external) standard. But who is so bold or so wise to assert and verify such a standard?

Finally, the sociopolitical context brings about contact among cultures, so that individuals have to adapt to more than one context. When many cultural contexts are involved (as in situations of culture contact and acculturation), psychological phenomena can be viewed as attempts to deal simultaneously with two (sometimes inconsistent, sometimes conflicting) cultural contexts, rather than by pathologizing colonized or immigrant cultures and peoples. These intercultural settings need to be approached with the same non-ethnocentric perspective as *cross-cultural* ones (Berry, 1985).

STUDIES OF PERCEPTION AND COGNITION

Initially (Berry, 1966), the link between ecology, culture, and behavior was elaborated into a framework in order to predict differential development of visual disembedding and analytic and spatial abilities between hunting-based and agriculture-based peoples. The first step was to propose that the "ecological demands" for survival that were placed on hunting peoples were for a high level of these perceptual–cognitive abilities, in contrast with people employing other (particularly agricultural) subsistence strategies. Second, it was proposed that " cultural aids" (such as socialization practices, linguistic differentiation of spatial information, and the use of arts and crafts) would promote the development of these abilities. As predicted, empirical studies of Inuit (then called Eskimo) in the Canadian Arctic and Temne in Sierra Leone revealed marked differences in these abilities. Further studies were carried out, and during the course of this empirical work the ideas became further elaborated into an ecocultural framework. In each case, a consideration of ecological and cultural features of the group were taken as a basis for predicting differential psychological outcomes in a variety of domains. For example (Berry, 1967, 1979), differential degrees of reliance on hunting and of social stratification (ranging from "loose" to "tight"; Pelto, 1968) and variations in child socialization practices (ranging from emphases on "assertion" to "compliance"; Barry, Child, & Bacon, 1959) were used to predict variations in the development of these functional abilities.

Further work on perceptual and cognitive abilities (aligned in part to the theory of psychological differentiation, particularly the cognitive style of field dependence—field independence; Witkin & Berry, 1975) resulted in three volumes (Berry, 1976; Berry, van der Koppel, Sénéchal, Annis, Bahuchet, Cavalli-Sforza, & Witkin, 1986; Mishra, Sinha, & Berry, 1996) reporting results of studies in the Arctic, Africa, Australia, New Guinea, and India.

The ecocultural framework has also been used to understand sources of variation in perceptual–cognitive development (Dasen, 1975; Nsamenang, 1992). This focus has clear relations to an increasing interest in cross-cultural psychology in indigenous conceptions of cognitive competence and in the cognitive tasks faced by people in daily life (e.g., Berry & Irvine, 1986; Berry, Irvine, & Hunt,

1988). In this work, it is argued that the indigenous conceptions of competence need to be uncovered; competencies are to be seen as developments nurtured by activities of daily life ("bricolage"), and as adaptive to ecological context. Understanding the indigenous conceptions, the cognitive values, the daily activities, and the contexts is an essential prerequisite for valid cognitive assessment. Once again, as for the cross-cultural and intercultural research strategies, these indigenous (within-culture) studies need to be carried out from a non-ethnocentric standpoint (e.g., Berry & Bennett, 1992).

DIMENSIONS OF ECOLOGICAL AND CULTURAL VARIATION

In order to conceptualize a number of possible human adaptations to varying habitats, a unidimensional ecocultural dimension was developed and operationalized (Berry, 1966, 1976) over the range of subsistence economic activities from hunters to agriculturalists. About the same time Lomax and Berkowitz (1972) found evidence for *two independent factors* of cultural variation over the ecological range, from gatherers through hunters to agriculturalists to urban dwellers: they called these "differentiation" and "integration." The first refers to the number and kinds of role distinctions made in the society, whereas the second refers to the "groupiness" or degree of cohesion among members of a society, to their solidarity, and to the social coordination of their day-to-day activities. While there are two independent dimensions, over the *middle range* of subsistence strategies the two dimensions are *positively correlated*. It is precisely at this middle range (hunters to agriculturalists) that my earlier (1966, 1976) conceptualization and operationalization took place. Thus, the unidimensional nature of my earlier ecocultural dimension was not fundamentally in error; it was just restricted in range. A more general conceptualization, able to take into account gatherers and urban societies, would need to adopt the two-dimensional view of ecological and cultural variation.

In a series of papers, Boldt and colleagues (Boldt, 1976; Boldt & Roberts, 1979; Roberts, Boldt, & Guest, 1990) have pursued the possibility that there are indeed two independent dimensions (see also Gamble & Ginsberg, 1981). They argue that "structural complexity" and "structural tightness" need to be distinguished. The first refers to the number and diversity of roles in society, which "should expand the range of courses of action available to an actor, and therefore, enhance choice and individual autonomy" (Roberts et al., 1990, p. 69). The second refers to the degree to which social expectations are imposed on individuals, which should "reduce an actor's autonomy by narrowing the opportunities for negotiating a preferred course of action" (ibid., p. 69).

This structural complexity–structural tightness distinction corresponds to the differentiation–integration distinction of Lomax and Berkowitz (1972). At the same time it breaks into two components the more general sociocultural indexes such as "cultural complexity" (McNett, 1970), "tightness-looseness" (Pelto,

1968), and the ecocultural index of Berry (1976). More specifically, for the eco-cultural index, it places the ecological variables of settlement pattern and mean size of local community together with the cultural variable of political stratifica-tion into one construct ("structural complexity"), but puts the other cultural variables of social stratification and socialization emphases on compliance into another construct ("structural tightness").

Triandis (1994) has introduced the concept of "cultural syndromes" that draws together some of these cultural dimensions. He has adopted the "tight–loose" and the "cultural complexity" notions and incorporated them into a framework linking them to the psychological dimension(s) of "individualism and collectivism." This framework moves the focus away from cognitive behaviors, toward social behavior, particularly to an interest in how, and how much, individuals become embedded in their social context. This area is now considered briefly.

STUDIES OF SOCIAL BEHAVIOR

While most use of the ecocultural framework has been in the study of percep-tion and cognition, it has also been useful to explore aspects of social behavior. For example, studies of social conformity (Berry, 1967, 1979) have shown that greater conformity to a suggested group norm is likely in cultures that are struc-turally tight (with high norm obligation). The relationship is robust, whether examined at the level of individuals or by using the group's mean score as the variable related to ecology (see Bond & Smith, 1996, for a review). A further example proposes links between ecocultrual indicators and the currently popular concepts of "individualism" and "collectivism" (Berry, 1993). It is suggested that individualism may be related to the differentiation (structural complexity) dimen-sions, with greater differentiation in a society being predictive of greater personal individualism. However, collectivism is proposed to be related more to the integration (structural tightness) dimensions, with greater integration predictive of greater collectivism. It is further suggested that when individualism and col-lectivism are found to be at opposite ends of one value dimension, it is because data are usually obtained in societies (industrial urban) where the two cultural dimensions (differentiation and integration) are strongly distinguished; if data were to be collected in other types of societies (e.g., hunting or agricultural) where the two dimensions coincide, then this value opposition or incompatibility may not be observed.

Current work (Georgas & Berry, 1995; Georgas, van de Vijver, & Berry, 2000) further extends this interest in social aspects of behavior. The first study sought to discover ecological and social indicators that might allow societies to be clus-tered according to their similarities and differences on six dimensions: ecology, education, economy, mass communications, population, and religion. The second study further examined ecosocial indicators across cultures and then sought evidence of their relationships with a number of psychological variables (such as values). Results showed that many of the indicators came together to form a single economic dimension (termed "Affluence"), and this was distinct from "Religion" in the pattern of relationships with the psychological variables. Specifically, across cultures, a high placement on Affluence (along with Protestant Religion) was associated with more emphasis on individualism, utilitarianism, and personal well-being. In contrast, for other religions, together with low Affluence, there was an emphasis on power, loyalty, and hierarchy values.

THEORETICAL ISSUES

Two basic assumptions of the ecocultural approach were articulated at the outset: universalism and adaptation. While no claim can be made that these two assumptions have been established, they have served as a useful and important heuristic in the field (see Troadec, 2001). One other theorectical issue has not yet been addressed: Is "culture" conceptualized as an "independent "or as an "organismic" variable in the framework? My answer (Berry, 2000) is that it is both.

To justify this view, it is helpful to recall the argument (Kroeber, 1917) that culture is "superorganic," "super" meaning above and beyond, and "organic," referring to its individual biological and psychological bases. Two arguments were presented by Kroeber for the independent existence of culture at its own level. First, particular individuals come and go, but cultures remain more or less stable. This is a remarkable phenomenon; despite a large turnover in membership with each new generation, cultures and their institutions remain relatively unchanged. Thus, a culture does not depend on particular individuals for its existence, but has a life of its own at the collective level of the group. The second argument is that no single individual "possesses" all of the "culture" of the group to which he or she belongs; the culture as a whole is carried by the collectivity, and indeed is likely to be beyond the biological or psychological capacity (to know or to do) of any single person in the group. For example, no single person knows all the laws, political institutions, and economic structures that constitute even this limited sector of his or her culture.

For both these reasons, Kroeber considered that cultural phenomena are collective phenomena, above and beyond the individual person, and hence his term "superorganic." This position is an important one for cross-cultural psychology because it permits us to employ the group–individual distinction in attempting to link the two and possibly to trace the influence of cultural factors on individual psychological development.

From the superorgainc perspective, which notes that culture exists prior to any particular individual, we can consider culture as "lying in wait" to pounce on new comers (be they infants or immigrants) and to draw them into its fold by the processes of cultural transmission and acculturation (see Figure 6.1). Hence, we can claim that culture is, in important ways, an *independent variable* (or more accurately, a complex set of inter-related independent variables).

These same two transmission processes, however, lead to the incorporation of culture into the individual, and hence culture also becomes an *organismic variable*. It is simultaneously outside and inside the individual. Being both "out there" and "in here" (Berry, 2000), the interactive, mutually influencing, character of culture–behavior relationships becomes manifest. This view is indicated by the feedback loop shown in Figure 6.1, where individuals are in a position to influence, change, and even destroy their ecosystem and cultural accomplishments.

METHODOLOGICAL ISSUES

The view that cultural and behavioral phenomena can be conceptualized and measured in their own right has some methodological implications. We can distinguish between two levels of observation (cultural/individual); we can also distinguish between two levels of analysis of the data obtained by such observations. In Figure 6.2, these two issues are presented in relation to each other. For each, the distinction between the cultural (population) level and the individual level is made, producing a classification of four methodological types of cross-cultural studies.

In the first type, the data are collected at the cultural level, usually by anthropologists using ethnographic methods, and are interpreted at that level, leading to the typical ethnographic report. These cultural observations can also be related to each other, comparing various customs or institutions across cultures, leading to holocultural studies (e.g., using the HRAF).

In the second type, the data are collected at the individual level (e.g., using interviews, questionnaires, etc.) with samples of people in a population. These data are then used to create scores for each culture, by aggregation, from the individual responses. Here the level of observation is the individual, but the level of analysis is the culture. Culture (or country) scores can claim to represent the population if individual data are from representative samples of individuals. Such country scores can be related to other aggregated scores, or to (independent) country indicators, such as GNP. These aggregated country scores are sometimes used in correlations with individual scores on very similar scales (e.g., in countries high on Collectivism, individuals usually score high on a Collectivism scale). This practice may lack sufficient independence in conceptualization and measurement to be entirely valid.

LEVEL OF ANALYSIS	LEVEL OF OBSERVATION	
	CULTURAL	INDIVIDUAL
CULTURAL	1. HOLOCULTURAL (e.g., HRAF)	2. AGGREGATION (e.g., Values)
INDIVIDUAL	4. ECOCULTURAL (e.g., cognitive style)	3. INDIVIDUAL DIFFERENCE (e.g., traits, abilities)

Figure 6.2
Classification of types of cross-cultural studies

In the third type of study, data are collected at the individual level and remain at that level for analysis. These are the common *individual difference* kind of studies used by psychology more generally. Often mean scores are calculated, or the relationships among scores (or other variables, such as schooling) are correlated or factor analyzed. When cross-cultural comparisons are made, they are usually of these mean scores, sometimes taken to represent only the sample, but also sometimes taken to represent the culture as a whole. If factors are produced, comparisons of the factors are made, usually to establish equivalence or provide evidence of bias. Studies of personality traits are of this type.

The fourth type represents a hybrid, combining elements of the first and third types. Here, cultural level findings (the first type, from ethnographic sources) are taken and examined for their relationships with individual level data (from the third type, individual difference studies). Sampling of cultures can provide a range of variation in contexts and allow the prediction of variation (similarities and differences) in individual psychological development. Since the two sets of data are independent of each other (due to their different levels of observation and analysis), it is valid to examine relationships between them. Examples of these are the ecocultural studies of cognitive style and conformity, mentioned earlier.

SUMMARY AND CONCLUSION

In this chapter, I have addressed the question of the origins of similarities and differences in human behavior across cultures. I have argued that we can go a long way to providing an answer if we adopt an ecocultural perspective, in which we assume that psychological processes are "universal" in the species and that behaviors are "adaptive" to context. Within such a framework, we can conceptualize cultural and individual behavior as separate phenomena: culture exists apart from particular individuals but becomes incorporated into all individuals through two transmission processes. Hence, culture is both an independent and an organismic variable in such a framework. Given this conception, it is possible to carry out empirical work at the two levels. Analyses can be conducted within levels (the classical ethnographic and individual difference studies), or cultural-level data can be used to predict individual and group similarities and differences in behavior. This last strategy is both "cultural" and "comparative," allowing for the "cross-cultural" understanding of human diversity.

REFERENCES

Aberle, D. F., Cohen, A. K., Levy, M. J., & Sutton, F. X. (1950). Funtional prerequisites of society. *Ethics, 60,* 100–111.

Barry, H., Child, I., & Bacon, M. (1959). Relations of child training to subsistence economy. *American Anthropologist, 61,* 51–63.

Bennett, J. (1976). *The ecological transition.* London: Pergamon.

Berry, J. W. (1966). Temne and Eskimo perceptual skills. *International Journal of Psychology, 1*, 207–229.

Berry, J. W. (1967). Independence and conformity in subsistence-level societies. *Journal of Personality and Social Psychology, 7*, 415–418.

Berry, J. W. (1969). On cross-cultural comparability. *International Journal of Psychology, 4*, 119–128.

Berry, J. W. (1975). An ecological approach to cross-cultural psychology. *Nederlands Tijdschrift voor de Psychologie, 30*, 51–84.

Berry, J. W. (1976). *Human ecology and cognitive style: comparative studies in cultural and psychological adaptation.* New York: Sage/Halsted.

Berry, J. W. (1979). A cultural ecology of social behaviour. In L. Berkowitz (Ed.), *Advances in experimental social psychology, Vol. 12*, (pp. 177–206). New York: Academic Press.

Berry, J. W. (1985). Cultural psychology and ethnic psychology. In I. Reyes Lagunes & Y. Poortinga (Eds.), *From a different perspective* (pp. 3–15). Lisse: Swets & Zeitlinger.

Berry, J. W. (1993). Ecology of individualism and collectivism. In U. Kim et al. (Eds.), *Individualism and collectivism* (pp. 77–84). London: Sage.

Berry, J. W. (1994). An ecological approach to cultural and ethnic psychology. In E. Trickett (Ed.), *Human Diversity* (pp. 115–141). San Friancisco: Jossey-Bass.

Berry, J. W. (1995). The descendants of a model. *Culture & Psychology, 1*, 373–380.

Berry, J. W. (2000). Cross-cultural psychology: a symbiosis of cultural and comparative approaches. *Asian Journal of Social Psychology, 3*, 197–205.

Berry, J. W., Dasen, P. R., & Saraswathi, T. S. N. (Eds.) (1997). *Handbook of cross-cultural psychology, 3 volumes.* Boston: Allyn & Bacon.

Berry, J. W., & Bennett, J. A. (1992). Cree conceptions of cognitive competence. *International Journal of Psychology, 27*, 73–88.

Berry, J. W., Bennett, J. A., & Denny, J. P. (2000). Ecology, culture and cognitive processing. Paper presented at IACCP congress, Pultusk, Poland.

Berry, J. W., Dasen, P. R., & Witkin, H. A. (1983). Developmental theories in cross-cultural perspective. In L. Alder (Ed.), *Cross-cultural research at issue* (pp. 13–21). New York: Academic Press.

Berry, J. W., & Irvine, S. H. (1986). Bricolage: savages do it daily. In R. Sternberg & R. Wagner (Eds.), *Practical intelligence: nature and origins of competence in the everyday world* (pp. 2271–2306). New York: Cambridge University Press.

Berry, J. W., Irvine, S. H., & Hunt, E. B. (Eds.) (1988). *Indigenous cognition: functioning in cultural context.* Dordrecht: Ninjhoff.

Berry, J. W., van de Koppel, J. M. H., Sénéchal, C., Annis, R. C., Bahuchet, S., Cavalli-Sforza, L. L., & Witkin, H. A. (1986). *On the edge of the forest: cultural adaptation and cognitive development in Central Africa.* Lisse: Swets and Zeitlinger.

Berry, J. W., Poortinga, H. H., Segall, M. H., & Dasen, P. R. (1992). *Cross-cultural psychology: research and applications.* New York: Cambridge University Press.

Boldt, E. D. (1976). Acquiescence and conventionality in a communal society. *Journal of Cross-Cultural Psychology, 7*, 21, 36.

Boldt, E. D., & Roberts, L. W. (1979). Structural tightness and social conformity. *Journal of Cross-Cultural Psychology, 10*, 221–230.

Bond, R., & Smith, P. (1996). Culture and conformity: a meta-analysis. *Psychological Bulletin, 119*, 111–137.

Boyd, R., & Richerson, P. (1983). Why is culture adaptive? *Quarterly Review of Biology*, *58*, 209–214.

Bril, B. (1995). Les apports de la psychologie culturelle comparative à la compréhenson du développement de l'enfant. In J. Lautrey (Ed.), *Universel et différentiel en psychologie* (pp. 327–349). Paris: PUF.

Dasen, P. R. (1975). Concrete operational development in three cultures. *Journal of Cross-Cultural Psychology*, *6*, 156–172.

Dasen, P. R. (1993). Theoretical conceptual issuer in developmental research in Africa: *Journal of Psychology in Africa, South of the Sahara, the Carribean, and Afro-Latin America*, *1*, 151–158.

Dasen, P. R., Berry, J. W., & Witkin, H. A. (1979). The use of developmental theories cross-culturally. In L. Eckensberger, W. Lonner, & Y. Poortinga (Eds.), *Cross-cultural contributions to psychology* (pp. 69–82). Lisse: Swets & Zeitlinger.

Feldman (1975). The history of the relationship between environment and culture in ethnological thought. *Journal of the History of the Behavioural Sciences*, *110*, 67–81.

Forde, D. (1934). *Habitat, economy and society*. New York: Dutton.

Gamble, J. J., & Ginsberg, P. E. (1981). Differentiation, cognition and social evolution. *Journal of Cross-Cultural Psychology*, *12*, 445–459.

Georgas, J., & Berry, J. W. (1995). An ecocultural taxonomy for cross-cultural psychology. *Cross-Cultural Research*, *29*, 121–157.

Georgas, J., van de Vijver, F., & Berry, J. W. (2000). The ecocultural framework and psychological variables in cross-cultural research. Paper presented at IACCP Congress, Pultusk, Poland.

Huntington, E. (1945). *Mainsprings of civilization*. New York: John Wiley.

Irvine, S. H., & Berry, J. W. (1988). The abilities of mankind. In S. H. Irvine & J. W. Berry (Eds.), *Human abilities in cultural context* (pp. 3–59). New York: Cambridge University Press.

Jahoda, G. (1995). The ancestry of a model. *Culture & Psychology*, *1*, 11–24.

Kroeber, A. L. (1917). The superoyenic. *American Anthropologist*, *19*, 163–214.

Kroeber, A. (1939). *Cultural and natural areas of native North America*. Berkely: University of California Press.

Lomax, A., & Berkowitz, W. (1972). The evolutionary taxonomy of culture. *Science*, *177*, 228–239.

Marin, G., Balls-Organista, P., & Chung, K. (Eds.) (2001). *Acculturation*. Washington: APA Books.

McNett, C. W. (1970). A settlement pattern scale of cultural complexity. In R. Narool & R. Cohen (Eds.), *Handbook of method in cultural anthropology*. New York: Natural History Press.

Mishra, R. C., Sinha, D., & Berry, J. W. (1996). *Ecology, acculturation and psychological adaptation: a study of Advasi in Bihar*. Delhi: Sage Publications.

Moran, E. (1982). *Human adaptability: an introduction to ecological anthropology*. Boulder: Westview Press.

Moran, E. (Ed.) (1990). *The ecosystem approach in anthropology*. Ann Arbor: University of Michigan Press.

Murdock, G. P. (1975). *Outline of cultural materials*. New Haven: Human Relations Area Files.

Nsamenang, B. (1992). *Human development in cultural context*. Newbury Park: Sage.

Paabo, S. (2001). The human genome and our view of ourselves. *Science*, *291*, 1219–1220.

Pelto, P. (1968). The difference between "tight" and "loose" societies. *Transaction, 5,* 37–40.

Roberts, L. W., Boldt, E. D., & Guest, A. (1990). Structural tightness and social conformity: varying the source of external influence. *Great Plains Sociologist, 3,* 67–83.

Segall, M. H., Dasen, P. R., Beroy, J. W., Pooring, Y. M. (1999). Human behavior in global perspective: An introduction to every-cultural psychology, 2nd edition. Needham Heights: Allyn & Bacon.

Steward, J. (1955). The concept and method of cultural ecology. *Theory of culture change.* Urbana: University of Illinois Press.

Tomasello, M., Kruger, A., & Ratner, H. (1993). Culture learning. *Behavioral and Brain Sciences, 16,* 495–552.

Triandis, H. C. (1994). *Culture and social behavior.* New York: McGraw-Hill.

Troadec, B. (2001). Le modèle écoculturel: un cadre pour la psychologie culturelle comparative. *International Journal of Psychology, 36,* 53–64.

Vayda, A. P., & McKay, B. (1975). New directions in ecology and ecological anthropology. *Annual Review of Anthropology, 4,* 293–306.

Vayda, A. P., & Rappoport, R. (1968). Ecology, cultural and non-cultural. In J. Clifton (Ed.), *Cultural anthropology.* Boston: Houghton Mifflin.

Werner, C., Brown, B., & Altman, I. (1997). Environmental psychology. In J. W. Berry, M. H. Segall, & C. Kagitcibasi (Eds.), *Handbook of cross-cultural psychology, vol. 3: Social behaviour and applications* (pp. 253–290). Boston: Allyn & Bacon.

Witkin, H., & Berry, J. W. (1975). Psychological differentiation in cross-cultural perspective. *Journal of Cross-Cultural Psychology, 6,* 4–87.

7. Semiotics of Culture in Scientific and Carnivalistic Guises: Michail Bakhtin and Yuri Lotman

Ivana Marková

In the past two decades or so the sociocultural approaches to the study of the human mind in psychology have often associated themselves with the semiotics of Michail Bakhtin. For example, Jim Wertsch links the semiotic approach of Michail Bakhtin (Wertsch, 1991, 1998) to that of Lev Vygotsky. He particularly dwells on the ideas of semiotic interdependence between language and thought at the individual and social planes. Both in Bakhtin's and in Vygotsky's works, this interdependence forms a precondition of the sociocultural analysis of the mind.

More recently, however, the cultural semiotics of the Moscow–Tartu school has attracted similar attention. Toomela (in press) links the Moscow–Tartu semiotics both to Lev Vygotsky's (1926, 1934; Vygotsky & Luria, 1930) and to Mark James Baldwin's (1904, 1906) ideas, focusing on the problems of culture and of individual/social interdependencies.

These intellectual associations between sociocultural approaches in psychology and Bakhtin's and Moscow–Tartu's semiotics raise a number of philosophical and epistemological questions. The issue is even more curious because Bakhtin's system on the one hand and that of the Moscow–Tartu school on the other are epistemologically diverse, although they deal with similar concepts like dialogue, culture, change, and oppositions, to mention but a few. Therefore, to my mind, if Vygotsky's sociocultural approach is intellectually associated with one of these two systems, it cannot be associated in the same way with the other system.

As yet, there have been very few attempts to compare and contrast Bakhtin's and Lotman's semiotic approaches to the study of culture (but cf. Grzybek, 1995; Reid, 1991; Titunik, 1976). For example, Grzybek draws attention to some differences between Bakhtin's and Lotman's concepts like *text* and *sign*. He also maintains that despite the theoretical differences between the two systems in the early period of the Moscow–Tartu semiotics, in the later period the Moscow–Tartu school became theoretically and conceptually closer to Bakhtin. Specifically, Grzybek claims that in the later stage, the Moscow–Tartu semiotics started viewing text as a generator of heterogeneous and multifaceted meanings in a similar manner as Bakhtin would have done.

In this chapter, although I cannot do justice to the comprehensive and complex nature of Bakhtin's and of Moscow–Tartu's conceptions of semiotics, I shall outline their respective epistemologies of language and culture. This in turn will make it possible to reflect on the differences between some common terms that both systems use, like "dialogue," "oppositions," "ambivalence," "change," and "dynamics."

THE BOUNDARY IN PLACE OF THE DEFINITION OF CULTURE

When Descartes (1637/1985) contrasted "example and habit," which for him at that time meant "culture," with rationality of the individual, he made a sharp division between what he thought was irrationality of the collective, i.e., culture, and rationality of the individual, i.e., reason (cf. Gellner, 1992). When in the nineteenth century the terms "culture" and "civilization" became part of the social scientific vocabulary, it was to make a division between the world of intellectual and moral progress on the one hand and that of uncivilized barbarians on the other (cf. Jahoda, 1992). When in the twentieth century "culture" became the common term used in psychology, it was to create the boundary between those approaches, which emphasized universals and cognitivism on the one hand and those which claimed the specificity of rational systems and of social knowledge in different cultures on the other. In still other contexts "culture" would be used to create the boundary between the psychology of humans and their construction of the sociohistorical environment on the one hand and of humans as biological and physiological organisms on the other hand.

The twentieth-century Soviet semiotics and cultural studies produced two significant, yet different, scholarly systems: the Bakhtinian Circle and the Moscow–Tartu School. These two systems are both based on the presupposition that it is primarily the human language and communication in their broadest senses that comprises culture. This does not mean to say, however, that culture is reduced to language and communication. Rather, human language and communication form boundaries between those phenomena that can and that cannot be subsumed under the concept of culture.

These simple observations focus attention on the fact that the term "culture" has been frequently used to mark the division between some systems in opposition, e.g., culture versus nature, culture versus reason, culture versus non-culture, and so on. What is foregrounded here is the boundary itself rather than the list of items that could or should be subsumed under each of the two components in opposition. Within each component of such antinomic pairs culture evokes different meanings.

For Michail Bakhtin (1895–1975), the main representative of the Bakhtinian Circle, the boundary is between phenomena that constitute *the dialogical world of humans* and phenomena that belong to the world of monological objects. Humans are by nature responsive, i.e., *dialogical*, whereas objects are nonresponsive, i.e., *monological*. The dialogically constructed and re-constructed social world is the world of multifaceted and multivoiced realities situated in culture. Any coherent system of signs, any text, a work of art, a piece of music, a historical interpretation, all of these have dialogical properties. They are products of human minds that are responsive, i.e., orientated to other human minds and to their cognition.

For Yuri Lotman (1922–1993), representing the Moscow-Tartu School, the boundary between culture and non-culture is created by the division between *the system of signs, which is structured and organized*, and between *chaos, random, and unsystematic conglomerates* (Lotman & Uspensky, 1978). Culture proposes itself to the individual as "a mediator and regulator of experience" (Godzich, 1978, p. 394) and it organizes and preserves information in the historical consciousness of the community.

Thus, in these two semiotic systems, the Bakhtinian and the Moscow–Tartu, the boundaries between what does and what does not constitute culture are defined with respect to different counterparts. The meaning of culture in each of these systems must therefore be conceived and interpreted differently and *only* with respect to what constitutes their counterparts.

In many respects, as already indicated, Michail Bakhtin and Yuri Lotman were concerned with similar issues: with dialogue, communication, opposition, ambivalence, change, novelty, and so on. Importantly, both systems emphasize the fundamental role of *antinomies or oppositions in human thinking*. Although the issues are similar, however, their conceptual presuppositions are different. Bakhtinian semiotics is based on dialogism, which, according to Bakhtin's own characteristic, is the epistemology of human and social sciences. In contrast, the Moscow–Tartu semiotics is based on information theory and on the Saussere theory of signs.

AESOPIAN LANGUAGES

Any intellectual enterprise takes place in specific social, historical, and political contexts. These contexts can play a decisive role in the researcher's activity. This is even truer if the researcher, living in a totalitarian regime, cannot create freely and must look constantly over his shoulder to see whether his ideas are still acceptable to the political regime. Both Bakhtin and Lotman lived in the Soviet Union during its highly repressive years, and the dominant ideology of totalitarianism imposed constraints on their work. They coped with the constraints in different ways, clothing their ideas in different guises. One could say, following Emerson (1997), that they both applied, in their own ways, the Aesopian principles according to which you should be prudent when dealing with those in power who can destroy you. While the epistemologies underlying their work are presumably consistent with their main views, a number of commentators have drawn attention to the fact that neither Bakhtin nor Lotman expressed himself without restraint as they might had done should the official orthodoxy have allowed that.

Each of these two semiotic systems has had a different history and influence both inside and outside the Soviet Union. Bakhtin's Circle was productive in the 1920s and 1930s, and its public appearance stopped with the Soviet persecution of its members in the early 1930s. Thanks to his life-long illness of osteomyelitis, which made him chronically disabled, Michail Bakhtin survived persecution and spent many years in relative isolation in the remote provincial town of Saransk where he worked as a college teacher. His work was "rediscovered" in the 1960s and 1970s, and the Moscow–Tartu School made a considerable contribution to its revival. Since then, both in Russia and in particular outside Russia, Bakhtin's ideas are winning more and more influence in the social sciences and humanities.

The Moscow–Tartu School started to be productive in the 1960s and 1970s when it became the "accepted" version of Soviet semiotics. The members of the Moscow–Tartu School have been talented scholars, with backgrounds in mathematics, cybernetics, linguistics, formal logic, and humanities. Yuri Lotman held an important academic position during the Soviet regime at a time that did not favor original thinking. In that context, the aim of the Moscow–Tartu School was to create a new science of cultural semiotics based on cybernetics, information theory, communication, and formal logic. After the original rejection of information theory and cybernetics in the Soviet Union, in the 1960s these fields became important in the development of technology in the socialist system competing, during the Cold War, with the capitalist West. The strict scientific basis of the information theory and cybernetics became therefore acceptable in the Soviet Union as a paradigm for the social science and humanities because it placed them, too, on the firm ground of science and information theory. In that context, scientific approaches were less threatening to the orthodox ideology than humanistic (i.e., "nonscientific") approaches. Lotman (1990, p. 4) describes the situation as follows:

Over the last few decades semiotics and structuralism in the Soviet Union as in the West have lived through testing times. Of course the experiences have been different. In the Soviet Union these disciplines had to endure a period of persecutions and ideological attacks, and this was followed by a conspiracy of silence or embarrassed semi-recognition on the part of official science.

Lotman continues, saying that neither persecution nor fashion was decisive in the creation of new scholarship and that it was the profundity of ideas that led to the development of semiotics as a scientific discipline in the Soviet Union. This scientifically based semiotics was transplanted into the cultural and historical studies, literature, art, and cinema.

Thus, scientific orientation and the use of scientific terminology of information processing of the Moscow–Tartu semiotics achieved to be viewed as being in line with the Soviet scientific mission. This enabled the Moscow–Tartu School to express many ideas that probably would not had passed otherwise. Emerson (1997) comments on this issue:

As Boris Egorov, a scholar of Lotman's circle in Tartu and later Petersburg and a legendary storyteller of Russian literary follies, wrote much later in his memoirs: "The party-minded orthodox were still dubious about Structuralism, and we were afraid that the new term *semiotics* would provoke even more fears. We began to reason by [Saltykov-] Schedrin's Aesopian principle: 'how might all this be expressed more obscurely?' Then the Moscow mathematician V[ladimir] A. Uspensky invented a splendid term, *secondary modeling systems*. Clever, and incomprehensible" (quoted by Emerson, 1997, p. 41).

After the Stalin era, the Party's ideology became more lenient and, considering that they were prudent, Soviet scholars could take advantages of the new opportunities in academia that were unthinkable before. Moreover, since Soviet semiotics was officially approved, it could penetrate into and have an influence on many spheres of intellectual life. Outside the Soviet Union it created interest at the time. Because the Soviet semiotics was based on familiar principles of structuralism and formalism, however, its influence did not last too long. After the 1970s many principles of the structuralist semiotics were rejected or at least overcome in the West. In addition, the abstract nature of the Lotman system did not appeal to many scholars (cf. Hymes, 1978) and thus the influence of the Soviet semiotics outside the Soviet Union decreased. Today, its impact outside Russia seems to be limited to the specialists in Slavic cultural and historical studies.

EPISTEMOLOGIES UNDERLYING BAKHTIN'S AND LOTMAN'S CONCEPTIONS OF DIALOGUE AND CULTURE

The Epistemology of Dialogism

Bakhtin's Dialogicality of the Human Mind and Dialogism

For Michail Bakhtin, the human mind is dialogical. The adjective "dialogical" in this context does not refer simply to dialogue but, above all, to the capacity of conceiving the social world as the world of various kinds of interdependence between the self and other. Dialogicality implies orientation toward other cognitions, ideas, meanings, and significations of others' ideas as well as toward those of one's own. Dialogicality is such a basic condition of human existence that we can talk about it as *an ontology of the human mind.*

The very capacity of having human consciousness is based on otherness. Each person lives "in a world of others' words" (Bakhtin, 1986, p. 143) and therefore the entire existence of the self is orientated toward others' words and others' world. They make the world in terms of others: "the limit here is not *I*, but this *I* in interrelationship with *other* personalities, that is, *I* and the *other*, *I* and *thou*"

(Bakhtin, 1986, p. 167). Dialogicality has developed together with the evolution of the human mind, and humans are therefore, born into a dialogically constructed social and cultural world. We begin life by learning others' words, the multifaceted world of others becomes part of our own consciousness, and all aspects of culture fill our own life. In brief, all symbolic activity of humans is founded on "dialogue" between different minds expressing multitudes of polyphonic meanings. We make sense of it, interpret it, reconstruct it, and they keep re-creating it.

Bakhtin spoke of dialogism (the notion "dialogism" came from the Marburg School of neo-Kantians and was probably first used by Rosenstock [1924]) as epistemology. Consequently, dialogism has become an alternative to the traditional individualistic theories of knowledge (Heen Wold, 1992). Bakhtin (1981) characterized dialogism as an epistemology of human cognition, communication, and, more generally, the human sciences, which are concerned with the study of symbolic thoughts expressed in language:

[D]ialogism is an epistemology in which one point of view is opposed to another, one evaluation opposed to another, one accent opposed to another. . . . this dialogic tension between two languages and two belief systems, permits authorial intentions to be realized in such a way that we can acutely sense their presence at every point in the work (Bakhtin, 1981, p. 314).

In contrast to the social sciences and humanities, natural sciences are concerned with the study of voiceless and reified objects, which need to be accurately described and explained. As Bakhtin said, natural sciences are monological because they examine things as if they existed only for the single human mind rather than for the mind in relation to other minds. Natural sciences are based on mathematical accuracy and on precision of measurement. In contrast to natural sciences, the social sciences and humanities are studying the social world of human dialogues, of texts and of polysemic and multifaceted meanings. Humanities and social sciences understand, transmit, and interpret discourses of others (Bakhtin, 1981). The concept of accuracy and precision in the social and human sciences is essentially different in kind from that of accuracy and precision in natural sciences. Accuracy and precision in the social and human sciences refer to the joint appropriation of cognition by different individuals in the attempt to understand the ways of overcoming the strangeness of cognition of the other person. This is achieved through *active* understanding, through mastering social environment, language, and any object that the individual cognition appropriates. Understanding, precisely because it is active, is evaluative. Understanding and evaluation, Bakhtin (1986, p. 142) argues, are part of an integral and unified action.

The human and social sciences always involve the study of one human cognition by another. Cognitions are in tension; they clash, judge, and evaluate one another. In other words, the human and social sciences are concerned with *dia-*

logical cognition. Bakhtin characterized dialogical cognition as a metacognition, as "the reflection of a reflection" (Bakhtin, 1986, p. 113). It always expresses different symbolic intentions, genres, and different communication activities.

Sources of Dialogicality

Bakhtin was well acquainted with the philosophical and religious movements of the 1920s, which placed emphasis on dialogue and on language. Among them was the religiously orientated neo-Kantian movement, flourishing particularly in the German town of Marburg. The neo-Kantians based their philosophy on the "dialogical principle," which involved the relationship between "I" and "Thou," that is, the relation of co-authors, whoever these might be. In addition to Hegelian philosophy, the dialogical principle came also from Judaism, and it was part of the Old Testament as the cultural communal spirit. The neo-Kantians (e.g., Cohen, 1919; Rozenzweig, 1921; Buber, 1958; Rosenstock, 1924) argued that the dialogical principle is established and maintained through speech and communication. Through communication people make their social world: they express their life experience, reality, emotions, and concerns. The dialogical approach placed considerable weight on the idea that the activity of thought creates human reality (e.g., Cohen, 1919). The dialogical principle of the neo-Kantians seemed to have been one of the most significant bridges connecting philosophy and religion in the early part of the past century.

Buber (1958) borrowed from Hegel the idea that there are two essential characteristics of human beings: first, that all human beings wish to be acknowledged as to what they are and what they should become; and second, that all human beings have the capacity to acknowledge others in this way. Buber pointed out many times that the dialogical principle follows from Jewish orthodoxy. Subjectivity is not individualistic but it is dialogical. His conception of "I–Thou" refers to the "sphere of between" individuals as an essential concept underlying human reality. This conception remained basically at the level of dialogue between human individuals. Another neo-Kantian philosopher, Franz Rosenzweig (1921), treated human dialogicality in a much broader way. Rosenzweig did not conceive dialogue simply as a mutuality between I and You but, above all, the communal world in which judgment, difference, and conflict prevail. "What would become of the I–Thou if they will have to swallow up the entire world and Creator as well? . . . For my and your sake, there has to be something else in this world besides-me and you!" (cf. Batnitzky, 2000, p. 253, note 44, letter of Martin Buber). Batnitzky (2000, p. 113) argues that Rosenzweig's approach to dialogue stems from his understanding of the Jewish–Christian relation, which is "never one of mutuality, but always one of absolute difference . . . judgement comes from difference, but without judgement, and thus difference, dialogue, and the potential for self-tranformation, would not be possible" (p. 159). It is the impossibility of consensus that is the basis of all dialogue, and specifically, in Rosenzweig's context, of dialogue between Judaism and Christianity. The relation between them strengthens and intensifies judgment of one another through tension, but, despite tension and hostility, it leads the way to redemption. Like Rozenzweig, Bakhtin also views dialogicality broadly, as a clash of ideas, as a heterogeneity and polyphony of voices. This broad conception of dialogicality is reflected in Bakhtin's dialogues between cultures and specifically between "official" and "unofficial" cultures (see later).

While it is well established that Bakhtin was inspired by the neo-Kantians and that he admired particularly Buber's work, other scholars place a significant emphasis on the influence of the Russian Orthodox Church "as a secret to all of Bakhtin's writing" (Mihailovic, 1997, p. 2). Mihailovic draws attention in painstaking detail to Bakhtin's life and writing, attempting to connect Bakhtin's work to the Johannine religious philosophy of the enfleshed and embodied word. The idea of dialogical struggle resulting in heterogeneity and polyphony in Bakhtin's work, Mihailovic argues, comes from the christology (ibid., pp. 18ff.) Dialogue must be viewed as a human binding, a contract that provides a moral and ethical order of the religious kind. That religion, Mihailovic argues, is for Bakhtin above all the Russian Orthodox Church.

Dialogue: To Be Means to Communicate

The ideas of the self-recognizing him- or herself in the other person (rather than in God) and of "I and thou," as co-constituting one another were explicitly elaborated by many thinkers since the eighteenth century, including Herder, Humboldt, Fichte, and Hegel. In psychology, this idea was essential for Baldwin, Vygotsky, and Mead, and it has become part of the contemporary developmental psychology of the self (Valsiner, 1989, 1999). Therefore, it is not original in Bakhtin. What is specifically Bakhtinian, however, is his insistence on the fundamental dialogicality of "I and thou," on its polyphony and infinity. The essential presupposition of otherness penetrates all Bakhtin's work, yet it is in his analysis of Dostoyevsky, where he lays bare the meaning of "I and thou":

I am conscious of myself and become myself only while revealing myself for another, through another, and with the help of another. The most important acts constituting self-consciousness are determined by a relationship toward another consciousness (toward a *thou*). . . . The very being of man (both external and internal) is the *deepest communion. To be* means *to communicate.* Absolute death (non-being) is the state of being unheard, non-recognised, non-remembered. . . . To be means to be for another, and through the other, for oneself. A person has no internal sovereign territory, he is wholly and always on the boundary; looking inside himself, he looks *into the eyes of another* or *with the eyes of another* (Bakhtin, 1984b, p. 287).

Without dialogue, there is no life.

Bakhtin and his circle understand dialogue in a broad sense, which means not only face-to-face verbal communication between persons but verbal communication of any type, for example, a book or any printed material. The word is always directed outside, toward someone else (Voloshinov, 1929/1973). At the same time, because each of us speaks and thinks idiosyncratically, the speech of others and their thoughts, when considered from one's own point of view, contains *strangeness*, which we try to overpower. We do this by appropriating the thoughts and speech of others. It is therefore the strangeness of others' thoughts and speech that enables communication and gives credit to it. Bakhtin's notion of strangeness between dialoguing cognitions is bound with a constant negotiation of tension. There could be no dialogue if participants were not opposed one to another through mutually experienced strangeness. Strangeness creates tension between them, and the tension is not bound to either of them but actually exists between them. Tension is ever present, whether participants strive for intersubjectivity or for dominance or for dialogical mutualities of any kind. Even if participants in dialogue are in a close intersubjective relation and share a great deal of knowledge, it is tension between different kinds of mutually interdependent antinomies that keeps their dialogue going. For example, since human speech is always double-voiced, it involves antinomies like "the constant combination of falsehood and truth, of darkness and light, of anger and gentleness, of life and death" (Bakhtin, 1984a, p. 433).

Dialogue for Bakhtin is always concrete, takes place in specific conditions, and has specific meanings in a particular situation. Therefore, dialogue, whether between people or between cultures, never includes indifferent and neutral words. Neutrality can be imposed only artificially, but ordinary speech is never neutral. Since words are always doubly orientated, i.e., toward the self and toward the other, they are always open to different interpretation and in this sense they are ambivalent. In addition, words are never neutral because their content is morally binding. It is the moral and ethical contract of a dialogical binding that is different in kind from the neutral exchange of information.

Epistemology of the Theory of Information

Lotman's Structuralism and the Semiotic Modeling of Information

Information theory and cybernetics together with the Saussurean semiotics provided an impetus for the Moscow–Tartu School in the early 1960s. The new science of Soviet semiotics followed the ideas of Ferdinand Saussure (1915), and thus from the start there was a fundamental difference between Bakhtin and Lotman. In contrast to Lotman, Bakhtin's Circle was critical of the Saussure semiotics (Voloshinov, 1929/1973; Bakhtin, 1986). The main reason for Bakhtin's criticism was the notion of code, which he contrasts with that of context. While a context is always open and unfinalized, the characteristic of a code is that it must be finalized. A code, Bakhtin says, is a deliberately killed context (Bakhtin, 1986, p. 147). Moreover, a code as a ready-made element of language is a "scientific fiction" depicting, often graphically, the speaker and the listener in alternating positions. In such depictions the speaker is presumed to be active while the listener is passive. Then they exchange their roles; the listener becomes the speaker and the speaker becomes the listener.

If applied to dialogue like an information-processing sequential model, speaker and listener are bound to one another by the sequences of utterances in which they alternate their positions and exchange information. This model is essential in all versions of the Moscow–Tartu semiotics, including the historical and cultural analyses (see below). While Bakhtin does not object to such depictions as partially corresponding to reality, "when they are put forth as the actual whole of speech communication, they become a scientific fiction" (Bakhtin, 1986, p. 68). What he means here is that true dialogicality presupposes *simultaneity* as its primary feature. It is about the mutual co-construction of dialogical contributions. *Sequentiality* in time is a consequence of so-defined simultaneity. Thus we could say that as a concept, simultaneity is primary to sequentiality.

Despite the fact that Bakhtin's epistemology of dialogism was sharply different from scientific monologism, Bakhtin rejected the idea that there might be an insurmountable barrier between the human and natural sciences (cf. Bakhtin, 1986, p. 145). To my knowledge, however, he did not put forward any supposition of their theoretical connection.

Lotman in contrast explicitly insisted on the notion of the universal science. He argued for a structuralist and monistic approach that can be applied both to natural and to social phenomena. In developing the idea of cultural dynamism and characteristically for his scientific attitude, Lotman turned to the study of dynamic processes in natural sciences like chemistry, biology, and physics. Specifically, he thought that Prigogine's and Stengers' concepts of determinacy and randomness in the general dynamics of the world were applicable to all sciences. According to Prigogine and Stengers, it is *the universal laws of equilibrium* that guide processes in balanced and unbalanced structures of whatever kind, whether in the natural or in the social world.

Lotman maintained that the general theory of dynamics can be applied to the study of history in which spontaneous and unconscious processes are intertwined with personal and conscious processes. The task of historical semiotics, in this approach, is to understand the mechanism of change and the mechanism of conscious choice. While determinacy and randomness coexist both in the natural and human sciences, in the natural sciences the phenomena of study continuously repeat themselves and are therefore relatively predictable. In contrast, consciousness, which is essential to human sciences, is always based on making choices and therefore it renders the phenomena of study much less predictable. By excluding choice and therefore unpredictability, we would exclude consciousness from historical processes. The laws of history differ from the laws of other sciences because they can be understood only if we take into account people-conscious activity and this includes semiotic activity (Lotman, 1990, p. 234).

Even consciousness, however, may have a different effect, depending on which of its two components, the social or the individual, is prevalent. Lotman follows Saussure in arguing that the former component operates as a discrete system of codes (like Sausserean *la langue*) in which the bearer of meaning is sign. The latter component operates as a continuous system of texts (like Saussure's *la parole*) in which the bearer of meaning is text. This latter component is dynamic and therefore less predictable than the former.

The Mechanism of Dialogue

Like Bakhtin, Lotman defined dialogue broadly, yet there are essential differences between their definitions. For Lotman, dialogue is a mechanism of translating information from one system of communication to another. Bakhtin (1986, p. 141) argued on the other hand that dialogue *is not* a translation from the language of another person into one's own language.

Translation assumes only sequentiality. It assumes that for each word in one language there is an equivalent in another language, that there is a one-to-one correspondence between my and your word. Take, for example, an automatic translation from one language to another. Messages chosen for automatic translation are usually simple in order to deliver information and no more than information. The process of understanding in translating messages goes like this. The machine translates the message, which we then read and transform into our own understanding, replacing the machine's words by our own words if they do not fit into our understanding. We do this on the basis of what we know about the situation to which the text refers, about the person who provides us with the message, what we know of his or her intentions, and so on. There can be no one-to-one correspondence between messages even if the process of translation is technologically improved. Dialogue is polysemic and polyphonic and will remain so unless humanity does not fall into an Orwellian kind of disaster. Understanding is actively co-produced moment by moment and is open to different possibilities of interpretation. We cannot escape mutuality of *my* understanding and *your* communicative intentions at any stage of *our* communication. In Bakhtin's kind of dialogue, participants jointly generate messages and share responsibility for any dialogical contribution.

Lotman's concept of dialogue is different. Being based on information processing, dialogue is a strict exchange. Each participant is responsible for his or her own contribution; there is a pause between contributions; after the pause, participants exchange their roles, from a position of speaker who transmits to a position of listener who receives. Dialogue thus consists of discrete sections with intervals between them (Lotman, 1990, p. 143).

In order to clarify his point about dialogue as "a strict sequence of transmission and reception . . . when one participant gives a 'message' the other pauses, and vice versa" (ibid., p. 144), Lotman gives an example from mother–baby "dialogues" as it was studied by John Newson (1979). What is interesting here is that Lotman interprets these mother–baby dialogues as examples of discreteness in information processing. Thus, he says that "Discreteness, or the ability to issue information in portions, is the law of all dialogue systems" (ibid., p. 144). Lotman imports this conception of the human dialogue from the theory of information.

One can take the same example of mother–baby dialogue, however, and argue for dialogicality. For instance, microanalyses of mother–infant interactions have shown the seamlessness of dialogical contributions, the nonexistence of discrete units, the mutual construction of messages and the joint responsibility for each contribution, and the simultaneous activity of both participants both in speaking and in listening (Marková, 1987; Collins and Marková, 1990).

But one may object to the latter kind of concept of dialogue by presenting a counterexample. Consider a dialogue on the telephone where we do not see one another and cannot interpret the message instantaneously; consider dialogue by e-mail, by ordinary post, and so on. Clearly, *that* is an exchange: I speak, there is a pause, and you reply. Such an argument of course holds true and cannot be denied. What is ignored in such counterexamples, however, is that only information exchange is possible and only because humans are dialogical. They are born with dialogicality, with the capacity of answerability in a mutual and simultaneous manner. It is because of this capacity that they can develop capacity for exchanging information, for mastering rules of politeness, of turn-taking and so on, which they then make explicit in exchange models. The latter models are mechanistic and they ignore historical explanation of dialogicality; indeed, they consider it irrelevant (Fodor, 2000).

Lotman does not have much to say about a concrete dialogue between people, being primarily concerned with dialogue in general terms, like in literary criticism and in cultural dynamism. He views all these phenomena from the historical and cultural perspective. In his treatment of dialogue in the article *Mechanisms of Dialogue* (1996), he emphasizes that the notion of translation of information from one system to another can be applied to any kind of communication, including cultural transmission. Rather than being concerned with interpersonal dialogue, the focus of Lotman's attention is a cultural dialogue, which he defines as the translation of semiotic signs through different periods of the history of culture. In the historical development, say, of literature, just like in a dialogue between people, one can isolate a continuous and a chronological line in which periods of intensity, i.e., of speaking, alternate with periods of calm, i.e., of responding:

[I]f we look at this immanent development as *one partner in a dialogue* [Lotman's emphasis] then the periods of so-called decline can be regarded as a time of pause in a dialogue, the time when information is being intensively received, after which follow periods of transmission. This is what happens in the relationships between units of all levels—from genres to national cultures (Lotman, 1990, p. 144).

Dynamics in the semiotic mechanism of culture is defined on the basis of time sequences, in which *movement* is followed by the period of *stability* (Lotman & Uspensky, 1978).

Lotman's description of the cultural dialogue in the history of Russian literature goes like this: At one stage in the history there may be an intensive literary creation while in the subsequent stage literature may be in a responding, rather than in a speaking mode. Lotman (1996) also implies that the dialogue is not a passive exchange of information. Rather, translation *demands effort* and is therefore more than mirroring of information by another system. In other words, it assumes the reverse process, that of reconstructing information. In this process, understanding goes together with non-understanding as well as with inadequacies in the transmission and reception of messages. These inadequacies in the transmission of messages must not be viewed as merely side-products of imperfections in the construction of actual information-transmitting mechanisms. Instead, both understanding and difficulties in understanding are complementary processes, and the presence of both enables functioning of the semiotic mechanism of culture. Lotman does not clarify the phrase "demanding effort" any further, however. His major concepts are those of information, information processing, code, system, level, hierarchy, and so on. Thus, one can say that his approach is rather weak on those dialogical features that make both the human dialogue and the dialogue metaphorically involving the mind of the individual and culture, essentially different from technological information processing.

Lotman applied the pattern of discrete sequences so described to dialogical relationships at all levels, from genres to national cultures. He documented his claims by examples from the world literature. For instance, for long periods of time Italy absorbed cultural currents from different European cultures, thus being in a responsive state, but the Renaissance was its speaking period. Another example is France. France assimilated ideas from the Reformation in various European countries—the philosophical trends from Bacon, Locke, and Newton; Italian humanism; the Mannerism from Spain—until, in the age of Enlightenment, France was speaking for herself. And so on.

Lotman's examples from the world literature are thought-provoking, yet one is left with a feeling that information theory with its rules of sequentiality and discreteness is far overstretched. Lotman's vivid descriptions of "giving" and "receiving" in world cultures are no more than analogies of information-processing models, which are too general to be treated as analyses of dialogues between cultures. Neither is it explored what kinds of forces affect the change of partners from "speaking" to a "receiving" mode and vice versa. Despite that, in many of his writing about Russian poetry, history, and culture, Lotman forgets about information theory and leaves the reader with the pleasure of experiencing the depth of his thoughts.

Culture Versus Non-Culture

Although Lotman accepted in principle the Saussurean opposition between synchrony and diachrony, in contrast to Saussure he studied synchronic structures in a diachronic manner, and hence his emphasis on dialogue as a sequential process. In this way he followed the linguists of the Prague School who had expressed their criticism of a purely synchronic approach early in the 1920s. Specifically, for Tynjanov and Jakobson (1928/1981), pure synchronism was only a scientific illusion because every synchronic system, in addition to being something here-and-now, has its past and future. Thus Tynjanov and Jakobson claimed that the opposition between synchrony and diachrony, i.e., the opposition between the concept of system and the concept of evolution, is not sustainable. Every system exists only as evolution and, on the other hand, evolution is inescapably of a systematic nature.

Lotman's conception of culture, too, addressed the problem of diachrony, i.e., the question of longevity and of cultural dynamism. Lotman and Uspensky (1978) defined culture as the whole human activity of working out, exchanging, and preserving information, which is composed of a number of individual systems. This very broad definition of culture as "the whole of activity," however, could dangerously imply simply *everything*, and the authors certainly wished to avoid such a position. Therefore, they posited culture as a historical process versus non-culture. Culture has structure and is systematic (the system of signs); it generates structuredness and organizes the world around humans. It creates a social sphere, or the *semiosphere* (Lotman, 1990), around people, just like biosphere is the world in which animals live. In contrast, non-culture is chaos, random, and unsystematic. Non-culture, however, for Lotman is not an independent entity but an important methodological tool that enables definition of culture. It forms an opposition to culture and must therefore be understood only with respect to a specific culture that it opposes and of which it is not part. While culture, because it is historically or diachronically structured, requires collective memory as an expression of its longevity, non-culture is characterized by forgetfulness. Nevertheless, non-culture is not rejected as useless. The non-culture or the non-systematic, while it is not part of the system, may be drawn into it in the process of cultural change. Lotman's (1976) example of such a process is a stone rejected by builders as superfluous or useless in their current building. This rejected stone, however, can become a cornerstone of another, future building. Thus, what is non-significant in the present culture can become important at the next stage of cultural development. This process of non-culture as being drawn into culture, however, seems to depend on chance rather than on active or consciously provoked processes.

Culture has structure and its organized into core and periphery (Lotman, 1976, 1992). The concepts of core and periphery are borrowed from structuralism and from information theory, but Lotman adapts them to his approach of cultural dynamism. The center of the cultural space is organized and relatively inflexible, monovalent and incapable of development. It plays an important role in a synchronic approach. It is the space of semiotic norms. Periphery, in contrast, is the space of semiotic practices. It is vaguely organized and ambivalent. It is more valued in diachronic approaches as a source of change. The more one moves from center to periphery, the more the cultural system, e.g., communication, becomes strained by tension between sometimes artificial norms and peripheral genres, e.g., in arts. For instance, marginal forms of culture can be drawn into conflict with the mainstream art. As Lotman points out, the avant-garde starts as a rebellious fringe and through negotiation of conflict it moves to the center, changing the semiosphere and becoming the object of thematisation and of dispute. Such shifts between center and periphery, without using this terminology, have also been observed by historians of art like Mukařovský (1936/1970) and by Gombrich (1960). They both argue that an individual's vision in art is largely determined by shared social representations and by collective vision and discuss conditions of shifts between fringe and center. These interdependencies between individual and collective vision are the subject matter of history or art, and Lotman's descriptions of actual events from culture and literature largely enrich the study of these dynamic movements.

OPPOSITION AND CULTURAL CHANGE

Opposition as Interdependence and as Difference

Observation that human rationality starts with oppositional thought pervades philosophical systems from ancient Babylonia, ancient China, and ancient Greece to the present ones (Marková, 2000; Moscovici & Vignaux, 1994). These philosophical systems, however, conceive oppositions in different manners, ranging from the wave-like continuities of Chinese Yin and Yang and Plato's and Aristotle's strictly separated dualisms to dialectic oppositions in the magical medieval thought, to take a few examples. Opposition is also one of the fundamental concepts both in Bakhtin's and in Moscow–Tartu's semiotics. The concept of opposition in these two systems has essentially different meanings, and these meanings are implied, again, by different underlying epistemologies on which each system is built.

For Bakhtin, dialogue is by definition ridden with a variety of interdependent oppositions. Among them, the most important one is the opposition between dialogical participants. Although the oppositional way of thinking between I and you saturates all of Bakhtin's writings, it is perhaps most clearly expressed in his analysis of Dostoyevsky's novels (Bakhtin, 1984b). Dostoyevsky, Bakhtin declares, created a completely new type of artistic thinking, which he calls *polyphonic*. Bakhtin's own thinking about dialogue is also polyphonic. Polyphony, for him, derives itself from a simple scheme: from "the opposition of one person to another person" or from *I to you* (ibid., p. 252). Within this scheme, polyphony saturates hidden and open polemics, parody, irony, hidden dialogicality, open and hidden rejoinders, collisions and quarreling, all of these ridden with tension, leaving always a loophole, thus exposing dialogue to openness of different interpretations—and therefore to novelty. A loophole for Bakhtin is a residual meaning leaving "the possibility for altering the ultimate, final meaning of one's own words" (Bakhtin, ibid., p. 233). Thinking and speaking are always open and undetermined because there can always be new interpretations of meanings depending on who is the other. It always involves negotiation of conflict and tension. "Nothing conclusive has yet been spoken, the world is open and free, everything is still in the future, and will always be in the future" (1984b, p. 166). In other words, where there is dialogue, there is a human activity. Words want to be heard and, similarly, ideas are live events and they want to be understood and answered by others from their positions. When dialogue ends, everything ends.

In contrast to Bakhtin, Lotman's concept of opposition is binary, related to the principles of binary coding in information theory and in linguistics. Binary oppositions are mutually exclusive. For example, in phonology, one member of the pair of oppositions is marked by the presence of a feature that the other lacks, e.g., voiced versus unvoiced. The concept of binary opposition is conceived here as one of the cultural universals. Thus, Lotman defined oppositions in terms of firm boundaries that

may separate the living from the dead, settled people from nomadic ones, the town from the plains; it may be a state frontier, or a social, national, confessional, or any other kind of frontier. There is an amazing similarity, even between civilizations which have no contact with each other, in the expressions they use to describe the world beyond the boundary (Lotman, 1990, p. 131).

Lotman viewed oppositions primarily as typologies or categories, dividing the world into "us" and "them," "culture" and "non-culture," "top" from "down," and so on. He quoted in this context from the Frankish chronicler who described the customs of the pagan Saxons and showed that pagan culture allowed the exact opposite of things that were not permissible to his own culture. This universal concept of opposition in the Moscow–Tartu school is basically the Saussurean concept of binary opposition and the notion of binary opposition as it figures in the information theory. For Saussure, the whole linguistics was based on the notion of opposition as difference. The problem with this typological approach is that, apart from identifying and describing oppositional types, it does not open itself to any conceptual analysis or to theoretical elaboration. Types and categories are ready-made, and once they are described as a part of structure, no continuation follows. Bakhtin explicitly rejected structuralism and its "mechanical categories" like "opposition" and "change of codes" (Bakhtin, 1986, p. 169).

Sergej Karcevskij (1927), in his study of the Russian verb, referring to Sausserean linguistics, observed that it became fashionable to affirm that linguistic values existed only in terms of their oppositions. But to talk about oppositions in terms of differences rather than interdependencies, Karcevskij maintained, is meaningless because it amounts to no more than saying that a tree is a tree because it is not a house, a river, or another object. Oppositions on their own lead to chaos as they are not part of any system. Instead, true oppositions, "true differentiation presupposes a simultaneous resemblance and difference" (Karcevskij, 1927, pp. 13–14).

Both Saussure and the Moscow–Tartu School sought general principles of systems and universal aspects of structures. While Saussure could account for the whole *system of linguistics* in terms of differences, Lotman could account for the whole *system of culture* in terms of differences. However, while Saussure thought that the general principles of language could be explained *without* the notion of language change, Lotman saw his major contribution in showing *how* cultural change and cultural dynamics take place.

One needs to emphasise that the idea that oppositional thought has different implications depending on whether one conceives oppositions as differences, i.e., as types and categories, or as dialogical counterparts. Types and categories separate objects, e.g., "us" from "them," "good" from "bad," "nature" from "culture." They freeze the complex and dynamic world by creating static frames into which objects are placed depending on the chosen criteria. They enable us to describe stable states of affairs.

The "same" oppositions, say "us" and "them," when considered as dialogical counterparts, *are* in dialogue and in tension. They are not separated one from another but dialogically conceived "us" and "them" are partners in communication who attempt to appropriate each other's meanings. "Them" impose the meanings on "us," "us" may impose the meaning on "them" or "us" may attempt to estrange "them," and so on. Dialogical oppositions are oppositions in communicative movement, and they themselves both change in the process. They thematize and diversify contents in question and are negotiated through oppositions conflicts and tension. They open up new avenues for dialogue.

Ambivalence Versus Monovalence

The difference between Bakhtin's and Lotman's concepts of opposition can be documented in various aspects of their work. I shall choose here one aspect only, that of *ambivalence* versus *monovalence.*

Bakhtin's analysis of the Rabelais carnival (Bakhtin, 1984a) is carried out in terms of a "dialogue" between the folk culture and the official culture in medieval France. This dialogue between the two cultures takes place through a feast, which temporarily suspends the entire official system and hierarchies in the Catholic Church. Bakhtin interpreted carnival, as others had done before him, as liberation from everyday conventions. Through turning them upside down, ironizing and rejecting them, folk culture expressed imagination and creativity, an attempt, in medieval France, to materialize the wish for freedom. Bakhtin interpreted laughter as liberation from fear of the sacred, of prohibitions, of the past and of power. In his words, carnival laughter "builds its own world in opposition to the official world, its own church versus the official church, its own state versus the official state" (ibid., p. 88).

Bakhtin showed here (Bakhtin, 1984a) the power of his notion of ambivalence. In reading Bakhtin's analysis of Rebelais, one feels as if Bakhtin chose the topic of the Renaissance carnival to exhibit his extravagance in the treatment of ambivalence as a dialogical concept. He could hardly find another topic, which could give him the same opportunity and satisfaction to display the idea of double-voicedness. Ambivalence saturates language, daily life, culture, and the human body, simply everything that has some human relevance. All ambivalent images that Bakhtin displays are dual-bodied and dual-faced and pregnant with their oppositions. They integrate affirmation and negation, the top and the bottom, convergence and divergence, not only as sequences of expressions but, above all, as expressions in their simultaneity. Among them, the simultaneity of life and death figures as most prominent. Bakhtin dramatizes his analysis to the extreme, presenting even dying as gay, depicting an individual body in throes of death and at the same time giving an image of another human body just being born. For him, where there is death, there is also change, renewal (ibid., p. 409). The image of birth is also ambivalent, showing that where there is birth there is also departure, these pictures culminating with the image of the birth-giving death (ibid., p. 352). Bakhtin presents variations of death in renewing the earth's fertility, the birth of Pantagruel, which caused his mother's suffocation (ibid., p. 408), and even death from laughter. There is also a sequence of the past giving birth to the future.

Ambivalence presents many opposite faces and intentionally distorted proportions (ibid., p. 410). The play with negation infiltrates all spheres of ordinary life. Men transvest as women, dresses are worn upside down or turned inside out, carnival shows walk backward, riding a horse facing its tail or standing on one's head (ibid., p. 411). Similar anti-logic is applied to the use of physical tools that would be turned inside out and utilized in the wrong way; household objects turned into arms, kitchen utensils and dishes became musical instruments, and so on.

Official and unofficial cultures are separated linguistically. Official culture is represented by Latin and by formalistic expressions, whereas folk or unofficial culture uses popular and festive language, which also represents a dual-bodied world: language always includes praise while abusing and it abuses while praising (ibid., p. 415). Folk culture uses dialects with all their comic aspects: "The dialects become complete images and types of speech and thought; they are linguistic masks. The role of Italian dialects in the *commedia dell'arte* is well known. Each mask features a dialect of the Italian language" (ibid., p. 469). Ambivalence makes impossible neutral words or expressions. The dual-bodied world and dual-voiced language are based on the fusion of opposites. Abuse is the other side of praise; the past gives birth to the future; everything is a two-faced Janus. Ambivalence denies any end, hierarchy, or absoluteness.

Ambivalence never changes into monovalence, but the two oppositions coincide in *the world of becoming*, in which there are no hard boundaries between objects, words, or cultures. Boundaries always change because "a tense dialogic struggle takes place on the boundaries" (Bakhtin, 1986, p. 143). Carnival transforms folk culture into official culture and official culture turns into folk culture.

As Lachman (1988, p. 128) expresses it, carnival culture and official cultures communicate in concrete rituals involving body and language, and this communication takes place through inversion and negation. Carnival ambivalence integrates and disintegrates cultures at the same time.

Although the brilliance of Bakhtin's treatment of carnival has never been denied, some scholars have raised questions about the historical authenticity of his analysis. For example, the possibility of applying his analysis to medieval Russia was questioned (for details, cf. Emerson, 1997). It was pointed out that unequal weight was given to official and folk culture, and, indeed, the question was raised as to how the existence of these two cultures could be connected in the consciousness of the medieval man (Gurevich, 1988). When reflecting on these questions we should also raise the query as to what it was that Bakhtin was doing in his carnivalesque.

A number of Bakhtin's interpreters have pointed out that one needs to see his analysis of Rabelais in the context of the totalitarian regime, which did not allow him to publish this piece for years. Why not? Could it be that the dominant Soviet "culture" recognized some similarities between the official medieval culture and its own official culture? Perhaps the official Soviet culture perceived some parallels between the descriptions of the grotesque medieval body and

the functional body, as exemplified by the drive to overfulfill quotas, by the Stakhanov movement, or by the disembodied folk body as heroicized in public monuments. Outfitted in folk dress, uniform, or work clothes, the functional body was secured against every sort of contamination: firmly entrenched in institutional hierarchies or the work brigade, it was separated from other bodies through competition and robbed of all sexual distinctions. In official Soviet culture, this ascetic body striving for higher ideals could be parodied only in one image: that of the inebriated citizen sobering up in the local drunk bar. Contamination, as the "despoiling" of one realm by another, was "cleaned up" in the Stalinist purges, to which language, literature, ideology, and the body (whether individual or collective) were subjugated. Under the banner of crude "naturalism" or "physiologism", official censorship cut short all attempts to represent the corporeal and the sexual; the work of the censor silenced authors like Pil'njak and Babel'. Bakhtin countered the official image of the body developed by Socialist Realism with his concept of "grotesque realism", which he introduced in his description of Rabelais's corporeal poetics and which also applies to a part of the avant-garde literature in the 1920s (Lachman, 1988, pp. 118–119).

Equally, Gurevich's question as to how the two cultures, "official" and "unofficial," could be connected in the consciousness of the medieval man could be answered by posing another question. How could the two cultures, "official" and "unofficial," be connected in the consciousness of the modern man living under the Soviet rule? They were connected, in both cases through the living ambivalence, through a constant internal dialogue with the self and through external dialogues that take place at schools, at work, often even in families. Bakhtin, it seems, understood better than did the historian that the dialogicality of the human mind and its Aesopian dialogical principles of ambivalence can counteract the schizophrenic existence of a divided man, whether in a medieval or in a modern culture.

Lotman (1976) recognized Bakhtin's contribution to the understanding of the phenomenon of ambivalence and he himself considered ambivalence to be an essential feature of cultural dynamism. Like Bakhtin, he considered the role of ambivalence in cultural change. However, in contrast to Bakhtin, he viewed univalence and ambivalence as strictly separate, arguing that it is the opposition of *univocality* versus *ambivalence* that gives rise to cultural change. For him, culture has two tendencies: on the one hand, it has a tendency toward stability and on the other, a tendency toward dynamism. The tendency toward stability leads to rigidity and monovalence. Internal univocality or homeostasis maintains a dynamically stable state by means of internal regulatory processes. However, Lotman pointed out, rigid synchronic descriptions, like those of Saussure, tend to gloss over structural imperfections that do not fit the ideal structure, and therefore they eliminate important informative factors like ambivalence. Imperfections, while they are characteristics of the text, are not a matter of the author's design, but of relatively small errors of the text producer. Imperfections or ambivalence of the text is essential to materialize the other tendency of culture, the tendency toward dynamism and diversification. Thus it is because culture tends to diversify that the lack of orderliness of non-culture provides flexibility and space for change (Lotman, 1976, p. 85). As an example of a creative imperfection, Lotman quotes from Puskin's poem *Eugenij Onegin*, showing that Puskin's error led to creative variations of images expressed in his poem. Lotman interprets incorporation of errors and of chaos into structure as an innovative aspect of change. Consistent with Lotman's overall views, here we have another example of how change occurs that is in some ways similar to the example of culture and non-culture becoming integrated. Both non-culture and non-intentional errors are assimilated integrated into the system and thus they both contribute to cultural dynamism.

Lotman presents a strict boundary between what belongs and what does not belong to the system. Despite this, it is not obvious from these examples how the dynamics of change is actually achieved. In general terms there are structures in which ambiguity is low and therefore the structures tend to remain in homeostasis. On the other hand, high ambiguity shows a tendency toward change. In this case, novelty is something accidental rather than something that is characteristic of agency or of an effort for change.

Change as Random and Change as Conflict

One needs to remember here Toomela's (in press) question as to what are the specific qualities of culture that make the human mind possible. In the context of the above discussion, my response to this question would be that one could equally pose the opposite question. What are the specific qualities of the human mind that make culture possible? What comes first and what comes second? As I understand, for both Bakhtin and Lotman, it is the mind that makes culture possible, although each gives us a different answer as to how this process takes place. Both systems have implications, epistemological, theoretical and methodological, for cultural psychology. They each emphasize language, communication, and semiotics as essential to culture, without identifying them with culture. However, each is based on a different kind of rationality.

Lotman's vision of history and of the development of ideas reflects a systematic effort at the development of the semiotics of culture as a scientific enterprise. Semiotics proceeds from form to content (Lotman & Uspensky, 1984). Thus, at the bottom of his grandiose system is form, a text that is to be decoded. This approach, from form to content, underlies Lotman's concept of universal rationality uniting all science. Culture is a system of relationships between the individual and the collective:

In this sense the relationship between man and the social group may be regarded as a communicatory dialogue: the social group reacts to the behavior or the individual, to a considerable extent regulates it and the individual reacts to the social group (and in general to the reality surrounding him) (Lotman & Uspensky, 1984).

The whole theory of dynamic cultural system is underlined by binary oppositions that are bound to one another in an asymmetric relationship. Perhaps most important among these asymmetric relationships is the difference between static and dynamic systems of culture. The gap between static and dynamics always creates tension, "like a magnetic field" (Lotman, 1990, p. 225). The opposition between these two poles is a condition for their existence; they cannot be detached one from the other. Any dynamic process involving human beings fluctuates between the pole of continuous slow change and a pole of conscious human activity. A slow change results in predictability and equilibrium, whereas conscious human activity results in randomness and disequilibrium. Chance and determinacy guide self-organizing systems, which are two possible states. When tension between the opposing structural poles decreases and the state of equilibrium obtains, predictability of future states increases. If the social historical and psychological tension reaches the point where the individual's representations of the world alter, unpredictability is more likely. We see that in his system, everything has its place, its logic, and its order: after an address there comes a response, a static state is followed by dynamics, after life there is death.

Bakhtin's cultural semiotics takes a very different direction. He finds rationality in dialogicality based on interdependent oppositions in tension, in heteroglosia, and in never-ending movement. While in Bakhtin's semiotics the change and dynamics are ever present, however, the term "change" does not belong among the main terms of dialogism or dialogicality. Change is presupposed in dialogicality but is not explicitly thematized. Dialogicality presupposes a double orientation, e.g., toward self and toward other, toward centralization and toward decentralization (centripetal and centrifugal forces), toward appropriation and estrangement, toward completeness and incompleteness. Change is presupposed and takes place in any concrete dialogue and in word meaning, because the text is always open to new interpretations.

In contrast to Lotman, Bakhtin'preoccupation is with ambivalence, polyphony of voices, with reflexivity, with the strangeness of the other, and with fractures between the self and other, as if he rejected anything systematic, predictable, and regular. Clefts, splits, polyphonies of various kinds penetrate all his work. Scholarly debates continue years after his death about authorship of books that he supposedly wrote under different names, leaving ambiguities about authorship and about interpretation of unfinished pieces and of his notes.

Bakhtin's concern is not with the change as a linear progress but with the change of the ideas in becoming, in variation, plurality and the multiplicity of perspectives, and with the constant internal incompletion. In notes he wrote in 1970–1971 he admits (Bakhtin, 1986, p. 155) that open-endedness of ideas is absolutely essential to his way of thinking:

. . . an open-endedness not of the thought itself but of its expression and exposition. Sometimes it is difficult to separate one open-endedness from another. It cannot be assigned to a particular trend (Structuralism). My love for variations and for a diversity of terms for a single phenomenon. The multiplicity of focuses. Bringing distant things closer without indicating the intermediate links (Bakhtin, 1986, p. 155).

Thus, in the end one returns to the question posed at the beginning of this essay. Vygotsky and Bakhtin or Vygotsky and Lotman?

Following Moscovici's (1998, p. 428) analysis of Vygotsky's and Piaget's work, one could say that Bakhtin, like Vygotsky, exemplifies "a Dionysian spirit of rupture, irregularity, conflict and the duality of psychic forces and of unforeseen novelties." Lev Vygotsky, like Levy-Bruhl, aimed to examine different cultural systems of collective rationality and their effect on the mind of the individual, whether of adults in Uzbekistan or in concept learning in children. Vygotsky's ideas are rich and novel, yet, Moscovici argues, comparing Vygotsky to Piaget, they leave us with an image of a magnificent torso:

but a torso nevertheless. A bit like one of Leonardo da Vinci's who wrote so much, who started works without completing them. The great temptation is to oppose Piaget and Vygotsky as controlled reason over passion, a managed life vs a disorganized existence, a normal career as against rebellion, the classical vs the romantic (Moscovici, 1998, p. 428).

As Moscovici maintained, Vygotsky lived during the time of storm of the Soviet revolution and its aftermath, and of one of the greatest tragedies of our time. Vygotsky died young. Bakhtin lived through the same time but he lived a long life, although in isolation.

Yuri Lotman, like Jean Piaget and unlike Lev Vygotsky, developed a magnificent system, driven by reason rather than by passion and by regularity rather than by unpredictability. Like Bakhtin, Lotman lived in the period of storm after the Soviet revolution. Unlike Bakhtin, he managed to sail through the storm with glory yet with dignity. Egorov (1997, p. 11), in his introduction to the edition of Lotman's *Pisma 1940–1993 (Letters 1940–1993)*, draws attention again to Lotman's Aesopian language. He emphasizes that although Lotman was an honest and brave man, the danger of censorship of his personal correspondence during the Soviet era forced him to use Aesopian language and to read between the lines. Despite this, Lotman's letters are livelier and include cheerful puns and imagination, which is missing from his scientific texts where, of course, he had to be even more careful.

Thus one can see that culture and ideology form and transform the individual just like the individual forms and transforms culture and ideology. Scientific effort requires genius, but genius is never free of culture and struggles of its time. The interdependence between these oppositions determines both the contents of thinking and the form in which these contents are expressed.

NOTE

I am grateful to Aaro Toomela for his comments and suggestions on the previous draft of this chapter.

REFERENCES

Bakhtin, M. M. (1981). *The dialogic imagination. Four essays by M. M. Bakhtin.* Ed. M. Holquist. Trans. C. Emerson and M. Holquist. Austin: University of Texas Press.

Bakhtin, M. M. (1984a). *Rabelais and his world.* Trans. H. Iswolsky. Bloomington: Indiana University Press.

Bakhtin, M. M. (1984b). *Problems of Dostoyevsky's poetics.* Ed. and trans. C. Emerson. Manchester: Manchester University Press.

Bakhtin, M. M. (1986/1979). *Estetika slovesnovo tvorchestva.* Moskva: Bocharov. Trans. V. W. McGee as *Speech genres and other late essays* (ed. C. Emerson & M. Holquist). Austin: University of Texas Press, 1986.

Baldwin, J. M. (1904). The limits of pragmatism. *Psychological Review, 11,* 30–60.

Baldwin, J. M. (1906). *Thoughts and Things.* London: Swan Sonnenschein & Co.

Batnitzky, L. (2000). *Idolatry and representation: The philosophy of Franz Rosenzweig reconsidered.* Princeton: Princeton University Press.

Buber, M. (1958). *I and thou.* Edinburgh: T. &T. Clark.

Cohen, H. (1919/1972). *Religion of reason: out of the sources of Judaism.* Translated, with an introduction, by Simon Kaplan. Introductory essay by Leo Strauss. New York: F. Ungar Publishing Co.

Collins, S., & Marková, I. (1990). Complementarity in the construction of a problematic utterance in conversation. In I. Marková, C. Graumann, & K. Foppa (Eds.), *Mutualities in dialogue.* Cambridge: Cambridge University Press.

Descartes, R. (1637). *Discourse on Method.* In R. Stoothoff and D. Murdoch (Eds.) (1985), *The philosophical writings of Descartes.* Trans. J. Cottingham. 2 Vols. Cambridge: Cambridge University Prees.

Egorov, B. F. (1997). O pismax Yu. M. Lotmana (About the letters of Ju. M. Lotman). In *Pisma 1940–1993.* Moscow: Jazyky Russkoj Kultury.

Emerson, C. (1997). *The first hundred years of Mikhail Bakhtin.* Princeton: Princeton University Press.

Fodor, J. (2000). *The mind doesn't work that way.* Cambridge, Mass.: MIT Press.

Gellner, E. (1992). *Reason and culture*. Oxford: Blackwell.

Godzich, W. (1978). The construction of meaning. *New Literary History, IX*, 389–397.

Grzybek, P. (1995). Bakhtinskaja semiotika I moskovsko-tartyskaja skola. In E. V. Permjakov (Ed.), *Lotmanovskij sbornik*. pp. 240–259. Moscow: IC Garant.

Gombrich, E. H. (1960). *Art and illusion*. London: Phaidon.

Gurevich, A. (1988). *Medieval popular culture*. Editions de la Maison des Sciences de l'Homme. Cambridge: Cambridge University Press.

Heen Wold, A. (Ed.) (1992). *The dialogical alternative*. Oslo: Scandinavian University Press.

Hymes, D. (1978). Comments on Soviet semiotics and criticism. *New Literary History, IX*, 399–411.

Jahoda, G. (1992). *Crossroads between culture and mind. Continuities and change in theories of human nature*. New York: Harvester Wheatsheaf.

Jakobson, R. (1982/1988). La théorie Saussurienne en rétrospection. In S. Rudy (Ed.), *Roman Jakobson selected writing, Vol VIII*, pp. 391–435. New York: Mouton.

Karcevskij, S. (1927). *Système de verbe russe*. Prague: Legiografie.

Lachmann, R. (1988). Bakhtin and carnival: culture as counter-culture. *Cultural Critique, 11*, 115–152.

Lotman, Y. M. (1976). Un modèle dynamique du système sémiotique. In Y. M. Lotman & B. A. Ouspenski (1976), *Travaux sur les systèmes de signes*. Traduits du russe par A. Zouboff. Bruxelles: Editions Complexe.

Lotman, Yu. (1990). *Universe of the mind. A semiotic theory of culture*. Trans. A. Shukman. New York: Tausis.

Lotman, Yu. M. (1992). Vmesto zaklucenija o roli slucajnuch faktorov v istorii kultury. In: Yu. M. Lotman, *Izbrannyje stati v trech tomax. Tom I*, pp. 472–479.

Lotman, Yu. M. (1996). Mekanismy dialoga. In Yu. M. Lotman. *Vnutri mysljascich mirov*. Moscow: Jazyky ruskoj kultury.

Lotman, Yu. M., & Uspensky, B. A. (1978). On the semiotic mechanism of culture. *New Literary History, IX*, 212–232.

Lotman, Yu. M., & Uspensky, B. A. (1984). *The Semiotics of Russian Culture*. Ann Arbor: University of Michigan.

Marková, I. (1987). *Human awareness*. London: Hutchinson.

Marková, I. (2000). Amédée or how to get rid of it: social representations from a dialogical perspective. *Culture & Psychology, 6*, 419–460.

Mihailovic, A. (1997). *Corporeal words: Mikhail Bakhtin's theology of discourse*. Evanston, Ill.: Northwestern University Press.

Moscovici, S. (1998). Social consciousness and its history. *Culture & Psychology, 4*, 411–429.

Moscovici, S., & Vignaux, G. (1994). Le concept de thêmata. In Ch. Guimelli, *Structures et transformations des représentations sociales*. Neuchâtel: Delachaux et Niestlé.

Mukařovská, J. (1936). *Estetická funcke, norma a hodnota jako socialní fakty*. Trans. M. E. Suino as *Aesthetic function, norm and value as social facts*. Ann Arbor: Michigan Slavic Contributions, 3, 1970.

Newson, J. (1979). The growth of shared understandings between infant and caregiver. In Bullowa, M. (Ed.), *Before speech: the beginning of interpersonal communication*. New York: Cambridge University Press.

Reid, A. (1991). The Moscow-Tartu school on Bakhtin. *European Journal for Semiotic Satudies, 3*, 111–126.

Rosenstock, E. (1924). *Angewandte Seelenkunde, eine pragmatische Übersetzung.* Darmstadt: Roetherverlag.

Rozenzweig, F. (1921). *Stern der Erlösung.* Frankfurt: Kauffmann.

Saussure, F. de (1915/1959). *Course in general linguistics.* Glasgow: William Collins.

Saussure, F. de (1910–1911/1993). Troisième cours de linguistique générale (1910–1911). *Saussure's Third Course of lectures on General Linguistics (1910–1911).* (From the notebooks of Emile Constantin). French text ed. by E. Komatsu; English trans. by R. Harris. New York: Pergamon.

Titunik, I. R. (1976). Bakhtin and Soviet semiotics. *Russian Literature, X,* 1–16.

Toomela, A. (in press). Culture as a semiosphere: on the role of culture in the culture–individual relationship. In I. Josephs & J. Valsiner (Eds.), *Dialogicality in development.* Westpont, CT: Ablex.

Tynjanov, J., & Jakobson, R. (1928). Problems in the study of literature and language. In *Roman Jakobson, Selected writings. Vol. III,* pp. 3–6. The Hague: Mouton, 1981.

Valsiner, J. (1989). *Human development and culture.* Lexington: D. C. Heath.

Valsiner, J. (1999). *The guided mind.* Cambridge, Mass.: Harvard University Press.

Voloshinov, V. N. (1929/1973). *Marxism and the philosophy of language.* Trans. L. Matejka and I. R. Titunik. New York: Seminar Press.

Vygotsky, L. S. (1926). *Pedagogicheskaja psikhologija.* Kratkii Kurs. Moscow: Rabotnik Prosveschenija.

Vygotsky, L. S. (1934/1996). *Myshlenije I rech.* Moscow: Gosudarstvennoe Social'no-Ekonomicheskoe Izdatel'stvo.

Vygotsky, L. S., & Luria, A. R. (1930). *Etjudy po istorii povedenija. Pbezjana. Primitiv. Rebjonok.* Moscow: Gosudarstvennoe Izdatel'stvo.

Wertsch, J. V. (1991). *Voices of the mind: a sociocultural approach to mediated action.* Cambridge, Mass.: Harvard University Press.

Wertsch, J. V. (1998). *Mind as action.* New York: Oxford University Press.

Part IV: The Role of Culture in Child Development

8. Making Sense in a World of Symbols

Katherine Nelson

The fundamental human universal is the use of symbols. As Deacon (1997) asserts, we are the "symbolic species." The question, "What does this mean?" is explored in this chapter.

Human development inevitably takes place within "worlds of shared meanings," where meaning is shared through the mediation of symbols. Such a world may vary from a small family context to a broad geographical, national, or societal context within which specific meanings are communally understood to be represented by specific symbolic forms, including but not exclusive to language, oral and written. Cultural meanings surround virtually every aspect of the child's experience. The central problem then is how human infants and young children, born into an interpreted, symbolically organized world, come to participate in its ways. How do children come to understand symbols? How do they begin to move into the myriad novel possibilities afforded by the semiotic world? What are the unique advantages that symbolic functions offer to the developing child? The problem for the child is twofold: (1) how to negotiate the symbolic world and to make sense of its people, places, things, and events prior to mastering its symbols; and (2) how to acquire the symbolic knowledge that is displayed all around, not least in the language used to communicate.

The focus throughout this chapter is on understanding the layered nature of symbolic functions and relations, which are more abstract and complex than most developmental (and philosophical) accounts assume. This complexity lies behind the great gap in cognitive functioning between our prehuman primate ancestors and our own species, as well as the great, often surprising, gap between the cognitive functioning of an infant and toddler and that of a child in the later preschool and school years. The gap is partially bridged by the acquisition of first words, but it is the sophisticated complex cognitive functions made possible by symbolic language that are of greatest significance to the child's (and adult's) transformed knowledge state. The key to understanding this transformation is to go beyond the simple idea that a symbol "stands for" something else to discover what is involved in a symbolic system of any kind, of which natural human languages are prime exemplars. The next section discusses the nature of symbols and symbolic systems, the evolutionary transitions from presymbolic hominid species to *Homo sapiens*, and the analogous transitions in modern human childhood.

SYMBOLIC SYSTEMS

The emergence of symbolic language is perhaps the central puzzle of human evolution. Deacon's (1997) theory of brain and language attacks this problem of the origins of symbolic structures in human life in a way that sheds considerable light on what may be involved in the child's approach to symbols. Deacon relies on Peirce's (1897) theory of semiotics (the science of signs) as the foundation of his theory of the evolution of human mind and language. In doing so, he emphasizes the abstractness of symbols as the primary quality that differentiates them from other signals, abstractness that is derived from the system of relatedness that defines a symbol. His discussion of symbols from this perspective differs from many other uses of the construct, but it most clearly relates to the symbolic nature of human languages and thus to the issue of what distinguishes human language and culture from other communicative and cognitive modes.

Three kinds of signs are identified in Peirce's theory: *iconic, indexical, and symbolic.* Iconic signs have some similarity with the objects that they represent; for example, a linedrawing of an apple or the color red may signify an apple for some purpose. A basic characteristic of signs of whatever type is their dependence on interpretation. Red alone could not indicate "apple" (as opposed to any other red thing) unless its reference were intended and recognized as such. Thus all signs are conventional to some degree. It may be that iconic signs were used to communicate through gestures or similar objects by prehuman hominid species. As later discussed, however, the developmental literature suggests that the use of similarity in sign/symbol relations is not easy for children to grasp, even after they have begun to learn some language. Thus, iconicity as a primary basis for early symbol use may be questionable.

Indexical signs are associated in some way with the object signified; they rest on basic kinds of associative learning. Human infants quickly learn associative relations, but although the indexical relation is based on simple associative learning, the use of an indexical sign for reference, as with the icon, implies intention to interpret the sign in a given way. To refer is not simply to recognize an association between objects, but to use some object or element as a sign for another to bring the other into attention for some purpose. Implicit here is the idea of reference as an intentional social act establishing joint attention, not an accidental association.

Infants come to understand the intentional indexical relation established through pointing during the first 15 months, and first words are learned soon thereafter (Tomasello, 1997). Theories abound regarding intentionality as a basis for interpretations of social actions and words, whether emanating from simulation of individual intentions, as an innate capacity of the human (perhaps primate) mind, or whether learned/acquired through social experience in infancy. Or perhaps intentionality is a multilayered construct and all three sources are in play (Zeedyk, 1996). Like convention, which it must precede, intentionality is essential to language learning.

Unlike icons and indexicals, which have natural associations with the things signified, in the Deacon/Peirce scheme *symbols* are arbitrary, with no natural connection or association with the thing signified, thus arbitrarily established by convention among people. This is a special but not uncommon use of the term *symbol*, within the theory of signs, and in its application to language and communication in general, although *symbol* is often not used by developmental researchers in this restricted way. In some cognitive and psychodynamic uses, symbols are viewed as being highly personal and affect-laden. In semiotic theory, however, the symbolic relation is always social, dependent on an interpreter knowledgeable about the conventional *system* of symbols. Symbols are not just related to elements in the real world on an arbitrary basis, but they relate to other elements in a system of symbols, as in human languages.

The creative potential inherent in such a system is a rich and powerful resource that humans are uniquely able to draw on. This creative potential is not specifically cognitive in an individual sense. Rather, symbols are inherently social in origin and use. When an individual constructs or uses symbols for personal functions (e.g., telling stories to oneself, using words to enhance memory), this is an *extension* of the original social construction of the relation and in effect treats the individual as two separate persons, one who tells the story or says the word (aloud or silently) and the other who interprets or uses it. The bottom line is that all semiosis is fundamentally social; an individual may participate in its construction through a social transaction process but usually the individual learns the symbol system through its use by others. Personalization of semiotic relations is necessarily a social constructive developmental process, as Vygotsky (1978, 1986) envisioned it.

The abstract basis of symbolic relations (e.g., morphosyntactic, semantic, pragmatic relations in linguistics systems) poses a difficulty for the learner but at the same time contains a potential for referential construction. The barrier to easy acquisition of complex abstract grammatical systems is recognized implicitly in many accounts of language learning, but it is not usually pointed out explicitly in discussions of children's encounters with symbolic forms of varying kinds, including word learning.

The complexities of symbols and symbolic systems may be approached by contrasting the Deacon version of Peirce's semiotic theory with ways that the symbolic relation has been traditionally viewed in its application to the acquisition of words by young children, almost always conceptualized in terms of an individual word functioning as a symbol for an individual object. Ogden and Richards (1923/1946) proposed an analysis of the problem in terms of a "semiotic triangle," showing the relation between a word (sign) and an object (or other real element—B and A, respectively in Fig. 8.1).

Given that the word is an arbitrary symbol, the connection with the object is problematic, and according to the standard analysis, its meaning is held to be mediated through a mental element (C) at the apex of the triangle. For example, the word *dog* is an arbitrary sign for a generally accepted natural category of

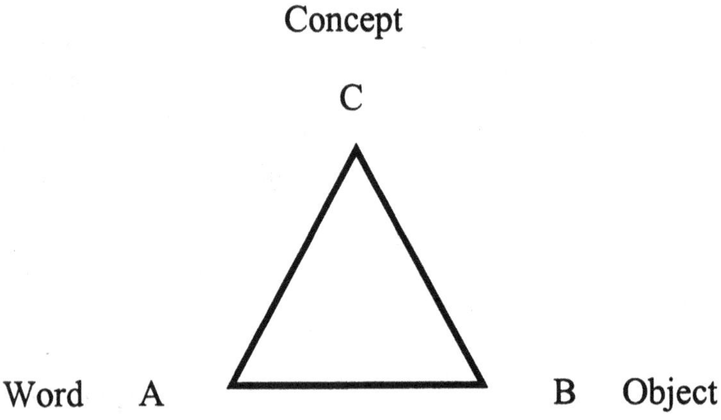

Concept

C

Word   A   B   Object

Figure 8.1
The semiotic triangle. The A–B relation is mediated through C, the object concept.
Adapted from Ogden and Richards (1946)

animals (a species), namely the DOG category. The word used to refer to the category, concept, specific animal, or species could be *chien,* or *cat,* for that matter;
it is arbitrary and conventional. In learning the word *dog* most toddlers learn
to *associate* it with a picture or with an instance of a real dog. Thus phonological
form comes to stand in an *indexical* relation to the animal signified; it is associated with the animal and through perceptual and conceptual generalization
processes becomes associated with like animals, indeed for many children
with animals of other species as well, such as all four-legged creatures (Nelson,
1974).

A problem with this analysis is that an individual who already has a concept
(a mental element that points to the object, as Millikan [1998] states) does not
also need a word in addition, at least not for individual cognitive purposes. The
idea or concept of the thing attended to already exists. The word is necessary,
however, for establishing joint attention, and particularly for sharing reference
and ideas between people under conditions where nonverbal reference in the
immediate context is ambiguous or impossible. This point underscores the fact
that words originate in social communicative situations; but at the same time it
raises the problem of how to bring about shared meaning. An individual may
connect the word and object via a mental element, but that element (or concept)
may differ from that incorporated within the conventional system of symbolic
meanings. This is a problem that the simple word–object relation tends to hide,
although the example of the child's overgeneral category of *dog* referred to previously is suggestive of it.

Indeed, the semiotic triangle is seriously incomplete and requires at least a
complementary triangle that shares the AB side with a different C at the adjoined
apex (see Fig. 8.2).

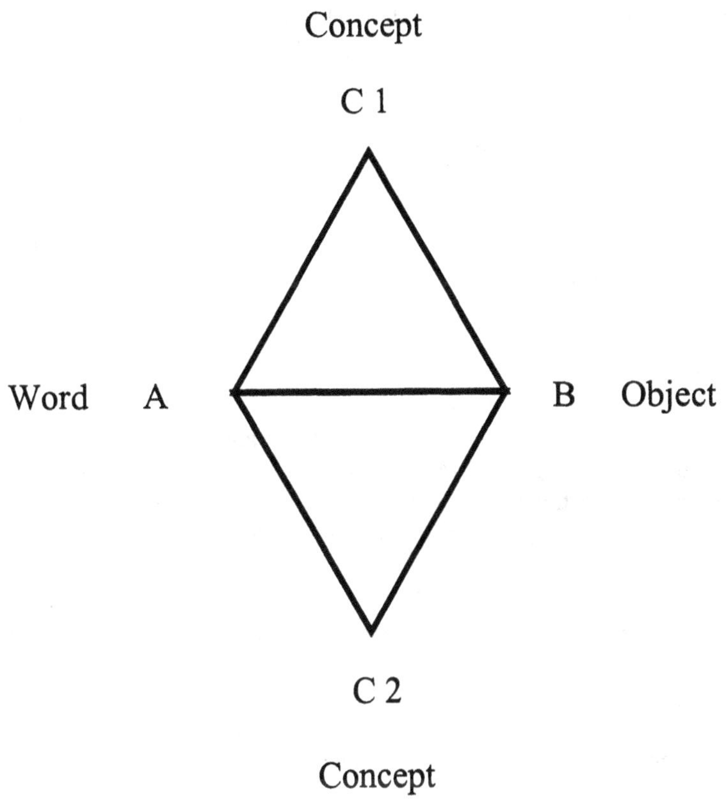

Concept

C 1

Word   A   B   Object

C 2

Concept

Figure 8.2
The expanded concept connecting the meanings of two speakers. Adapted from
Nelson and Shaw (2002)

This figure reveals that the problem is one of *coordinating* concepts, for example, the child's concept with the adult's (Nelson, 1985; Nelson & Shaw, 2002), but as just noted the child's concept (based on pragmatic experience) may differ radically from the adult's conventional one (based on experience with language). The basic problem illustrated in Figure 8.2 is this: how can the same concept come to be associated in the minds of both speakers to the same arbitrary symbol? Here we see that the conventional symbol involved in the word–concept relation rests on the conventionality of the *concept–meaning* as well as the conventionality of the word form.[1]

More significant to our understanding of the symbolic relations, the conventionality rests on the place of the form and meaning within the system of meanings in the language as a whole (Quine, 1960). Association and perceptual/ conceptual generalization (the processes by which the child extends object–word use) do not establish the word as a *symbol* within a system of conventional abstract symbols, where meaning is derived from the system as much as from the original referent of the word. For example, the lexical system that embeds the word *dog* involves relations to other categories of *animals*, such as *cat, horse,* or *tiger,* as well as hypernyms (e.g., *mammal*) and hyponyms (e.g., *collie*). The word *dog* learned on its own in the absence of these contrasting categories establishes it as an index only (an association), not as a symbol.

Deacon (1997) claims that the unique contribution of human cognition was to evolve a mode of learning that involved *systems of abstract symbols.* In support of this claim he points out that indexical relations exist between sign tokens and objects in the world in a one-to-one relation. Deacon explicated the difference between indexical signs and symbolic relations in a way that I have adapted and simplified in Figure 8.3.

Level 1 (A in Fig. 8.3) shows one-to-one relations between word and object that may be succeeded by the generalized category of object (b), based on perceptual/conceptual generalization, but still an indexical relation of word to general category. A transitional relation (c) may be established next among the indexical tokens (words) that *represent the relations existing among the objects in the world.*

For example, the fact that different foods are presented at different meals may lead to a recognition of the *relation among the names* of these foods (which were learned individually and indexically). Thus, different kinds of fruit (apples, oranges, etc.) are recognized as being related, and their names (*apple–orange–banana*) form an indexical group. This transition may lead to the establishment at the higher sign–token level of a pattern of related symbols, a *symbolic system* that recodes at a more abstract level relations that exist at the indexical and real-world level. Thus, patterns established among signs through relations in the world can be recoded in terms of sign–sign relations. *Apple–orange–banana* can be recoded as *fruit* (Nelson, 1985).

Next, the *fruit* pattern of relations may be related to the *sandwich* pattern to form a more abstract *food* hierarchy that exists only symbolically and is not represented *as such* in the real world, but only through the symbolic system[2] (Figure 8.3D). In Deacon's analysis, symbols thus "take off" from their relations in the real world, initially established through indexicals, to become recoded within a symbolic system wherein new relations may be formed among elements, categories, and relationships. Indeed, this is the very basis of a complex language system, relating abstract categories of elements to one another to form sentences and semantic relations. These two types of systematic symbolic relations of traditional grammar were termed *syntagmatic* (combinatorial) and *paradigmatic* (substitutable) by Saussure (1959/1915). Note that for Saussure the relations were held to exist within the language as a whole system, *langue* in Saussure's term, in contrast to *parole,* language as it is used. Then the question is "how can the child discover this abstract system that is not displayed as such in the real world?"[3]

A. Word-object

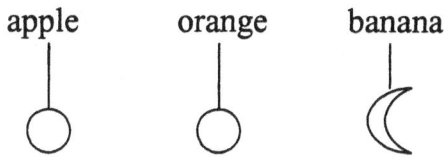

B. Indexical

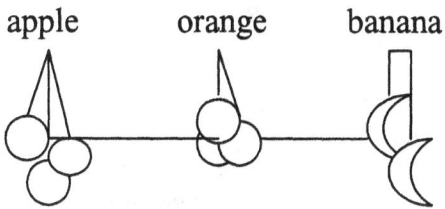

C. Transitional

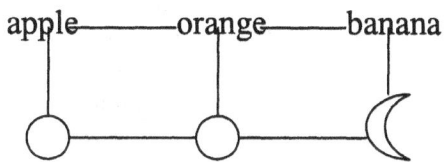

D. Symbolic

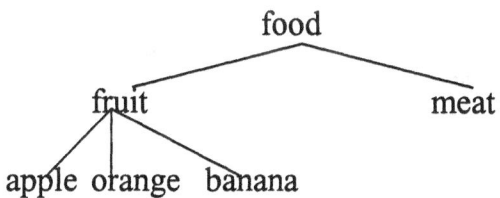

Figure 8.3
Semiotic relations based on Deacon (1997; adapted from Figure 3.3, p. 87). (The word–object level is added to Deacon's levels in this version, and object–object relations are noted at the indexical level, not only at the transitional level, to accord with my understanding of the developmental analogue to Deacon's account.)

Deacon proposes that the symbolic system depends on recoding at successively higher levels of *patterns of relationships*. His basic claim is that these relations depend in the first instance on the learning of indexical tokens initially, and that the learning of vast numbers of these relations is necessary before the symbolic system can be *discovered* at the individual level; it cannot be itself learned from the outset. Thus, the child's initial matching of words for objects to his/her own experientially based concepts of the familiar objects is a necessary step. This is a critical point: the symbolic relation is not accessible to learning from real world relations, but must be discovered in the pattern of *tokens* that represent the pattern of items being mapped. Crucially, for understanding children's progress in this domain, the analysis implies that learning a word is not equivalent to learning a symbol but is necessary to moving to the stage of symbolic acquisition.

Deacon (1997, p. 379) states: "Even a small, inefficient and inflexible symbol system is very difficult to acquire, depends on significant external social support in order to be learned, and forces one to employ very counterintuitive learning strategies that may interfere with most nonsymbolic learning processes." These learning strategies involve focusing on relations among names rather than on the real things named. Much of the language that children learn even very early is abstract in this sense, although children do not grasp the abstraction at first acquisition. According to Deacon, it is necessary to begin from the indexical within any domain, before it is possible to move from the higher-order system to identify a new relation or transformation within the system. Once in command of a word, its place in varying levels of relationships (indexical, symbolic) may become salient in the uses of the word by others in natural discourse. Experience with different examples of such uses, as when parents make the relation between different animals explicit, including their inclusion as animals, no doubt aids the process of recognition of higher levels.

Becoming a symbol user thus appears to be a complex developmental problem. An analogy with the evolutionary problem is suggestive. Hominid ancestors (probably *Homo erectus*) using vocal signals to communicate simple commands or to indicate places, people, or things could learn a small set of differentiated signs, much as *Bonobos* are learning in the experimental situations arranged by Savage-Rumbaugh and her colleagues (Savage-Rumbaugh, Murphy, Sevcik, Brakke, Williams, Rumbaugh, 1993). Of course *Homo erectus* had to invent this set in the absence of a preexisting system of such signs. Each such sign can be established and then learned by others *indexically*, that is, as an associate of the thing indicated. But this is a limited relation of word to thing, without the potentials inherent in the relations among words in a symbolic system. How an index becomes a symbol (in the Deacon/Peirce sense) is at the heart of the long process of symbolic development in evolution or in development.

Most contemporary theories of children's word learning are not addressed to the semiotic problems discussed here, and thus many proposals are non-solutions, resting implicitly on assumptions about universals of concepts as well as language. The solution must involve the child's discovery of conventional *meaning* within a symbol *system*. The paradox here is that symbols must be learned individually, but their semiotic meanings emerge within conventional systems of symbolic relations. Not all word learning and use are symbolic; what is learned as an indexical word–object associate is not a true symbol but an index masquerading as a symbol; symbolic relations may remain complex and opaque to the young child for a number of years.

There is good empirical evidence (originally presented by Piaget, 1929) that young children, and even some adults (Homer, Brockmeier, Kamawar, & Olson, 2000), treat the word–object relation as indexical rather than symbolic, that is, that the word is an inalienable *symptom* of the object and is not at all arbitrary. For example, when asked if a dog could be called "cow," a young child will deny this possibility on the grounds that "dog" is its inalienable name, a property of the thing analogous to fur. This notion was termed *nominal realism* by Piaget. We may conclude from this and related evidence that in at least some, perhaps most, cases very young children are *using a symbolic code (words) in a non-symbolic mode*.

The problems of interpreting the symbolic status of children's words is illuminated by our finding that even 20-month-old toddlers command a range of words that for adult users clearly have symbolic, rather than or in addition to indexical, functions, for example the words *brother, doctor, toys, animals, party*, or *night* (Nelson, Hampson, & Kessler Shaw, 1993). Children presumably learn these words as indexicals, referring to specific people, items, or events. It may be many years before they are understood as symbols within a conventional system of relationships. Indeed, Piaget (1929) presented evidence that children did not understand a kin term like *brother* in terms of its relational implications until well into the school years. These examples have supported our claims that children typically engage in "use without meaning," that is, without symbolic meaning. They may use terms pragmatically, and to reference situations or relations, without having yet formed the abstract system that gives the term its complex meaning within a system of symbolic relations (Levy & Nelson, 1994; Nelson & Shaw, 2002). Thus far, the consideration of symbol learning has been theoretical and abstract. In the next section I examine the developmental problems of children experiencing the world with and without language more closely in the light of Deacon's analysis and in relation to the cognitive change theory proposed by Donald (1991, 2001).

DEVELOPING TOWARD A SYMBOLIC WORLD

Infants and young children experience a world of shared activities that are arranged by adults. Although parents and their children share the places, people, and things in this world, and participate in the same events, they have very different experiences there. Adults live in a semiotic world where virtually everything they do and touch has layers of significance, based on histories and relationships that cannot be apparent to the naïve child. Adults also know and constantly update their knowledge through the medium of language and other symbolic forms, through newspapers, radio, television, computers, and talk. Most important, adults know that there are worlds beyond the horizon that they have never experienced but that they can learn about through linguistic and other media; and they know that other people have had different experiences and may look at the same events in different ways. They know that some representations are not true, but are fictional or false. That is, they know the difference between imagining and doing, between fantasy and reality, between my experience and someone else's. They know all this because they have grown up in and live in a symbolic world, but their 2-year-old children do not yet know any of this.

In contrast, children emerging from babyhood only know what they themselves have experienced from an individualistic or, more properly, an undifferentiated point of view. Over the first year the infant slowly emerges from total dependence on adults to active exploration of the world. Our knowledge of this process is gained from the perspective of the observer; there is no certain way to obtain the perspective of the infant, who can communicate only through action and nonlinguistic vocalization. The objective description of the sensory and motor capacities of the infant and young child, together with sensitive and empathic observation, can, however, provide the foundation for imaginative understanding of what experience of the world from the standpoint of infancy might be. It is not asocial; the world the child experiences is fundamentally social, but the child's experience is not differentiated into self and social others. There is no distinction between what really happened and the child's emotional response to what happened. Fonagy and Target (1997) term this early mentality a state of *psychic equivalence,* wherein infants and young children experience the world as a place where everything, including their own feelings, dreams, and imaginings, are part of a single experiential reality. The child's emotions and representations about experience in the world are all that they have to rely on; there is no alternative knowledge or perspective. The sense that I wish to convey here is of a one-centeredness, a one-perspective reality. Emerging from this undifferentiated state of psychic equivalence depends on access to the differentiated understandings of adults, which are communicated most effectively through language and thus depend on the child's becoming capable of using language for this purpose.

Because of the parallel problems in evolution and development, highlighted by Deacon's analysis, it is helpful to think of the psychic state of the young child as in some ways equivalent to our evolutionary ancestors prior to the emergence of symbolic language in *Homo sapiens.* Although we have no good way of knowing what such experience was like—even less so than with our own children, who share our world—we have clues from present-day primates with whom we share an evolutionary past. The effort to understand their mental states can provide some insights into what it is that the child is engaged in in coming to grips with the symbolic world and how he or she is attempting to make sense.

Yet human life is very different from that of other primates; many, including Deacon, have written and speculated about just what makes the difference, in essence what changed the trajectory of evolution from its biological course to an explosive cultural evolutionary course. The analogy with present-day children is what I wish to pursue, as they too discover symbols with their potential for expanding the world beyond that of the child's own direct experience of it, in the process unlocking the windows into other minds, and other ways of experiencing. It is not that the evolutionary account applies directly to the developmental problem; the evolutionary problem is to explain how humans came to invent symbols in the first place, whereas the developmental problem is how a child already surrounded by symbols learns to interpret them. But both problems involve the dramatic shift from pre-symbolic to symbolic communication and cognition.

One approach to the evolutionary question has been explored by Donald (1991, 2001) in terms of levels of representation that evolved from the basic primate mind and culture to the modern "hybrid mind" based on external and internal symbol systems. This scheme has developmental resonance (Nelson, 1996), particularly so with the semiotic mediation theory of Vygotsky (1978, 1986). In very brief outline, Donald describes four levels of mental representation that have evolved through transitions in hominid evolution, each accompanied by the emergence of more complex cultures. A major advantage of Donald's theory is its close consideration of mental change in relation to both brain evolution and cultural change.

The story here begins with the basic primate level of event representations, or as Donald puts it, the episodic mind. This is a level that enables the memory of episodes and general events, observable in the lives of monkeys and apes, as well as in our own human lives. There are significant limitations to this mental level, however, in that such memory is not accessible to voluntary recall, and thus to reflective thought. It leaves the ape mind locked into its own immediate experience, even though surrounded by a rich social environment; access to prior experience in this state is confined to situations relevant to the present.

In the developmental analogue, infants experience a series of mostly familiar and routine events that are represented in terms of perceptual and motoric schemas or scripts, for example, the feeding scenario, the bathing scenario, the changing and dressing scenario, the going to the park scenario; within these scenarios emotions are bound up with activities (Nelson, 1986). Each of these has its own signals and signs that indicate things to come within it. Scenarios and scripts thus enable the infant to anticipate and participate in the adults' world of caretaking and games. Whereas much linguistic communication may surround the child within and outside of these routines, its meaning for the infant lies in its affective tone, not in its symbolic import.

In the evolutionary scheme according to Donald, a major transition took place with the emergence of *mimesis* in early hominid cultures some two to three million years ago, enabling new levels of precise motoric imitation, self-cued recall of prior experience, and delayed practice of imitated or innovative motoric skills. Mimesis makes possible the sharing of knowledge on a broader scale than the simple social learning of ape cultures. It involves showing and deliberate modeling and practice. It supports a broad variety of individual and social activities that modern humans, adults as well as children, engage in, with or without being accompanied by language (e.g., dance, play, construction of tools, building, sports, and so on). These first two levels of mental representation and accompanying communicative forms (including gesture and nonlinguistic vocalization) remain important parts of our modern human capacities. As Donald emphasized, mimesis in combination with event representations provides much of what we think of as human intelligence.

Mimetic skills emerge in infant development toward the end of the first year, and toddlers readily imitate words, gestures, and actions of all kinds. Imitation provides for a level of communicating with others, as well as learning skills from others. The toddler equipped with these levels of functioning is able to join in with peers and adults in novel as well as familiar activities. These skills also enable young children to engage in play with toys, typically modeling their actions on those of an adult partner or older peers. While not yet fully understanding the significance of the language used, toddlers employ mimetic skills to acquire first words and to interpret the meanings of adult utterances (Nelson, 1996).

The second major transition in Donald's evolutionary scheme, which accompanied the emergence of our species, *Homo sapiens,* was the invention of complex oral language and symbolic imagery, the basis for the establishment of the complex cultures of all preliterate societies, historical and present-day. In the ancestral culture this capacity was employed in the construction of myths and narratives of all kinds that had the function of providing cultural coherence (Carrithers, 1991). For the child, of course, the acquisition of complex oral language is of major significance, and the emergence of narrative-making between the ages of 2 and 5 years has been extensively documented (Nelson, 1996). It can now be seen that the problem in the light of Deacon's analysis is how to move from mimesis and the acquisition of indexicals to complex language and its use for the social construction of narrative.

The final transition in Donald's scheme took place in historical time through the establishment of external memory systems, especially the phonetic alphabet and eventual widespread literacy. This level has advanced the extendability of cultural knowledge to an extraordinary degree. However, it lies beyond the developments considered here.

It should be noted that each of these transitions has precursors in the preceding periods. Other primates imitate, although they do not use imitation as precisely and extensively as humans do; *Homo erectus* presumably evolved oral speech that later enabled the development of true symbolic language; and early *Homo sapiens* used cave paintings, sculptures, and other external forms that served as memory evocations prior to the invention of written language. Nothing arrives *de novo*, in evolution or in development, but always builds on prior forms. The problem for developmental analysis is to trace how one level enables the child to bootstrap to the next level of functioning. At the same time, we can appreciate the contribution that each level makes to the child's intelligent activity, as well as to the present-day adult's everyday life, which continues to draw on event representations and mimetic skills, as well as language and literacy. Donald terms this complex of levels the modern "hybrid" mind where experience can be represented simultaneously and in parallel in different ways.

The different potentials offered by each of these levels of both internal (private) and external (shared) representational systems suggest how children in early development, who lack the symbolic systems of language and literacy, may be negotiating within a social world that is now almost totally dependent on symbolic forms. From this point of view we can imagine what it is to have an episodic/mimetic mind rather than a fully hybrid mind equipped with symbolic forms and interpretants. This conceptualization formed the basis for a theory of how the transition to the latter kind of mind takes place in human development (Nelson, 1996). To reiterate, however, these developments differ from the evolutionary process specifically in taking place within a culture thoroughly saturated with symbolic systems of all kinds. The most obvious problem for the contemporary event-mimetic child of 1 to 2 years of age is the problem of how to learn a symbolic language without a symbolic base to start with. Donald views mimesis as a necessary prelude to true language, and, as noted, children are able to use mimesis to acquire their first (indexical) words.

FROM INDEXES TO SYMBOLS

So long as the symbolic relation is viewed as a simple matter of "standing for" some thing in the real world, rather than as a function of an abstract system of relations, it has been easy for theorists to postulate ways in which children may come to grasp this relation. Indeed, as previously noted, most traditional accounts have been based on individualistic constructions of symbols, in play, fantasy, and in words. For example, Piaget (1962) viewed the onset of the semiotic function in terms of the child's production of symbolic play, as well as the construction of idiosyncratic symbolic associations with words. The use of objects as symbols is as characteristic of our cultural worlds as is the use of words as symbols. For example, both the religious and the political world depend on systematic interpretation of symbolic objects. Perhaps on this basis, most investigators refer to the toddler's use of toys or other objects in play as *symbolic*, implying that the toy is a symbol of the real object, for example, when the child lays a doll in a doll bed and covers it with a cloth.

A number of people have questioned whether the child is using the doll symbolically, standing for herself or for a baby, in a symbolic relation where she herself represents a mother (Huttenlocher & Higgins, 1978; Tomasello, Striano, & Rochat, 1999). Tomasello and colleagues explored toddlers' ability to use one object to stand for another and found that children below the age of 2 years are not able to do this and do not spontaneously produce symbolic actions with objects (such as using a stuffed sock as a doll). The alternative interpretation of the toddler's play schemes is that the toddler is acting out familiar event scripts, where the focus is on the action and activity, not on the relation of the objects to a pretend symbolized world of rules and relations. This interpretation is consistent with the young child's dependence on event representations and mimetic activities. Vygotsky (1978) proposed that children below the age of 3 years did not engage in symbolic play because such play necessarily involved an imaginary world with systems of rules, and it was not until 3 years that the children in Tomasello's studies used objects in ways that would be interpreted as symbolic. Vygotsky's position seems to align well with Deacon's theory of symbol systems and with the present account of development of symbolic relations.

DeLoache (1990) has investigated children's ability to use a model as a representation of full-size room in order to locate objects, and in a vein similar to Tomasello, finds that children below 3 years of age are not successful on these symbolic tasks. These studies highlight the ages of 2 to 4 years as ones that are critical to the acquisition of symbolic insight in the domain of object–object relations, but insight that arises only gradually over this period. The relation of objects to other objects, in play or in communication, apparently has its own complexities. It may even be that understanding the symbolic relation in language is a prerequisite to understanding what would appear to be a more "basic" object–object symbol system.

Studies of how abstract words and categories are learned and used during the years beyond the first acquisition of object words may shed more light on how symbol systems are learned than either symbolic play, model studies, or object word studies. Lyons' (1977) distinction between *reference, denotation*, and *sense* with respect to word meaning reflects some of the same distinctions brought out by the semiotic triangle(s) of Ogden and Richards (1946; see Figure 8.1), but comes closer to the analysis derived from Peirce. Lyons viewed reference as the direct relation between a word and its referent (AB in Figure 8.2), with denotation representing the conceptual level (C), and sense the relations between words within semantic and syntactic systems of the language—the symbolic level. We proposed a developmental trajectory related to this scheme for the analysis of children's early vocabularies (Nelson, 1996; Nelson & Lucariello, 1985). Based on an analogy with Lyons, we claimed that children initially used their words referentially to refer to particular objects in particular contexts (Deacon's indexical). We claimed that they next discovered the concept mediation relation, what Lyons refers to as denotation, allowing the extension of words to new contexts where the conceptual meaning applies. The sense relation as defined by Lyons depends on the relation of words to each other, in categorical relations or semantic fields, essentially the symbolic system. We proposed that children did not discover or move to this level until a later point, first during the preschool years, but for some purposes (e.g., taxonomic categories) not until the school years.

Shaw (1999) applied Lyons's reference–denotation–sense scheme to children's learning of abstract mental state terms, *think* and *know*, where reference is obscure, and thus the relation of the term to real world elements or to conceptual categories is difficult to locate; it may, in fact, not exist as such. Shaw (1999) defined the beginning state of the acquisition of these terms as uses in pragmatic discourse contexts, thus broadly indexical to particular contextual conditions. This "indexical" phase of using the terms was characteristic of the great majority of uses by children between $2^{1}/_{2}$ to 4 years of age. Some transitional uses were observed, where children used the terms to refer to knowing or thinking in different temporal or spatial contexts, for example, in the past or the future.

Although parents used the terms in symbolic or sense relations by relating terms for knowing and thinking within the same utterance or making an explicit distinction between them, their children with one exception (out of 24) did not give any evidence of having related the terms within an abstract semantic system of mental state terms by the age of 4 years. The meanings of these mental state words are exceptionally difficult to learn because of their obscure reference. Children learned to use many related terms (e.g., *remember, guess*) in pragmatic contexts, but they did not apparently relate them in a system of mental state symbols. This is consistent with evidence from experimental studies of children's understanding of mental terms (Moore, Bryant, & Furrow, 1989), which shows that they do not reliably distinguish between meanings of these terms until the early school years.

Children's construction of higher-order categories such as *food, clothes,* and *animals,* which are abstract symbols referring to categories of symbols (e.g., *apple, coat, jaguar*), have a long history in the developmental literature. I proposed (1983; 1985) that children first formed "slot-filler" categories on the basis of observation of items that go together as substitutes in real-world events (thus relying on event representations) and subsequently use the symbolic forms provided by adults to recode these (indexical/transition) categories into symbolic systems, that is, into true taxonomic categories. This process maps onto the transition proposed by Deacon. Studies of children's list-learning, word association, and category-clustering provided evidence for this progression (Lucariello & Nelson, 1985; Lucariello, Kyratzis, & Nelson, 1992). This is an example of how a child may bootstrap from event representations and associated indexical concept–word links to a more abstract, symbolic system through the experience of words used by adults in the events that serve as the knowledge source of categorical construction. It should be noted that the transition from slot-filler categories to abstract taxonomic categories takes place somewhere between the ages of 4 and 7 years, aided by instruction in school (Nelson, 1996).

Taken together, children's early use of relational nouns such as *brother* (Nelson, Hampson, & Kessler, Shaw, 1993), their slot-filler category use of taxonomic terms (Lucariello, Kyratzis, & Nelson, 1992), and Shaw's (1999) study of mental state terms provide further support for the proposal made by Levy and Nelson (1994) that children progress in word learning through a phase of "use without meaning," that is, without symbolic meaning. They easily acquire abstract words imitatively during the preschool years, often called "fast mapping," and use them in appropriate discourse and syntactic contexts, but do not immediately move on to generalizing to new contexts of use or to evidence of symbolic meaning within a system of related words where meanings are derived from relations within the system and not just from relations to real world objects and events.

Shaw's (1999) study of children's understanding of mental state terms also supports Deacon's claims about symbolic uses being dependent on indexical uses within any domain (in contrast to an assumption that symbolic insight is a general across-the-board achievement). In her study, children used terms indexically in specific pragmatic contexts long before they related the terms within a system of related but distinguishable meanings. The fact that they appeared to attain conceptual meaning as a transitional phase is consistent with Deacon's claims as well. But it is notable that for mental terms like *know* and *think* the pattern of relationships "in the world" (i.e., in the minds of interactors) is difficult to establish, making the symbolic relations especially hard to discover, but essential to the meaning of the words themselves. Indeed, the pattern of relationships is not "in the world" in any real sense, but in the symbolic language and the conceptual system, thereby established from it.

Overall, the empirical studies of early words, taxonomic categories, and mental state terms (Lucariello, Kyratzis, & Nelson, 1992; Nelson, 1983, 1996; Nelson & Lucariello, 1985; Nelson & Shaw, 2001) support on the developmental level the claims made by Deacon about the abstract status of symbolic relations, and their dependence on the discovery of a system of relations among tokens established initially on a more concrete level, a level that connects objects, words, and the concepts of communicators. Thus, although the symbolic system depends absolutely on the tutorials of language users to establish initial word–world relations, the symbolic system that the conventional *langue* incorporates must be *discovered* by each individual language user as these lower-level relations accumulate within a domain of use. Experience with language is obviously important in this movement, and expert language users are important models of how symbolic versions of the world are constructed, but ultimately the symbolic level is achieved on the individual mental level through reconstruction, recoding, and transformations that result from recognition of abstract symbolic patterns. Social construction of symbols is only in fact possible because it is based on individual minds that can support it.

THE POINT OF SYMBOLIC SYSTEMS: WHAT IS THE USE?

The previous section suggests just how complicated it may be to acquire a symbolic system, to fully enter into the abstractions that constitute the semiotic world of human cultures, a move that is highly dependent on the achievement of complex language. Given a language environment and social support, human children are motivated to make this move, although it takes several years to accomplish. They are then able to enter into the rich, complex communication between and within individuals that enables sharing social knowledge, personal ideas, and feelings, as well as creating new conceptual systems out of old symbolic structures.

Some mastery of the system of linguistic forms and categories is essential to the comprehension and production of complex syntax characteristic of children's language abilities at about the age of 3 to 4 years. This level of mastery may be thought of as the transitional stage discussed in the previous section, in which indexicals form systems reflective of those exhibited in the world, but not yet decontexted from that use, as exemplified in the uses of the mental state terms at what Shaw (1999) termed the denotation level. Levy's analyses of person, tense, and temporal–causal terms suggest that grammatical forms may be understood and systematized in the same way (Levy, 1989; Levy & Nelson, 1994). Although grammatical relations are abstract, they are not more abstract than semantic relations, for example, the distinction between *know* and *think*. There is a good deal of evidence that children acquire patterned phrases from use in pragmatic contexts and use these as scaffolds for further construction, as well as the abstraction of systematic relationships (Lieven, Pine, & Baldwin, 1997). Symbolic systems are not all acquired in the same way by all individuals. The symbolic level is not achieved in language all at once and certainly not instantaneously. Rather, small parts of the semantic and syntactic systems are organized in patterns that with frequent use become transformed into abstract systems of relations that may lend themselves to a deeper level of understanding and greater possibilities of transformation and articulation.

The advantage of a complex symbolic system for understanding experience in a new way can be seen especially in narrative construction and comprehension (see Nelson, 1989). As Donald (1991) claimed, narrative is the natural product of language, universal across cultures. In the child's entry into the semiotic world, narrative is an important scaffold. This is most apparent in two arenas of developmental research: personal memory-based narratives and stories. Narratives about the child's lived experience are often co-constructed by parents and their children "on-line," beginning when the child is 2 to 3 years old and able to engage in short conversations. Typically parents take the bits and pieces contributed by the child and weave a narrative around them. By this means, parents assist young children in constructing stories about their own past lives (Fivush & Hamond, 1990; Hudson, 1990). Even more frequently they present their children with anticipations of future happenings, although talking about the future is less well documented than talk about the past (Benson, 1994; Lucariello & Nelson, 1987; Nelson, 1989; Presler, 2000). Both kinds of temporally displaced talk depend on children's emerging capacity to use the symbolic resources of language to reconstruct in their own minds an imaginative production collaboratively constructed with another. Narratives often use the language construction to explain why something happened the way it did or to anticipate something that has not yet happened or to create a made-up reality (a fiction). The narrative form requires experience to understand its structure and its rules. At the same time experience with such talk enables the child to gain greater control over the symbolic resources of language. It is not surprising that such talk becomes common around 3 years of age, as children are coming to use and understand the symbol systems of their language and the constructions they make possible.

The practice of engaging children in narratives about their past experience is related to the onset of autobiographical memory and the offset of what is termed "childhood amnesia" (Fivush, 1994; Nelson, 1993). Autobiographical memory represents a new function of memory not present in the early years of life, specifically related to the child's emerging concept of self. The very concept of a continuing self appears to be a social construct that depends on symbolic constructions. Entering into the narrative of the child's past, both near and far, enables the child to establish a continuity of the self across time, a continuity that exists wholly in the imaginative, symbolic sphere, supported by the rules and scaffolding of parental representations, which in turn are supported by the rules and scaffolding of the surrounding and embedding culture (Nelson, 1997, 2000). The same symbolic structures support an imaginary construction of the self's future, existing only within an imaginary extension of a symbolic world with rules.

These experiences of self in the past and future and self in relation to parental expectations and rules bring about a newly emerging conception of self that may be termed the "cultural self." This self recognizes continuity over time and differentiation of one's own private experience from that of others, and it also has begun to situate itself within a "community of minds" (Nelson, Henseler, & Plesa, 2000), that is within a social–cultural world that extends beyond the family and the everyday world. As we have argued, "theory of mind," that is, understanding that actions derive from mental states, that mental states may differ from states in the real world, and correspondingly that others' mental states may differ from one's own, depends on symbolic insights. This claim is implicit in our interpretation of children's understanding of mental state terms, as found in the Nelson and Shaw (2001) study. Empathy with another and interpretation of intentionality on the basis of familiarity with action patterns may provide a good event/mimetic basis for anticipating others' actions, reactions, and interactions, as observed in children at around 1 to 2 years of age. An articulation of mental states is a symbolic project, however, involving an abstract system of relations and terms that are not accessible in the concrete world of experience (Nelson, Plesa, & Henseler, 1998). It is not surprising that children do not reveal knowledge of these complex relations until 4 years of age (Astington, Harris, & Olson, 1988; Nelson, 1996).

Narratives of experience, as well as stories of fiction and fact, incorporate in symbolic form accounts of actors' mental states, causal relations between these and actions, and explanations of people's motivations and behavior. These are of obvious use in coming to share the perspectives of others on shared and non-shared experiences. Furthermore, stories, oral or written, video or pictured, fiction or fact, take the child beyond the everyday world and thus help to situate the child within a larger context, where not everything can be anticipated from one's own prior experience and where often new rules apply and new explanations of events are called for. Stories represent complex events in a dramatic format that has its own structural rules. They do not simply refer to an event, but reconstruct it anew.

Children's responses to narratives in early childhood lend support to the model of development that grows out of the analysis of the acquisition of symbolic systems. For example, children often insist that a storybook be read over and over again, until they are able to recite the text almost flawlessly, and they will correct the adult reader if a mistake is made. What is the explanation for such an approach to stories? Following Deacons' clues, it seems likely that the associations made within the text need to be repeated until they can be recoded, not just into an account of the narrative, but to form new personally meaningful associations of an abstract form. In these cases the text displays a symbolic construction from which the child must reconstruct an indexical relation to his or her own understanding of the world. Miller and her colleagues (Miller, Hoogstra, Mintz, Fung, & Williams, 1993) provide a beautiful example of a child who uses repetitions of "Peter Rabbit" to imaginatively construct associations with his own life experiences and emotions.

Similarly, when 3- to 4-year-old children begin to tell made-up stories of their own, these typically have the exact same abstract structure time after time. Girls typically tell stories about princesses and marriage, whereas boys tell tales of superheroes fighting off one disaster after another (Nicolopoulou & Weintraub, 1998). It is plausible that these children are learning and practicing the abstract symbolic systems (relations of royalty, marriage rules, etc.) of these specific domains. The same symbolic types appear in improvisational play.

Play as narrative in action can serve as a transition toward narrative in verbal form. Children's play seems to follow a trajectory toward understanding patterns and transformations of reality that has similarities to their move toward symbolic systems in language, and is similar as well to their emerging understanding and construction of narrative. In play, children begin with concrete world relations and represent them in action at what can be termed an "indexical" level. Play begins on a pragmatic, concrete level, mimetically repeating everyday experience and marking it as "not real." Then, with the help of the use of forms that bridge the transition, a move to symbolic systems may begin. As children approach the 3- to 4-year-old age, they begin to construct imaginary worlds with other children, transforming reality and following rules derived from symbolic sources such as fairy tales or superhero tales. Thus a new level of relations removed from everyday life emerges at what we could term the true symbolic level. This level is a social and cultural construction adopted by children to their own uses, laying open the possibility of articulating the elements in the systems of rules. The analysis of play in terms of the kinds of symbolic development described in this chapter has considerable potential and would place in perspective the earlier play developments usually (and mistakenly from this perspective) termed symbolic. Further analysis in this domain, however, would take us far afield from the purposes of the present chapter.

Out of these varied practices in symbolic construction, communication, and narrative in the early childhood years come abstract, removed from concrete reality, understandings about the world and its people. For one, there is the understanding that there is a remote personal past and a remote personal future that exist only in the imagination of the tellers about these things. For another, there are distinctions between fact and fiction. And of great significance, there exist permeable boundaries between people so that one can know another's thoughts through talk about them. These are critically important, uniquely human, achievements of the preschool years.

CONCLUSION

This chapter has presented the following main points: Symbols, as discussed here, are not only referential indexes, one thing standing for another, but are arbitrary, conventional, and embedded within abstract systems of related symbols, from which they derive meanings beyond what they may stand for in the concrete world. Recent research shows that even the "stand-in" relation of one object for another is difficult for young children to grasp. The development of symbolic language appears to lead the ability to use objects or models in this representational way. Symbolic systems are the source of new abstract creations beyond the concrete worlds of direct experience. These open up for the child new understandings of the self and the social world.

Experience in acquiring and using symbolic systems in oral and imagery form prepares for the acquisition of literate, logical, and systematically organized cultural knowledge systems. The discovery of symbolic systems of all kinds, the comprehension and productions of narratives of the self and of other people, and the understanding of abstract explanations of how people and the world work are enormous achievements in early childhood. Fortunately, children do not need to do all the constructive work themselves but are the beneficiaries of cultural knowledge and symbolic forms represented in the social world in which they live. Children must do the work of symbolic discovery, but their guides are all around them, bathing them in patterns waiting to be discovered.

NOTES

1. Werner and Kaplan proposed a theory of the symbol–object problem in terms of the mother–child construction of the symbol that is similar to the enlarged triangle solution but that does not take the child beyond the single relation based on shared meaning through the intimacy of the mother–child bond (Werner & Kaplan, 1963).

2. The claim that higher-order categorical relations are abstract and not apparent in the real world, thus necessitating construction by the child through intermediate slot-filler categories, was made by Nelson (1983), but this claim has been widely ignored and/or denied. It is an inherent property of Deacon's analysis.

3. This question, of course, is the basis for Chomsky's (1965) claim of the inadequacy of the data to the learning problem of the child, leading to the conclusion that grammar must be built-in. This led, in turn, to claims of Universal Grammar, modern linguistics, language acquisition studies, and all that has followed. Deacon's analysis is specifically aimed at providing an alternative to Chomsky's account.

REFERENCES

Astington, J. W., Harris, P. L., & Olson, D. (Eds.). (1988). *Developing theories of mind.* Cambridge: Cambridge Universtiy Press.

Benson, J. B. (1994). The origins of future-orientation in the everyday lives of 9- to 36-mo-old infants. In M. M. Haith, J. B. Benson, R. J. Roberts, & B. Pennington (Eds.), *The development of future-oriented processes* (pp. 375–408). Chicago: University of Chicago Press.

Carrithers, M. (1991). Narrativity: Mindreading and making societies. A. Whiten (Ed.), *Natural theories of mind: evolution, development and simulation of everyday mindreading.* (pp. 305–318). Oxford: Blackwell.

Chomsky, N. (1965). *Aspects of a theory of syntax.* Cambridge, Mass.: MIT Press.

Deacon, T. W. (1997). *The symbolic species: the co-evolution of language and the brain.* New York: W. W. Norton.

DeLoache, J. S. (1990). Young children's understanding of models. In R. Fivush & J. Hudson (Eds.), *Knowing and remembering in young children.* New York: Cambridge University Press.

Donald, M. (1991). *Origins of the modern mind.* Cambridge, Mass.: Harvard University Press.

Donald, M. (2001). *A mind so rare: the evolution of human consciousness.* New York: Norton.

Fivush, R. (1994). Constructing narrative, emotion, and self in parent-child conversations about the past. In U. F. Neisser, R. Fivush (Ed.), *The remembering self: construction and accuracy in the self-narrative* (pp. 136–157). New York: Cambridge University Press.

Fivush, R., & Hamond, N. R. (1990). Autobiographical memory across the preschool years: Toward reconceptualizing childhood amnesia. In R. Fivush & J. A. Hudson (Eds.), *Knowing and remembering in young children* (pp. 223–248). New York: Cambridge University Press.

Fonagy, P., & Target, M. (1997). Attachment and reflective function: their role in self-organization. *Development and Psychopathology, 9,* 679–700.

Homer, B. D., Brockmeier, J., Kamawar, D., & Olson, D. R. (2000). Between realism and nominalism: Learning to think about names and words. *Genetic, Social and General Psychology Monographs, 127,* 5–25.

Hudson, J. A. (1990). Constructive processes in children's event memory. *Developmental Psychology, 26,* 180–187.

Huttenlocher, J., & Higgins, E. T. (1978). Issues in the study of symbolic development. In W. A. Collins (Ed.), *Minnesota Symposium on Child Psychology. 11*, pp. 98–140. Hillsdale, NJ, Erlbaum.

Levy, E. (1989). Monologue as development of the text-forming function of language. In K. Nelson (Ed.), *Narratives from the crib* (pp. 123–170). Cambridge, Mass.: Harvard University Press.

Levy, E., & Nelson, K. (1994). Words in discourse: a dialectical approach to the acquisition of meaning and use. *Journal of Child Language, 21*, 367–390.

Lieven, E., Pine, J. M., & Baldwin, G. (1997). Lexically-based learning and early grammatical development. *Journal of Child Language, 24*, 187–219.

Lucariello, J., Kyratzis, A., & Nelson, K. (1992). Taxonomic knowledge: what kind and when. *Child Development, 63*, 978–998.

Lucariello, J., & Nelson, K. (1985). Slot-filler categories as memory organizers for young children. *Developmental Psychology, 21*, 272–282.

Lucariello, J., & Nelson, K. (1987). Remembering and planning talk between mothers and children. *Discourse Processes, 10*, 219–235.

Lyons, J. (1977). *Semantics* (Vol. 1). Cambridge: Cambridge University Press.

Miller, P. J., Hoogstra, L., Mintz, J., Fung, H., & Williams, K. (1993). Troubles in the garden and how they get resolved: A young child's transformation of his favorite story. In C. A. Nelson (Ed.), *Memory and affect in development* (Vol. 26, pp. 87–114). Hillsdale, N.J.: Lawrence Erlbaum.

Millikan, R. G. (1998). A common structure for concepts of individuals, stuffs, and real kinds: more mama, more milk, and more mouse. *Behavioral and Brain Sciences, 21,* 55–100.

Moore, C., Bryant, D., & Furrow, D. (1989). Mental terms and the development of certainty. *Child Development, 60,* 167–171.

Nelson, K. (1974). Concept, word, and sentence: Interrelations in acquisition and development. *Psychological Review, 81,* 267–285.

Nelson, K. (1983). The derivation of concepts and categories from event representations. In E. Scholnick (Ed.), *New trends in conceptual representation: challenges to Piaget's theory?* (pp. 129–149). Hillsdale, N.J.: Lawrence Erlbaum.

Nelson, K. (1985). *Making sense: the acquisition of shared meaning.* New York: Academic Press.

Nelson, K. (1986). *Event knowledge: structure and function in development.* Hillsdale, N.J.: Lawrence Erlbaum.

Nelson, K. (1989). Monologue as the linguistic construction of self in time. In K. Nelson (Ed.), *Narratives from the crib* (pp. 284–308). Cambridge, Mass.: Harvard University Press.

Nelson, K. (1993). The psychological and social origins of autobiographical memory. *Psychological Science, 4,* 1–8.

Nelson, K. (1996). *Language in cognitive development: the emergence of the mediated mind.* New York: Cambridge University Press.

Nelson, K. (1997). Finding oneself in time. In Y. G. Snodgrass & R. L. Thompson (Eds.), *Annals of the New York Academy of Sciences.* New York: New York Academy of Sciences.

Nelson, K. (2000). Narrative, time and the emergence of the encultured self. *Culture and Psychology, 6,* 183–196.

Nelson, K., Hampson, J., & Kessler Shaw, L. (1993). Nouns in early lexicons; evidence, explanations, and implications. *Journal of Child Language, 20,* 61–84.

Nelson, K., Henseler, S., & Plesa, D. (2000). Entering a community of minds: a feminist perspective on theory of mind development. In P. Miller & E. S. Scholnick (Eds.), *Feminist development: regendering developmental psychology.* New York: Routlege.

Nelson, K., & Lucariello, J. (1985). The development of meaning in first words. In M. D. Barrett (Ed.), *Children's single word speech.* Chichester, England: Wiley.

Nelson, K., Plesa, D., & Henseler, S. (1998). Children's theory of mind: an experiential interpretation. *Human Development, 41,* 7–29.

Nelson, K., & Shaw, L. K. (2002). Developing a socially shared symbolic system. In E. Amsel & J. Byrnes (Eds.), *Language, literacy and cognitive development.* Mahwah, N.J.: Erlbaum.

Nicolopoulou, A., & Weintraub, J. (1998). Individual and collective representations in social context: a modest contribution to resuming the interrupted project of a sociocultural developmental psychology. *Human Development, 41,* 215–235.

Ogden, C. K., & Richards, I. A. (1923/1946). *The meaning of meaning.* London: Routledge & Kegan Paul.

Peirce, C. S. (1955/1897). Logic as semiotic: the theory of signs. In J. Buchler (Ed.), *The philosophical writings of Peirce* (pp. 98–110). New York: Dover Books.

Piaget, J. (1929). *The child's conception of the world* (Tomlinson, J. & A., Trans.). New York: Harcourt, Brace & World.

Piaget, J. (1962). *Play, dreams, and imitation in childhood.* New York: Norton.

Presler, N. (2000). *Pre-writing memories: from anticipatory discourse to children's personal narratives.* Unpublished Ph.D. Dissertation. City University of New York Graduate School, New York.

Quine, W. V. O. (1960). *Word and object.* Cambridge, Mass.: MIT Press.

Saussure, F. d. (1959/1915). *Course in general linguistics.* New York: The Philosophical Library.

Savage-Rumbaugh, E. S., Murphy, J., Sevcik, R. A., Brakke, K. E., Williams, S. L., & Rumbaugh, D. M. (1993). Language comprehension in ape and child. *Monographs of the Society for Research in Child Development, 58,* 3–4.

Shaw, L. K. (1999). *The development of the meanings of "think" and "know" through conversation.* Unpublished Ph.D. Dissertation, City University of New York Graduate Center, New York.

Tomasello, M. (1997). Joint attention as social cognition. In C. Moore & P. Dunham (Eds.), *Joint attention: its origins and role in development.* Hillsdale, N.J.: Erlbaum.

Tomasello, M., Striano, T., & Rochat, P. (1999). Do young children use objects as symbols? *British Journal of Developmental Psychology, 17,* 563–584.

Vygotsky, L. S. (1978). *Mind in society: the development of higher psychological processes.* Cambridge, Mass.: Harvard University Press.

Vygotsky, L. S. (1986). *Thought and Language.* Cambridge, Mass.: MIT Press.

Werner, H., & Kaplan, B. (1963). *Symbol formation: an organismic-developmental approach to language and the expression of thought.* New York: Wiley.

Zeedyk, M. S. (1996). Developmental accounts of intentionality: toward Integration. *Developmental Review, 16,* 416–461.

9. Development of Symbol Meaning and the Emergence of the Semiotically Mediated Mind

Aaro Toomela

There are two fundamentally different ways of explaining mental development. According to one view, development can be understood as a quantitative growth in information-processing capacity and in domain-specific knowledge. According to the other view, mental development proceeds through a series of qualitative changes. This latter view also postulates the emergence of novel ways of mental organization in the process of a child's interaction with the environment. There is no consensus, however, on the question of how such qualitative changes should be understood and whether they can be ordered into a series of domain-general stages. In this chapter, I suggest that human mental development is characterized by qualitative general-stage-like changes. These changes are related to the development of language and semiotically mediated thought. In developing these ideas, I rely on the theoretical inheritance of cultural–historical psychology in the form in which it was established by Vygotsky.

I have argued previously that the cultural–historical perspective needs to be elaborated at three hierarchical levels of analysis (Toomela, 2000a). The first and most general level of analysis can be called *a theory of functional systems*. The second level of analysis concerns general principles of the emergence and development of the human mind. According to cultural–historical psychology, specifically human attributes of mind result from the emergence of semiotically mediated mental processes. Semiotically mediated processes, in turn, develop in the social interaction of individual minds (see Toomela, 1996a, 1996b, in press for an analysis of semiotic mediation).

Finally, at the third, most specific level of analysis, two further issues need to be investigated. First, according to cultural–historical psychology (Vygotsky & Luria, 1994; Vygotsky, 1996), semiotic systems develop. To understand the semiotically mediated mind, it must be understood how symbols, especially their meaning, develop. Second, it must be understood how semiotically mediated processes emerge with the synthesis of nonmediated, "natural," mental processes.

These three levels of analysis are in hierarchical relationships. This means that rules of each lower (more general) level of analysis apply to each higher (more specific) level of analysis. At the same time, each higher level of analysis is defined by additional constraints and rules, which do not apply to the more general levels (see Baldwin, 1906, for a thorough analysis of the idea of hierarchy).

THE FIRST LEVEL OF ANALYSIS: CAUSE, EXPLANATION, AND THE THEORY OF FUNCTIONAL SYSTEMS

The Rationale for Discussing the Question of Explanation

Every scientific inquiry has a goal to understand better the thing or phenomenon under study. That understanding is, in essence, a description of possible *causes* and *explanation*, of the subject of inquiry. It is important to realize that both of these basic notions, cause and explanation, may have different meanings (e.g., Lakoff & Johnson, 1999). The specific meaning of cause and explanation that underlies scientific research constrains the ways in which the subject matter of investigation is conceptualized. I suggest that the most common understanding of cause that (usually implicitly) underlies most of "modern" psychology has a very limited scope and cannot lead to an explanation of the thing or phenomenon.

Cause and Explanation

The understanding of the concept of cause has a long history. Historically, the most influential analysis of the notion of cause was proposed by Aristotle, according to whom (Aristotle, 1941a), there are four kinds of causes of a thing: a *material cause*, the elements of which an object is created; a *formal cause*, the expression of the essence; an *efficient cause*, the means by which it is created; and a *final cause*, the end for which it is:

All the causes now mentioned fall under four senses [. . .] but of these some are cause as the *substratum* (e.g., the parts), others as the *essence* (the whole, the synthesis, and the form). The semen, the physician, the adviser, and in general the agent, are all *sources of change* or of rest. The remainder are causes as the *end* and the good of the other things [. . .] (Aristotle, 1941a, p. 753).

Description of all these kinds of causes can be understood as an understanding or an explanation of a thing (e.g., Aristotle, 1941a, Book I, Chapter 2). Causation in much of modern psychology, however, is seen only as efficient causation (e.g., Bem & Looren de Jong, 1997; Lakoff & Johnson, 1999). Such restricted understanding of causation leads only to the search of "laws," which in essence are names for regular co-variations of events. So, for example, an explanation of why a dog salivates when eating his food can be a law of nature like "Whenever a mammal gets food in its mouth it salivates" (Bem & Looren de Jong, 1997, pp. 19–20). But, if we ask now whether we really have *explained* why a dog salivates, then not only Aristotle, but also many psychologists, especially from the end of the nineteenth and the beginning of the twentieth century, would say—no. First, the "law of salivation," mentioned above, is wrong. Dogs do not salivate when they take water with a very low concentration of food into their mouth (cf. Pavlov, 1927, 1951). In addition, Pavlov demonstrated that for explaining salivation we must analyze which parts of the body are used for that act (salivary glands, receptors, different parts of the brain, i.e., material cause) and the relationship between the parts (formal cause). In addition, we must take into account the sources of change (different kinds of food as an efficient cause) and the purpose of the act, enhancement of digestion (final cause).

Most of modern psychology seems to search for only efficient causes. For example, the leading theory of personality declares that personality is understood as a structure of five factors: neuroticism, extraversion, openness, agreeableness, and conscientiousness. These five factors emerge in the factor analysis of answers to a large number of questions about oneself. The authors of this approach suggest that the issue of the structure of personality traits is resolved through this procedure (McCrae, 2000). What they have actually done, however, is to observe that some answers to the items in the Personality Inventory tend to be correlated. Overall, they have identified five clusters of such correlations. And after finding such regularities, they "explain" that regularity with a name. So, neuroticism becomes an explanation to why certain answers tend to be correlated. And extraversion becomes an explanation to why answers to other items are correlated. I think we still cannot explain neuroticism or extraversion. We have identified phenomena, but they need an explanation.

Many other similar examples can be found in psychology. I present only a few here. Children's word learning is "explained" by taxonomic assumption, which says that when hearing a novel word, children have a bias to assume that that word refers to a category of objects (e.g., Markman, 1990). We still cannot explain how that assumption (or several other assumptions) works. What are its components and what relationships between those components are necessary for such a bias to emerge. Children's thinking is "explained" by theory theory, which claims that young children possess "everyday" theories that are "coherent systems of knowledge that *organize and structure* everyday thinking" (Wellman & Gelman, 1998, p. 529, my emphasis). So, it seems that there is some Mister Theory that, as an efficient cause, organizes thinking? And there is no need to explain what these theories are and from where they came—they are innate.

In sum, I am arguing that the modern prevailing trend in psychology to "explain" mental phenomena through the identification and naming of efficient causes cannot lead to an explanation of mental phenomena. Fortunately, the perspective on how to study mental phenomena was not thus limited in scope at the beginning of scientific psychology. The broader view, later named the *theory of functional systems* in cultural–historical psychology, was explicitly described by Wilhelm Wundt more than a century ago. To understand mind, a psychologist must describe: (1) psychical elements; (2) psychical compounds; (3) interconnection of psychical compounds; (4) psychical developments; and (5) psychical causality and its laws (Wundt, 1897, p. 27). As can be seen, the list of aspects to be described is quite similar to the kinds of causes proposed by Aristotle, with the exception of explicitly requiring the study of *development* in addition to the description of other aspects of causality. Indeed, in changing things or phenomena, it is also necessary to describe how novel elements or parts are created and from where and how they emerge before it is possible to synthesize those parts or elements into a more complex thing or phenomenon. The theory of functional systems that underlies cultural–historical psychology differs from the Wundtian approach in details. There are some principles worthy of attention, however, that were not explicitly described by Vygotsky or Luria, founders of cultural–historical psychology. These aspects can be found in the works of other psychologists preceding or contemporary to Vygotsky.

The next part of this chapter describes the theory of functional systems and elaborates it, using works of several other scholars. (It should be mentioned that almost all of those principles can also be found in the general systems theory by von Bertalanffy [1968]. I want to emphasize the role of the earlier psychologists who not only had described the same principles before von Bertalanffy but who also had applied their general "metatheoretical" ideas in psychology. Correspondingly, the following description is based on the works of psychologists only.)

The Theory of Functional Systems

According to the theory of functional systems, to understand mental phenomena, it is necessary to describe three of their complementary aspects: the components it is made of; the specific relationships between the components that comprise a whole or structure of the phenomenon; and development, how the phenomenon emerges and changes in time (Luria, 1969; Vygotsky, 1994).

There are two characteristics of *components* that should be described. First, the *quality* of a component, the description of what a component is and in what relationships it has a potential to be involved (e.g., Hobhouse, 1901; Koffka, 1935; Köhler, 1947; Vygotsky, 1994; Werner, 1948; Wundt, 1897). Second, the *quantity*, the number of components, is important (e.g., Hobhouse, 1901). Thus, it is important to realize that systems are made of certain kinds of components. It may be possible to build similar systems from different elements. For example, the same idea can be expressed with different words in different languages. But to build certain systems, such different components must share some qualities. There are ideas, for example, that can be expressed only by using some forms of symbols. Even though there can be infinitively different kinds of symbols, they must be symbols to express the idea of an atom or solar system, or any other idea about phenomena humans cannot perceive directly through sense organs

(Toomela, in press). It is obvious that quantity is also important here. To express different ideas, we must have many different words.

Next, to understand systems as wholes, specific *relations* between the components must be described because the same components can be organized into very different systems (Koffka, 1935; Köhler, 1947; Vygotsky, 1994; Werner, 1948). The same words in different order, for example, can convey very different meanings. "Aaro Toomela is writing a chapter" is not the same as "A chapter is writing Aaro Toomela."

With the emergence of specific relations between components, a qualitatively new *whole, a higher-order system*, emerges. Properties of a whole cannot be reduced to properties of its elements. None of the components "Aaro," "is," "writing," "a," "chapter" will convey the meaning of "Aaro is writing a chapter." All systems—which are wholes from distinguishable but not separable components—have two complementary aspects, which I call *dynamic possibilities* and *topographical constraints* (see also, for a similar distinction, Lewin, 1935, who differentiated psychodynamic and topological descriptions of a structure; Koffka, 1935, who differentiated processes and conditions; and Köhler, 1947, who differentiated dynamic and topographical factors of structures, respectively). *Topographical constraints* exclude certain forms of function of a system or restrict processes to the possibilities compatible with topographical conditions. *Dynamic possibilities*, in turn, characterize all different combinations of components that satisfy the same topographical constraints of a system. In other words, at a specific level of analysis, a whole may remain the same ("the same" is defined by topographical constraints) despite the reorganization of relationships of components of a system (dynamic possibilities) at a more detailed level of analysis. For example, it is possible to create many different words from a limited number of sounds or letters. Dynamic possibilities for creating different words are almost infinite. But a whole is still topographically constrained. There are forms of function that words cannot have in principle. We can make a plan of a house with words, but we cannot build a real house from words. We can name different food with words, but we cannot eat words.

Finally, the *development* of a system must be described. Before describing general principles of development as understood in the theory of functional systems, I will explain why it is absolutely necessary to analyze all systems developmentally for explaining them. There are two complementary reasons. First, every system is built from specific components. Even though the same idea can be expressed in different languages, the systems of different languages are in many respects different. Some people understand one language and some people another language. That understanding is determined by what specific components are the material causes of the language (vocabulary) and what specific relations exist between those components (syntax or grammar). In other words, it is possible to build similar systems from different kinds of components. But such systems can never be identical in every respect. Thus, to understand a system, *components specific to that system must be described* (see also Baldwin, 1906). Second, there is an extremely important principle to be understood: *When a component is included into a system, both the properties of the new whole and the properties of the component change* (Hobhouse, 1901; Koffka, 1935; Köhler, 1947). An example, often used by Gestalt psychologists and Vygotsky is that of a molecule of water. Elements of the molecule, hydrogen and oxygen, burn or support burning. The composite whole, H_2O, however, can be used for extinguishing fire. The components after inclusion into a molecule cannot behave in a way they could before the inclusion into a whole. Similarly, in a study of the developed human mind we cannot separate the role of culture from the role of biological factors. The developed human mind is a whole in which we find both "cultured biology" and "biologized culture."

So, for explaining a system, its specific components must be described. But how can we tell what are the components if their properties have changed after the inclusion into a whole? In a whole, all components have a common faith due to properties of the whole that cannot be reduced to the properties of its components. Thus, to know what the components of a system are, they must be described before they enter a hierarchically higher order whole. That is the question of development. To understand a whole we must follow its emergence. Otherwise we can never be sure of which components it is built. And without distinguishing (not separating!) components of a system, we cannot explain the system.

Thus, one goal of developmental analysis is to identify what are the true components of a system. The other goal of developmental analysis is to understand the emergence of new components. The latter aspect of developmental analysis can be summarized by a definition of development by Heinz Werner (see also Hobhouse, 1901, for a similar idea). That definition is known as an orthogenetic principle (Werner, 1978):

[. . .] it is an orthogenetic principle, which states that wherever development occurs it proceeds from a state of relative globality and lack of differentiation to a state of increasing differentiation, articulation, and hierarchic integration. (pp. 108–109)

That definition, of course, cannot explain development; it does not state why development takes place or how differentiation takes place. But that definition is useful for understanding from where the new elements emerge—they emerge from existing elements in the process of differentiation. What makes differentiation possible? I suggest that differentiation becomes possible when there is a system with a sufficient number of components. The notion of *dynamic possibilities* (see above) implies that lower-order components can be combined in different ways and the emerging whole can still have the qualitatively same form (defined by *topographical constraints*). If there are only two components to combine, the number of combinations is limited to the number of different kinds of relations that may emerge between components (two sounds may give us two combinations that both can be words, "on" versus "no," for example). The maximum degree of differentiation of a system is limited to the number of possible combinations of its components. Vocabulary, for example, is in many languages differentiated into nouns, verbs, adjectives, and so on. Two words cannot differentiate into three or more classes. Thus, a vocabulary must be larger for such a differentiation to become possible. What is also important here is that all these grammatical categories are words. Thus, differentiation has taken place within the topographical constraints of a word in general. Through differentiation, novel components emerge that *are characterized by additional topographical constraints*, which do not apply to the lower level (see Baldwin, 1906, for an elaboration of that idea).

There still is no explanation as to why differentiation takes place. That question is answered in general terms by Munro (1992), who differentiated two aspects of systems—structure and process. According to Munro, "structure" defines what a thing *is*, and "process" defines what things *are doing*. It is important that "processes at any level n operate on structures at level $n - 1$" and "processes at level n have the potential to become structures supporting processes at level $n + 1$" (p. 117). In a less formal form, a similar idea has been discussed by Vygotsky (1926, 1984a) in his analysis of the role of activity in child development (see also Leont'ev, 1981). According to Vygotsky's idea, the activity of a child (usually in interaction with social others) leads to a reorganization of the environment. New organization can be internalized as knowledge. Through the process of internalization the system or structure of a mind changes (see Toomela, 1996a, for an analysis of the notion of internalization). Such change in mental structure allows a child to become involved in more complex activities that, in turn, lead to a more complex reorganization of the environment.

In sum, development can be understood as the process of emergence of novel elements through differentiation of a system at a certain level of topographical constraints. Through differentiation, a new, more restricted level of topographical constraints within the broader level of constraints emerges. Through the synthesis of differentiated components, a hierarchically higher-order structure can be synthesized.

Summary

To explain a phenomenon it must be described in a certain way. According to the theory of functional systems, an explanation is a description of a phenomenon that includes descriptions of: (1) components of the system (quality and number); (2) relationships between the components and properties of a whole that emerges in the synthesis of components (topographical constraints and dynamic possibilities); and (3) the development of a system (which, in turn, includes the description of elements before they enter the whole and the description of differentiation through which novel components emerge).

SECOND LEVEL OF ANALYSIS: GENERAL PRINCIPLES OF THE EMERGENCE AND DEVELOPMENT OF THE HUMAN MIND

The theory of functional systems outlines principles that can be applied to every field of science—these principles are not specific to psychology (cf. von Bertalanffy, 1968). Thus, another, more specific level of analysis is necessary to understand how such general principles are applied to the study of the mind. Before going on to the detailed analysis of the symbol meaning development, an intermediate level of analysis is necessary to define some basic psychological notions.

Stage of Mental Development

According to the theory of functional systems, development is, by definition, hierarchical. It follows that not every change in a system is developmental. There is a consensus in psychology that the mental system changes in time. It does not follow, however, that the mental system develops. Theoretically, it is possible that the mental system changes with age only quantitatively. It is also possible, however, that the mental system truly develops. In the latter case, it should be possible to find hierarchically emerging qualitatively different mental systems in different age periods. True hierarchical development, however, may take different forms. One possibility is that all such hierarchical changes are local and task and process specific. There is a lot of empirical evidence supporting the idea of local development (e.g., Siegler, 1994, 1996; Siegler & Crowley, 1991). The other form of mental development is the development over general stages that characterize the whole mental system.

Usually a domain-general stage is understood as pervasive, characterizing the whole mental system. If that is the case, then the idea of a general stage and the idea of local development should be mutually exclusive. As the empirical evidence for local changes seems to be convincing, either there are no general stages in mental development or a general stage cannot characterize the whole mental system in all points of time. I have proposed another way to define a general stage (Toomela, 2000b):

[. . .] a stage of mental development is a realization of the developmental potential that is absolutely constrained by topographical characteristics of a genetic level of structural development (p. 35).

According to my view, which follows the principles of the theory of functional systems, domain-general and local developmental changes are related to different aspects of a mental system. Local changes are true changes of the system of mind. Global changes, in turn, are not directly related to the changes of a system. Rather, global changes are changes in *topographical constraints* on local development. It means that all local developments can be classified under a limited number of domain-general stages. In principle, a general stage can characterize the whole system of mind. But that is a theoretical special case of the realization of the potential for development in any general stage. Usually, mind is heterogeneous, which means that an individual has mental systems at different stages of development in different domains of knowledge.

My definition of a stage of mental development is not constructed on the basis of theoretical analysis alone. If proposed on the basis of theoretical analysis alone, it would be a philosophical construct, which may or may not have any relevance to the understanding of changes in mental development because:

[. . .] no formula for progress from mode to mode, that is, no strictly genetic [from *genesis*, A.T.] formula in evolution or development, is possible except by direct observation of the facts of the series which the formulation aims to cover or by the interpretation of other series which represents the same or parallel modes (Baldwin, 1906, p. 20)

The third part of my chapter on the development of symbol meaning includes several empirical examples of the definition of a stage as a topographical constraint. That is already another, more specific level of analysis. Before going further, however, I briefly describe relationships between general stages and age. In principle, the only limitation to the development (both local and global) is the order of changes. Changes in a system of mind that are supposed to be hierarchical must always be ordered; some changes are possible only after some other, hierarchically lower, changes have occurred. But mental development is in addition constrained biologically by the maturation of the brain.

The possible role of biological maturation in mental development was defined already in the 1920s. According to Vygotsky, the founder of the cultural–historical school of psychology, mental development is characterized by critical and stable periods. In critical periods new domain-general possibilities are created, and in stable periods these possibilities are realized in specific domains (Vygotsky, 1935, 1967, 1984b). The ages at which critical periods begin are determined by the maturation of the nervous system. The potential created by the maturation of the brain can be realized only when appropriate social–cultural stimulation is available for the child (Vygotsky, 1929).

Vygotsky (1984b) proposed that there are six critical periods, which begin at birth, at the first year, at the third year, at the seventh year, at the thirteenth year, and at the seventeenth year of life, respectively. Recent studies on genetic variability, brain growth, and electrophysiological maturation (Cardon, Fulker, DeFries, & Plomin, 1992; Epstein, 2001; Fulker, Cherny, & Cardon, 1993; Hudspeth & Pribram, 1990, 1992; Thatcher, 1991, 1992, 1994; Thatcher, Walker, & Gindice, 1987), together with behavioral–development data (see Toomela, 2000b, and the analysis below), suggest that it is possible to differentiate eight critical periods. Six of them overlap with those proposed by Vygotsky. Together with the additional two critical periods there are eight ages around which rapid growth and maturation of the brain begin: birth, sixth month, first year, and eighteenth month, third year, seventh year, twelfth year, and eighteenth year of life. Between each of these periods are periods of relatively slow growth and maturation.

Mechanism of Mental Development

Without understanding *how* development proceeds, any theory of development, both local and domain-general, has little explanatory power. Especially problematic is the proposition of general stages in development without an explanation of how short periods of change from one stage to another ground continuous local developments (cf. Siegler, 1996). The possible mechanism for development was already proposed by Vygotsky, according to whom development results from the *activity* of a person in the environment (e.g., Vygotsky & Luria, 1994; Vygotsky, 1926). In principle, mental development can be understood as the construction of hierarchically more and more complex and informative representations about a world (Vygotsky, 1996). In essence, representations contain information about regularities, predictable events, in the environment. In the always-changing world the regularities are not obvious. Rather, regularities are created by a child in repeated interactions with the environment, in activity. Experiencing such regularities in activities, a child constructs representations of them. It is important that a child at the beginning of mental development is not able to observe all possible kinds of regularities in the world. In the very beginning of development, for example, there is the mother's breast as a source of food, warmth, and other physical characteristics of the world, but there are no cultural values, prejudices, or understanding of social order, and so on.

A child builds representations in the course of activities. These representations differentiate and, after differentiation, constitute a basis for the synthesis of the hierarchically next level of development, which allows representation of information that was not available at the previous level of representational development. For example, a child before understanding language is not able to represent knowledge about culture and society. Understanding of language, on the other hand, does not emerge from nothing by some *deus-ex-machina* mechanism. Language is a special category of objects that can be created and manipulated by persons. A child learns how to create and manipulate objects before acquiring language. In the interaction with social others, a child experiences regularities in their behavior and constructs a special, differentiated from other objects, class of objects that refer to other objects, i.e., symbols. After that development, a child becomes able to experience and represent entirely new kinds of regularities that are in the environment, regularities that are created by symbols.

A specific case of the development through activity was proposed by Nelson (Lucariello, Kyratzis, & Nelson, 1992; Nelson, 1988, 1996). In her *slot-filler theory*, she suggested that taxonomic categories are learned by children in the process of interaction with environment, in experiencing structurally similar events with different constituents. In recurrent events, different objects may occur in the same functional slot (different clothes put on on different mornings appear in the same structure of dressing in the morning; different food eaten on different mornings appears in the structurally same activity of eating in the morning, etc.). Observation of the regularity by which perceptually different but functionally similar objects appear in the structurally same situation allows children to construct hierarchically higher-order taxonomic category representation of such objects.

Nelson's theory rests on the basic notions of paradigmatic and syntagmatic relations between words (Nelson, 1996). By *syntagmatic* is meant the relationship that a linguistic element has with other elements in the stretch of language in which it occurs; by *paradigmatic* is meant the relationship it has with elements with which it may be replaced or substituted. Thus, slot-filler theory suggests that children construct taxonomic categories by experiencing paradigmatic relationships between words, which refer to substitutable objects in the structure of recurrent events in daily activities.

It must be mentioned, however, that the syntagmatic and paradigmatic relationships also characterize nonlinguistic elements and nonlinguistic events. In principle, a very young child may learn a category "source of food" by observing and participating in activities of getting milk from a breast and getting milk from a bottle. Breast and bottle are in paradigmatic relationships in the structure of feeding activity. There is no necessity to have words for a breast and a bottle to understand and represent their functional similarity.

The ideas outlined above suggest a general mechanism of development: development proceeds from actively creating and participating in syntagmatically organized events to representing paradigmatically related objects in syntagmatic structures. Representations of a paradigmatic category, in turn, allow the creation and participation in a new kind of event from where a hierarchically higher-level paradigmatic relationship can be experienced and represented. This "mechanism" of development, however, would be quite useless without explicitly defining what exactly develops and in what kinds of activities children are involved when constructing hierarchy of representations. These are questions for a more specific level of analysis, described later in this chapter.

What Develops? Concept and Representation

One of the basic assumptions of the theory of functional systems is that it is possible to explain a system satisfactorily only in terms of itself. For example, it would not be productive to study the development of concepts when concepts are defined—as they usually are—as something that mediates the link between words and the things they refer to. What follows from such obscure definition quite naturally is the situation that characterizes the field: there are many theories and little consensus on how to understand concepts and conceptual structure (cf. Komatsu, 1992). Mental development, as studied in this chapter, is the development of representations. *Representation is* defined here as *a (neurally based) system of sensory attributes that emerges in the interaction of an organism with the environment.* Representations are components of mental systems.

Relating representations to sensory attributes defines the starting point of development. Development is always continuous; it cannot begin from *tabula rasa.* A child is born with certain capabilities for registering and reacting to the events in the environment. There is only one way that the brain, the material basis for mind, can get information from the environment: through receptors, the system of which is innate. There are two kinds of photoreceptors (rods and cones) for transforming light into neural signals for vision; there are receptors for transforming changes in air pressure to signals of sound. There are receptors for registering pressure on skin, temperature, pain, position of the body in respect to space and position of body parts in respect of each other, receptors for odors, receptors for taste, and receptors for internal events like hunger, thirst, or lack of oxygen. Because there is no other way that the brain can get information from the environment, all representations must be built from basic qualities mediated by receptors. These qualities are *sensory attributes.* Some sensory qualities are not directly encoded by receptors but still can be classified as sensory attributes. These are sensory qualities that are encoded by innate mechanisms at a low level of sensory analysis. In the visual system, for example, the sensory attributes are form or shape, color, movement, and depth (cf. Livingstone & Hubel, 1988). So all sensory qualities that are processed by "hard-wired" innate mechanisms are classified sensory attributes here.

I suggest that all mental development can be understood as differentiation and hierarchical reintegration of systems of sensory attributes. Basically it is possible to differentiate two general kinds of representations, directly sensory-based representations and symbols. Symbols are developmentally secondary; they refer to sensory-based representations (or to other symbols). Remember, all symbols (usually words) are nothing but very specific systems of sensory attributes. So symbols are developmentally continuous to nonsymbolic representations. And we can see that there is no need to put some mysterious "something" to mediate symbols (words) and things they refer to. Concepts need not be "between" a word and an object, because words are systems of sensory attributes similar to systems of sensory attributes representing objects or phenomena in the environment. Rather, concepts can be understood as *properties* of symbols. These properties are defined by what a symbol is (representation of physical events like sounds or visual patterns) and what relations a symbol has with other representations, both symbolic and sensory-based. So, for example, the concept of a "unicorn" is a system of symbols where the word-form *unicorn* is a component related to other components, i.e., other symbols (animal, four legs, one horn, mythical, etc.). All we need to understand the concept of unicorn is to describe the system of relationships a *unicorn* has with other symbols.

THIRD LEVEL OF ANALYSIS: THE DEVELOPMENT OF SYMBOL MEANING

This chapter is specifically dedicated to the question of how culture and the social–cultural environment are related to the mental development of a child. Correspondingly, the main issue here is to understand better the development of symbol meaning and the relation of symbols with semiotically mediated thinking. It would be insufficient, however, to describe only the development of symbol meaning because symbols develop only after major developments in non-symbolic, sensory-based mental organization. To understand symbol development, it is necessary to understand where it begins.

The following differentiation of stages is based on the principles of the theory of functional systems. I have tried to explain stage-like mental development by indicating, as much as I could, the possible mechanisms of change as well as the results of developmental changes—what components characterize each level of development, in what order novel components differentiate, and what novel representational systems can be built from the differentiated components.

Prelinguistic Stages of Development

First Stage

I have suggested elsewhere (Toomela, 2000b) that prelinguistic development proceeds over three general stages. First, a child has innate, biologically determined sensory abilities. These abilities allow only the grasping of *independent sensory attributes*. All mental operations at the first stage of development are thus constrained by a topographical constraint—all operations are based on individual sensory attributes. Basically, if there is a possibility to react only to individual sensory attributes then, for the behavior to be coherent, such attributes must be directly related to activities. Activities where reactions are directly related to sensory attributes are called *reflexes*. That stage begins at about the tenth gestational week.

It is noteworthy that all following development is also constrained by the quality of basic components of representations. From individual sensory attributes it is possible to build only hierarchically higher-level systems the properties of which are defined by the qualities of its components and by the relationships between those components. All representations, even the most complex (e.g., electric field, democracy), are sensory-based developmentally.

Second Stage

The second stage begins around birth. At the second stage of development it is possible to *connect individual sensory attributes with each other into microsystems*. In these Microsystems, perception of one attribute in the environment leads to the activation of another attribute in the same microsystem of representation. That possibility is connected to an increasing choice of reactions toward the environment. With the covariations in appearance of sensory attributes, it is possible to connect already established patterns of reactions—reflexes—with new sensory inputs. In this way, conditioned reflexes develop. Microsystems of sensory attributes at the second stage are constructed on the basis of covariations between attributes. A relationship between the color and shape of an apple, for example, is represented similarly by a relationship between a ring of a bell and the smell of a food in a pavlovian experiment on conditional reflexes. These kinds of representations differentiate in the next stage.

Third Stage

Around the age of 6 months, the third stage begins. At the third stage a special class of microsystems of sensory attributes differentiates. It is a class of representations that corresponds to *objects in the environment*. Actions toward objects as separate entities become possible. Correspondingly, a child is increasingly able to plan its actions; the child's behavior is much less under the control of direct sensory information.

The third stage is still highly constrained in the kind of information that can be represented. All possible representations at that stage of development may contain information about only single sensory attributes, representational microsystems of sensory attributes based on covariations between attributes, and objects in the sensory world. There are still constraints on the system. First, there is no differentiated information about the situations, i.e., relations between objects. And second, there is no way to build representations about a world beyond the senses, for example, about electrons, electric fields, the solar system, and so on. The reason for that topographical constraint is that there is only one way that sensory attributes become synthesized into representations of environment. Such syntheses emerge only when a child experiences regularities directly through the senses and in direct contact with the environment. To understand that there is more in the environment than can be registered directly by sensory organs, it is necessary to be able to understand that perceptually the same environment can have different, sometimes contradictory meanings. So, for example, for understanding that the earth is moving around the sun it is necessary to give entirely different meaning to the representation of the Earth we perceive as stationary and the sun we perceive as moving. And there is no direct way to see or touch the heliocentric structure of our planetary system.

Emergence of Symbols and the Role of Social–Cultural Relationships in the Development of Representations

The third stage is thus limited by one way of information processing, by only one way of how objects and situations can be represented. To become able to represent aspects of a world beyond our senses, we must be able to attribute different meanings to the same objects and phenomena. This can be accomplished by acquiring another system of representations that describes exactly the same sensory world by a different mechanism. This other system is a system of *symbols.* I have analyzed in more detail elsewhere how the development of symbols allows representation of information about a world beyond the senses (Toomela, 1996a, 1996b, in press). Briefly, symbols are sensory microsystems that refer to other sensory microsystems, which, in turn, refer to objects and phenomena in the sensory environment. If symbols were only reflections, redescriptions of sensory representations, there would be no possibility to represent knowledge about a world beyond the senses. But there is an extremely important qualitative difference between symbols and their referents (which are sensory representations of objects and events, not directly objects and events in the external world). Referents of symbols and possible relationships between these referents correspond directly to the experiences of the structure of external events. The relationships between a symbol and its referent, as well as the relationships between symbols, are determined by entirely different rules, rules of social relationships, rules of communication. So a representation of a fire, for example, may include visual and tactile sensory attributes of fire. Because we can experience fire only in certain conditions, our representation of fire is limited to actual experiences of it. But it is possible to experience a symbol for fire, a sound pattern of "fire" in situations where fire never occurs. We can say "fire" while swimming in the middle of an ocean or while looking into the dark mouth of cave of ice. In this way we can bring the sensory representation of fire, which is activated by a symbol that refers to it, into contexts and situations where it can never exist physically. Symbols thus give qualitatively new meanings to sensory-based representations.

Thus, symbols allow representation of information that cannot be perceived directly through senses. Such new information, however, does not emerge in the process of social interaction or in the process of connecting symbols with arbitrary referents by itself. Rather, the development of symbols creates only a potential for representing qualitatively novel, nonsensory, information. That potential must be realized in *semiotically mediated thinking.* Thus, symbols can be understood as mental tools for constructing nonsensory representations (see more on that issue, Vygotsky & Luria, 1994; Vygotsky, 1996). As with external tools, the kind of job that can be performed with a tool depends on the nature of the tool. To understand what can be done with mental tools—symbols—it is necessary to understand that symbols develop and their structure changes hierarchically in ontogenesis.

Next I describe how symbols develop. This development is social–cultural; it is possible only in the environment where special kinds of sensory objects, symbols, are used for communication. In the development of symbol meaning we can observe how culture enters an individual mind.

Stages of Word Meaning Development

The description of the next stages of representational development follows the same schema. First, the approximate age when a stage begins is stated. Next, what differentiates at that stage and what is the possible mechanism of differentiation are defined. After that, topographic constraints of the stage are defined and meanings that can be represented at that stage are characterized. In this way every stage is characterized both negatively (what cannot be represented) and positively (what can be represented and what operations become possible). Finally, the categories that are encoded with symbols are briefly discussed. That discussion allows readers to connect ideas presented in this chapter with the enormous number of studies and theories about categorization and conceptual structure that have been conducted mainly in adults.[1]

Fourth Stage. Relationships Between Objects. Syncretic Symbols

The fourth general stage of representational development begins around the age of 1 year. What differentiates next in the system of representation is the ability to represent *relationships between objects*. Now it becomes possible to analyze objects intellectually and give them novel functions. One specific and most important possibility that emerges at the fourth stage is the potential to distinguish symbols (which basically are sensory objects too) from other sensory objects.

Children around their first birthday can be involved in a variety of activities. One special activity is social interactions with other people, usually the parents. In that early social interaction the next differentiation takes place. At the previous stage it became possible to represent objects. Now a special kind of object representations differentiates. This is a category of symbols, or objects that refer to something else.

There is evidence that first symbols—words—are really differentiated from nonsymbolic representations. It has been found that linguistic input, particularly input that provides an object label, facilitates nonlinguistic categorization. Interestingly, in infants around the age of 15 months, the same kind of facilitation of nonlinguistic categorization emerges with linguistic and nonlinguistic input. A segment of instrumental music has the same effect as a word (Roberts, 1995; Roberts & Jacob, 1991). Thus, 15-month-old infants are at a stage where symbols differentiate from nonsymbolic objects.

It can be hypothesized that that differentiation follows a general syntagmatic-to-paradigmatic shift, which is the general mechanism of development. First, children can observe that in some situations—situations of social interaction from an adult perspective—there are auditory objects[2] that are used in different contexts but still covary with some invariant across situations. From the adult perspective there are words that are used to refer to some particular aspect of the environment. From the developing child's view there are slots for auditory objects that are filled with different auditory objects with the same function, function to covary with something in the environment in the situation of the social interaction. This interpretation is in agreement with a suggestion that the beginning of symbolic development lies in general perceptual and cognitive mechanisms that process covariation information. These mechanisms underlie anticipations about how the social world works and about the means for directing attention to and maintaining it on a topic (Gogate, Walker-Andrews, & Bahrick, 2001; Roberts, 1995). In addition, there is evidence that children indeed may differentiate a slot for a word as a tool for directing attention in general. It has been found that naming of an object directs 10- to 14-month-old infants attention independently of whether the word is understood (Baldwin & Markman, 1989). Thus, "wordness" differentiates independently of specific word meanings.

As all stages in development, the stage of syncretic symbols is topographically constrained. That constraint is caused by the *number* of symbols that can be simultaneously activated (number is one characteristic of the components of a system that determines the characteristics of the whole; see above). First-acquired words are used independently each other. So the meaning of first words is fully constrained by the external context in which they are used (see, e.g., Barrett, 1995, for a review of empirical data). In addition, the constraint to use only one word at a time poses limits on symbol meaning. In observing covariations between certain auditory patterns and invariants across situations a child still has many ways in which to establish a connection between auditory pattern and an invariant. It can be reminded here that mental structure is usually heterogeneous. The development of representations of objects does not lead to representation of all correlated sensory attributes as objects. Similarly, some sensory attributes may stay independent in a sensory system (e.g., muscle lengthening while checking a knee/reflex seems to be represented independently of other sensory attributes even in adults). First symbols, correspondingly, can refer to all three lower levels of representations. So, what exactly is chosen by a child to be a referent of a word is idiosyncratic. Sometimes it is an object, sometimes a pattern of correlated attributes, sometimes a single sensory attribute.

There is another quantitative constraint on word meaning. In the beginning of the development, the size of a child's vocabulary is very small. The first function of a word in social interaction is to direct some other's attention to a specific "place" in the situation. With limited vocabulary a child may be forced to use learned words in novel ways to extend their reference. In a developed vocabulary, the possibilities for such extensions are constrained. Nouns usually refer to objects and can be extended to other objects; verbs refer to actions, and adjectives to properties. It is important that such word classes be defined within the system of language because grammatical categories do not overlap totally with sensory categories. Nouns, for example, may also refer to actions ("jumping"). So different categories of words are defined in respect to each other. Using only one word at a time does not allow that differentiation to take place. Correspondingly, first single words may have extensions that are inappropriate according to an adult model. The same word form can be used as a noun, verb, or adjective.

So, words are first learned as context-bound and later they become "decontextualized." One interesting phenomenon in children's early use of words is that references of first words change unpredictably. Sometimes their meaning is underextended when compared to the adult model, sometimes it is overextended, and sometimes there is a partial overlap together with partial overextension, and sometimes there is a total mismatch in reference. In other words, relations between words and referents are not systematic in young infants (e.g., Barrett, 1995; Nelson, Hampson, & Shaw, 1993). The reason for such heterogeneity might be that the establishment of relations between a word and referent is totally guided by three lower levels of sensory representations and absolutely unconstrained linguistically. With every new word a child constructs a novel reference. Without linguistic constraint there is no guide whether a word should refer to some object or to sensory attribute, for example. A choice of a referent may be guided by some simple mechanism like frequency of covariation between a word and invariant in the situation. If, by chance, a word will be connected with a single sensory attribute, it can easily be overextended. Mismatch may emerge for the same reason when sensory attribute is not specific to some object (like color which is not specific to objects, versus shape, which can be very object-specific). If some covariation of sensory attributes that crosses the borders of objects becomes a referent, underextension follows because such covariations may exist even only in one specific situation. Underextension may also follow when some unusual sensory attribute, like vibration, happens to become the real referent of a word.

In sum, first words may refer to any of the lower sensory levels of representation independently of a grammatical class of the word according to the adult model. The only systematic function such undifferentiated words can have is the possibility to direct attention to some specific "place" in the actual situation of communication. That is the topographical constraint of the fourth stage of development.

Fifth Stage. Symbols for Objects and Object-Specific Properties. Prototypes

The fifth stage of representational development usually begins around the age of 18 months. The essence of development at this stage is the differentiation of nouns from other words. It has been found that before the age of about 16 months in a forced-choice situation children's attention is about equally divided between "taxonomic" choices and functional choices or distractors even when a novel word is used as an input parallel to looking. After that age, however, words direct children's attention more and more to "taxonomic" choices, that is, objects from the same category (Oviatt, 1982; Waxman & Hall, 1993). In the present context it is important to understand what underlies "taxonomic" choices in young children. If my theory is correct, then the basis of taxonomy can be only some already achieved stage of representational development. Indeed, there is evidence that the taxonomy of objects is based on one sensory attribute, shape. In addition, the tendency to categorize objects with a similar shape into one category when a word is used emerges around the age of 18 months. The shape bias increases after that age in agreement with the idea of differentiation in a word-referent system (Jones

& Smith, 1993; Jones, Smith, & Landau, 1991; Landau, Smith, & Jones, 1988, 1998; Smith, Jones, & Landau, 1992). Thus, children have reached a stage where relations between novel words and their possible referents become systematic, predictable.

There seems to be little information on the possible mechanism of how exactly the differentiation in a system of symbols develops. Nevertheless, the study by Tomasello and Akhtar (1995) indicates that the mechanism of change may be related to external activities, as my theory predicts. They found that 27-month-old children learn a new word for whichever element is new in the discourse context. In addition, which of the possible referents of a novel word, an object or an action, is chosen by a child as a referent depends on social–pragmatic information rather than some internal cognitive or linguistic mechanism. In addition, there are other empirical findings that are in agreement with the idea that the mechanism of differentiation is related to differentiation of functional slots in the syntagmatic structure, which can be filled with objects in paradigmatic relationships. Namely, if children learn a differentiation of a category through experiencing certain objects that can substitute one another in certain slots then what is learned in the beginning must depend on actual experiences with actual objects. A "rule" why certain objects "go together" should be learned after a category is constructed from actual experience. Different studies have demonstrated that combinatorial rules of grammar for verbs are acquired verb-by-verb during social interactions (Braunwald, 1995; Olguin & Tomasello, 1993; Theakston, Lieven, Pine, & Rowland, 2001; Tomasello, 1992). Even more, it is possible that correct grammatical context is acquired item-by-item not only with verbs but with all word classes (Nelson, 1995). Thus, acquisition of grammatical classes truly develops; it is not based on some innate grammar, which defines grammatical classes, or by some general rule.

Symbol meaning at the fifth stage is topographically constrained. The reason for that constraint is, again, quantitative limitation on the number of symbols that can be combined. First symbol combinations include only two words (e.g., Fenson, Wale, Reznick, Bates, Thal, & Pethick, 1994). Even after children become able to construct expressions from more than two words, their expressions are constrained for some time so that every predicate is associated with a unique external argument and every external argument is associated with a unique predicate (Borer & Wexler, 1992). Perhaps the most extensively studied concrete example of young children's quantitative limitation on the structure of expression is the observation that young children before the age of about 3 years tend to omit subjects from their expressions even when subjects are grammatically necessary (Bloom, 1990, 1993; Hyams & Wexler, 1993; Valian, 1991; Valian, Hoeffner, & Aubry, 1996). Even though some authors suggest that omission of a subject is caused by different grammar of young children, all authors seem to agree that quantitative performance and comprehension limitations play an important role in this phenomenon.

The consequences of such quantitative constraint are relatively obvious: it is not possible flexibly to describe relationships between objects or phenomena with two-word combinations "decontextualized" from immediate experience. Take, for example, a situation such as "Dog bites me." Using two words, we cannot understand what happens. "Dog bites," "Bites me," and "Dog me" are not sufficient for understanding a situation, a relationship between objects. Theoretically it is possible to express that situation with only two words or even with only one word. A word can be connected with every lower-level representation; it is theoretically possible to have a single word for a system of correlated attributes that includes some attributes of a dog, some attributes of myself, and some attributes specifically related to a dog biting me (sharp pain, for example). In this way we could construct a word "dogbitesme." (A word form expressing that situation would probably be "dog" or "bites" or "pain" or whatever adults would use in such a situation). But such composite words are rare. Mainly because relations between objects are much less perceptually invariant across time than objects themselves. If learning word meanings in early stages is guided by detecting frequency of covariations, then relations between objects are usually not referents of words.

On the other hand, however, a possibility to combine words allows them to differentiate, and it becomes possible to develop different classes of words. There is increasing evidence that such differentiation emerges around the age of 2 years. It has been found that 23-month-old children have a grammatical class of noun they can recognize from syntactic cues (Tomasello & Olguin, 1993), but they still do not have a grammatical category of verbs (Olguin & Tomasello, 1993). Distinction of nouns from adjectives and first signs of the emergence of the grammatical category of adjective can be found in 21-month-old children (Waxman & Markow, 1998). The picture that emerges from different studies suggests that first nouns differentiate from other grammatical classes and after that step-by-step other grammatical classes differentiate when contrasted with differentiated nouns. So, it has been found that it is easier for young children to extend a novel adjective within object categories and the nouns that describe them (Hall, Waxman, & Hurwitz, 1993; Klibanoff & Waxman, 2000; Waxman & Markow, 1998). Further, in young children names for colors are not represented independently from objects. The limited object-color knowledge, rather, appears to be stored as a verbal association of an adjective with nouns that refer to objects (Davidoff & Mitchell, 1993). Finally, the same principle applies to the development of verb meaning: children's concepts of motion verbs, for example, are initially particular and limited to knowledge of situations in which and entities to which they can apply (Gallivan, 1988).

There is also some evidence that adjectives may also differentiate by a mechanism similar to that by which differentiation of noun categories is accomplished, in the social–pragmatic context of communication. Novel adjectives can be extended over object category boundaries when a property of object is pragmatically forced to be invariant over situations (cf. Waxman & Klibanoff, 2000).

Also, when experimenters create a situation where an invariant is a function of a word instead of a shape, novel nouns are extended on the basis of functional similarity (Kemler Nelson, Frankenfield, Morris, & Blair, 2000; Kemler Nelson, Russell, Duke, & Jones, 2000)

So, theoretically, at the fifth stage of representational development it should be possible to find symbols referring to categories of objects (category is mainly defined by shape) and object-specific properties. As the possible combinations of words are quantitatively constrained we should not find symbols that refer to relationships between objects or symbols that refer to properties of objects that are defined by a relationship to other objects (like bigger or stronger, which require comparison of objects). It must be mentioned that it is not an easy task to support that proposition because forms of words acquired by children from adults may refer also to relationships between objects and relational properties of objects by an adult model. Nevertheless, there is a lot of evidence that the meanings of such words in young children do not overlap with adult systems of meanings. It has been found, for example, that "behind" for 3-year-old children means "occluded from sight"; it does not refer to the relationship of objects (Johnston, 1984). Similarly, use of spatial locative words develops so that source and path words are used at the earliest ages studied (17 to 23 months), whereas words for goals develop later (Stockman & Vaughn-Cooke, 1992). So, words that refer to object-specific characteristics develop before words that define relationships of an object with other objects. Also very interesting are findings from studies of verbs meaning development. It has been found that verbs for self-actions are acquired earlier than verbs for observed actions. In addition, verbs that encode characteristic movements (e.g., "walk," "run") are extended to encompass observed actions earlier than verbs that encode change (e.g., "get," "open") (Behrend, 1990; Huttenlocher, Smiley, & Charney, 1983; Huttenlocher, Smiley, & Ratner, 1983). My theory suggests a possible explanation for that difference. Self-actions are specific to objects that perform actions, whereas observed actions require also representation of relationships between objects. It is, of course, possible to represent and understand relations between objects at the fourth stage of representational development. But it should not be possible to represent relations between objects in language where the number of words that can be combined is only two.

There is one important aspect in the development of symbol meaning. At the stage of development of syncretic symbols, symbols refer to categories that are idiosyncratic. There are no systematic boundaries that define categories. At the fifth stage, symbols can refer to categories. The most important characteristic that underlies categorization is that of shape of objects. Shape is probably the most pervasive basis for categorization because it differentiates object categories best. Nevertheless, other sensory attributes or attribute patterns may also underlie category structure if that pattern is sufficient to differentiate object categories. Categories referred to by symbols at this stage are in essence *prototypical*.

Prototypical, or *basic-level*, categories are the most inclusive level of categorization at which objects have numbers of attributes in common, whereby they share a similar shape and a similar pattern of motor movements[3] with the objects (Mervis & Rosch, 1981; Rosch, 1978). It is a well-established finding that boundaries of prototypical categories are not clear. Theoretically, the reason for ambiguity in category boundaries emerges for two reasons. First, categories are not restricted by their functional roles. There are many categories that can be perceptually similar but have different functions. Take, for example, dolls and children. Dolls share a similar shape with human children, and most of the motor movements related to handling dolls are also shared with human children. But human children are differently related to other objects when compared with dolls. That makes dolls and human children representatives of different categories. That relational information is not available for linguistic categorization because of the topographical constraints of that stage as described above. And second, categories of objects are also defined by attributes that are not available to the senses. Without breaking a doll and a child for direct comparison of their internal structures, it would be hard to understand why children sometimes must use a toilet or eat but why dolls do not have such needs. In other words, boundaries of prototypical object categories are permeable because there is no mental mechanism available to categorize objects into classical categories defined by individually necessary and collectively sufficient attributes.

In sum, symbols at the fifth stage of representational development are differentiated into nouns that refer to shape-based prototypical categories of objects and other classes of words that encode object-specific properties (including object-specific actions, locations, changes, etc.). Differentiation of other classes of words is facilitated by the linguistic context of already differentiated nouns. It becomes possible to differentiate by linguistic cues whether an object or its properties are referred to by a symbol. The fifth stage of development is topographically constrained so that relationships between objects and relational properties of objects are not encoded with symbols. That information can be communicated by young children, but only in the immediate sensory context where the relational information is directly available.

Sixth Stage. Symbols for All Sensory-Based Representations. Exemplars

The sixth stage begins around the age of 3 years. At that stage, differentiation of symbols continues. Symbols encoding relationships between objects and symbols encoding properties of objects independently of them differentiate. So, for example, it has been found that by the time children are 5 years of age, novel adjectives systematically direct attention away from shape (Landau, Smith, & Jones, 1992). Knowledge on control for all verb types and with different infinitive types develops considerably between the ages of 3 and 5 years, but an adult level of knowledge is still not available (Eisenberg & Cairns, 1994). In addition, it has been demonstrated that there is an appearance-function shift in the interpretation of object names between the ages of 3 and 6 years (Merriman, Scott, & Marazita, 1993). It is important that function in the last-mentioned study was clearly defined as a relationship between objects; it was not possible to represent functions like a function of a target object to hold a ball, to leave tracks, or to make shapes by the proprioceptive system alone. Thus, an appearance-function shift is a shift from object-specific characteristics to relational characteristics of objects. There is also evidence that children after the age of about 3 years are increasingly able to express and explain relationships between objects. It has been found, for example, that 2-year-old children in most cases do not justify their choices in a forced-choice categorization procedure, whereas most 4-year-old children respond meaningfully in the same situation (Hall, Waxman, & Hurwitz, 1993). Difficulties in giving meaningful explanations in such abstract experimental situations characterize even older preschool children (Smiley & Brown, 1979).

Thus, there is evidence that children develop an ability to use language out of the immediate sensory context to express relations between objects and relational characteristics of objects. I have not found any studies that could be used as examples for the syntagmatic-to-paradigmatic mechanism of differentiation of new classes of symbols. Theoretically, it can be suggested that children observe how properties of objects appear independently from particular objects. That observation is supported by a social communication where the same words for object properties are used by linguistically more competent others in different situations where objects vary but properties remain invariant. In this way a slot for relational properties and relations between objects probably are constructed and, step-by-step, filled with paradigmatically replaceable symbols for relations.

At the sixth stage it becomes possible to represent all objects, events, and phenomena in the sensory world symbolically. Still, the stage is topographically constrained. There are symbolic tools that allow the construction of complex theories about the world, even about the world beyond the senses. But there are no mental tools, as yet, that would allow us to demonstrate the validity of such "prototheories." All thinking is based on knowledge about events experienced in everyday activities. That knowledge is insufficient for understanding real properties of objects that remain beyond the reach of the senses. The reason for that limitation is that for understanding the nonsensory world it is necessary to detach observed objects or events from their everyday sensory context. Physically it is impossible to do that. It is possible to analyze objects totally outside the sensory context only with symbols, which can be used entirely out of or even in contradiction to sensory experiences. It is easy to say, for example, "I am a tiny frog with an Empire State Building in my pocket." But such a situation can never be observed in real life. Such expressions, of course, can be constructed already at the sixth stage of representational development. But for systematically analyzing objects abstracted from reality, it is necessary to create an abstract background or frame of reference that allows comparison and analysis of different abstracted expressions about the phenomenon meaningfully. That abstract context, the context of metalanguage, differentiates at the next stage.

The reason topographic constraints emerge may still be quantitative. For defining both the abstract frame of reference and the ideas that are to be analyzed in that context, it is necessary to create a symbolic system where several ideas are simultaneously involved in one basic scheme. The number of ideas that can be simultaneously processed by a child is limited in a 7-year-old and even in older children (Richardson, 1992).

So, children at this stage should be able not only to describe different situations with symbols but also to use such expressions for thinking, for understanding the world around them. There are many findings that demonstrate that thinking of children before the age of about 7 years is guided by everyday experience that can easily be translated into sensory experience. Many of such findings will be discussed in the next section where differences between "everyday" and "scientific" thinking are analyzed. Just a few examples are presented here. Chao and Cheng (2000), for example, demonstrated that pragmatic reasoning rules that are directly related to everyday experiences emerge earlier than explicit formal rules that are domain-independent. Deductive reasoning in the preschool age is, accordingly, based on context-sensitive rules. Similarly, it has been demonstrated that 6-year-old children are not able to construct domain-independent frames of reference in solving economic problems (Thompson & Siegler, 2000). Explanations, described in the latter study (Table 1, p. 666), are characteristic to everyday experiences. An abstract idea of profit-seeking, for example, is explained in terms of everyday activities. A seller sells products "so that he could get a little more money . . ." Money is something you can touch and put into your pocket. Profit is an abstract idea that is not necessarily related to real money.

New representational possibilities that differentiate at the sixth stage allow the use of symbols for encoding categories with a different structure. In addition to object-specific characteristics, relational or functional characteristics of objects can be involved in constructing categories. All sensory objects and phenomena can be differentiated from one another. Even perceptually entirely similar objects can be differentiated from each other in language through encoding relations between objects. Every object or phenomenon can be defined as an individual through its position in space or time, for example. Two entirely similar coins, for example, can be categorized into different categories of "money in my pocket" and "money in your pocket." In this way, *exemplar-based* categories can be built.

Boundaries of such categories are fuzzy. There are, again, two reasons for this. First, as in the previous stage, it is not possible to represent nonsensory attributes of objects, which may make externally similar objects categorically different. The difference between a doll and a child can be represented now because it is possible to understand that a doll's and a child's internal structures should be compared to understand the differences between them. These internal structures, however, can be represented directly through the senses. But it would be impossible to differentiate between a radioactively contaminated apple and an uncontaminated apple. To the senses, these apples can be identical.

The other reason for permeable category boundaries lies in the possibility that the same object can be observed in different situations and, correspondingly, can be categorized of into different categories. Aaro, for example, can be categorized on the basis of appearance in different situations as a citizen (for the state), as a father (for my daughter), as a husband (for my wife), as a (hopefully) respected teacher (for my students), as an incompetent boy (for my parents), or as an ugly old man (for teenagers). All these classifications are correct. And it is obvious that problems arise immediately when it is necessary to categorize Aaro simultaneously in more than one way. An incompetent boy cannot be a respected teacher. It would be confusing for a student to visit the teacher at his home and to observe a mother teaching the teacher what to wear in the evening. Exemplar-based categories constructed on the basis of everyday experiences can categorize the same object into contrasting categories. The boundaries of such categories are thus obscure.

In sum, symbols at the sixth stage are differentiated into symbols for objects, object-specific properties, relational properties, and relations between objects. It becomes possible to describe all objects, situations, and phenomena in the sensory world by symbols. Symbols encode exemplar-based categories. The sixth stage is topographically constrained so that it is not possible to represent real nonsensory properties of objects and phenomena. Language allows us to refer to possible nonsensory information (a god, intentionality of nonorganic objects, etc.), but there are no mental tools for analyzing the validity of such claims about nonsensory forces and properties.

Seventh Stage. Symbols for Nonsensory Characteristics of the World. Classically Defined Categories

The seventh stage begins around the age of 7 years. At this stage of representational development metasymbolic systems differentiate from other symbolic systems. A metasymbolic or metalinguistic description of a symbol system creates a frame of reference against which it is possible to map different statements about the same objects or phenomena. The essence of that mapping can be understood as construction of (scientific) experiments. The same object or phenomenon is studied under different experimentally constrained situations. All observations from different experimental situations where the context is systematically varied allow us to build and validate representations about a nonsensory world.

The differentiation process can be observed in the development of metalinguistic awareness. The results of many studies (Ferreira & Morrison, 1994; Gombert, 1992, 1993a, 1993b; Roberts, 1992; Tulviste, 1988b, 1993) can be summarized as follows. Metalinguistic awareness has two forms. First, preschool children have already acquired a procedural knowledge of how to use language and of how not to use language. They can recognize ungrammatical sentences, repeat grammatically defined categories of sentences (like subjects), count words in sentences, transform spoken sounds to graphic forms in writing, and so on. That level of metalinguistic awareness is called "epilinguistic" by Gombert and "tacit" by Roberts (see references, above). The second form, called "metalinguistic" by Gombert and "explicit" by Roberts, is developmentally secondary; it develops on the basis of epilinguistic-tacit knowledge. True metalinguistic awareness develops after the age of 7 years. True metalinguistic knowledge is characterized by an ability to explicitly verbalize the underlying reasoning behind one's judgment in an organized way—in other words, an ability develops to describe language with language.

The mechanism of such differentiation is documented very well by Nelson in her slot-filler theory (see above, Mechanism of Mental Development). Nelson has demonstrated how taxonomic categories differentiate in the process of experiencing paradigmatically related objects in the context of syntagmatically structured everyday activities. After differentiation, these paradigmatically defined categories are connected with symbols, symbols that encode superordinate categories. It is important that superordinate terms are *defined in language and not in the world.* It means that the taxonomic relation is a relation among words, not among things (Nelson, 1988). Indeed, taxonomically defined categories cross the boundaries of objects in the immediate sensory contexts, and they are also defined so that it is possible to include into a category objects or phenomena never experienced directly. A taxonomic category "mammals," for example, includes kangaroos and whales, which are perceptually very different and almost never appear in the same context (with the exception of drowned kangaroos in the ocean, perhaps). The category "mammals" is defined in language. And who are the subcategories and exemplars who belong to that category are defined in language.

Thus, taxonomy is another case of metalinguistic awareness; it is an example of language about language. It is interesting that human culture has created a special environment where paradigmatic symbolic relations are made especially salient. That environment is formal schooling. There is an ample evidence from cross-cultural research and from studies of the effect of schooling on children that formal schooling is related to qualitatively different way of thinking (Artman & Cahan, 1993; Cole, 1996; Luria, 1974, 1979; Tulviste, 1988a).

The most important development related to schooling is, according to my theory, not the acquisition of a huge amount of novel facts about the world but rather the acquisition of an ability to think purely at the symbolic level, that is, to think so that direct links to the sensory world can be totally ignored when necessary. It is very interesting that symbols, which still basically are patterns of sensory attributes, can now be systematically combined without constraints. At the same time, and this is the very basic fact about symbols, the symbols that are combined in whatever way are still connected with direct sensory representations and, through them, with the reality of the external environment. That relation can be direct (a symbol refers directly to some sensory level of representation) or indirect (a symbol is defined with the help of other symbols). But even the indirectly defined symbols are related to the sensory world. This is because it is logically impossible to develop symbols that are defined by other symbols without first having at least some symbols that encode sensory representations. So, since all symbols can eventually be connected to the external world, it becomes clear how it is possible to give entirely new meanings to the same objects.

It can be suggested that that is the only way it is possible to represent the world that is not available to the senses. The essence of giving new meaning to the same object is the relation of the object into some (taxonomic) category that is based on some nonsensory but real connection between objects. Different metals and water, for example, can be categorized as "substances that conduct electricity." It is also important that such categorization needs explicit theoretical explanation—what is electricity, how can it be recognized, and how can it be explained? The latter description, in turn, must be directly related to the conditions of the world available to the senses. If there is something we call electricity, then it must be possible to construct devices that react to it so that changes in the environment caused by electricity become visible or available to other senses. The requirement to systematically define the nonsensory phenomenon and explicitly define when, in what conditions, and how a hypothesized phenomenon must cause events in the sensory world differentiates representations at this stage from the representations of the previous stage.

It is possible to represent the world beyond the senses systematically at this stage. The representations are still topographically constrained. It is hard to find empirical evidence for the reason of the constraint, but it can be hypothesized that, as at previous stages, the constraint is quantitative. At this stage a special symbolic context is differentiated that allows analysis symbolically of all aspects of the sensory world and to construct representations about the nonsensory world. The possibilities of mental operations are constrained so that all nonsensory and sensory phenomena encoded representationally at this stage are explicitly related to only one "correct" abstract symbolic frame of reference. In schools, for example, the only correct answer to the question of what is the relationship between earth and the sun is that earth is moving around the sun. This is despite the fact that from the standpoint of a person living on earth the sensory analysis leads to the opposite answer, that the earth is stationary and the sun is moving. Obviously both of the answers are correct, but only when they are explicitly related to different contexts when one or the other answer is correct. To do that, it is necessary to organize the known facts about objects or phenomena into one system of representation together with interconnected different abstract backgrounds that define different correct answers to the same question. It can be hypothesized that such an amount of information cannot be processed simultaneously at this stage of development. Such explicit connection of representations with more than one context differentiates only at the next stage of development.

An entirely new kind of symbolic relationship is represented at this stage. It is possible to solve problems coded by symbols entirely independently from direct sensory experiences. One kind of such mental operation is syllogistic reasoning. The overall picture from developmental studies of syllogistic reasoning (Bara, Bucciarelli, & Johnson-Laird, 1995; Gigerenzer & Regier, 1996; Jorgensen & Falmagne, 1992; Markovits, 1993; Markovits & Vachon, 1990; Morris, 2000; Sloman, 1996a, 1996b) is as follows. Different studies are in agreement with the idea that there is more than one way to solve syllogisms. Many syllogistic tasks can be solved by preschool children. But, strictly speaking, the thinking of preschoolers is not syllogistic; their ability to solve syllogistic problems is related to actual everyday knowledge. Syllogisms that contain information that contradicts everyday experiences confuse children. Syllogistic reasoning that relies only on the formal-logical structure of the task develops gradually only after the age of 7 years.

A brilliant study on the development of formal-logical reasoning was conducted by Chapman and Lindenberger (1992a, 1992b). They hypothesized that children may solve transitive inference tasks in two ways: by constructing some concrete spatial representation of the task structure or by approaching the task formally as a purely linguistic exercise. They asked children to justify their solutions to the task and differentiated children into two groups on the basis of whether the justification was formal-logical or not. It appeared, as these researchers predicted, that children who did not use formal-logical justifications sometimes had accurate memory for premises. But in many cases their memory for premises was inaccurate. In addition, many children who gave nonformal justifications were not able to solve the problem correctly. Children who justified their solutions formal-logically, in turn, were always absolutely correct both in memory for premises and in solutions. Thus, the formal-logical way of solving syllogistic problems leads always to correct answers. That formal-logical processing relies on exact verbatim symbolic representation of premises.[4]

So, formal-logical reasoning must be coherent, and different ideas about the same phenomenon must be in a certain logical relationship to make correct and valid inferences from premises. There are studies on the development of representation of astronomical phenomena, for example, that are in agreement with the idea that novel knowledge about the nonsensory world involves a novel interpretation of the same external observations. The observations themselves do not change. If children observe that the earth is flat, then it remains flat for their vision even when they learn that actually the earth is a sphere. In developing a novel understanding, children first experience new interpretations of everyday phenomena, usually with the help of a teacher. Teachers' explanations lead to a change in interpretations. That change is first incoherent and directly related to specific facts. Only later (and not always) a coherent representation of novel knowledge is constructed (Kikas, 1998; Vosniadou, 1992; Vosniadou & Brewer, 1992).

With the differentiation of one invariant formal-logical frame of reference for representations, it becomes possible to define categories "classically" (cf. Aristotle, 1941b). Things or phenomena either do or do not belong to the category, and it is not possible to belong to a category in different degrees, as it was possible at previous stages of representational development. All birds are birds, and penguins and robins are birds at the same degree. There are many empirical demonstrations by which robins and penguins are usually perceived as belonging to the category at a different degree, that is, robins are more birds than penguins. It has even been claimed (and accepted by many) that "Most, if not all [sic!], categories do not have clear-cut boundaries (Rosch, 1978, p. 35)." If we would assume, following such statements, that it is not possible to define clear-cut categories, we would be seriously wrong. Biologically, for example, it is possible to be pregnant or not to be pregnant. Various degrees of pregnancy are purely quantitative within the qualitatively clear-cut category of the state of pregnancy. If we say "All humans are mortal," then we have defined a clear-cut category— it is not possible for a human being to be more or less mortal or not mortal at all. Formal-logical symbolic representations allow the construction of categories that are absolute. If people still feel very often that categories are fuzzy, then they simply operate at a more primitive developmental level, where it is not possible to construct categories in respect to one single frame of reference and to build a category that is defined by all its essential characteristics, both sensory and non-sensory. When philosophers try to refute such a position, they would probably indicate that by constructing a clear-cut category, we can be wrong. Yes, but so what? We are talking about representations. And representationally a category can be defined absolutely, even when no such category in the real world corresponds to that representation.

In sum, at the seventh stage of representational development, a possibility differentiates to describe language by language, or metalinguistics. It becomes possible to systematize very different sensory-based observations into one frame of reference and, through analyzing experiences in that formal-logical frame of reference, to construct representations about the nonsensory world. Symbols at that stage encode classically defined categories with clear-cut boundaries. The seventh stage is topographically constrained so that it is not possible to construct representational systems where the information that the same thing or phenomenon can belong to different categories in different frames of reference is represented.

Eighth Stage. Symbols for Differentiated Nonsensory Contexts. Categories Defined as Hierarchical Systems

The eight stage of representational development begins around the age of 12 years. The differentiation that becomes possible at this stage is the differentiation of different formal-logical frames of reference in which the same object or phenomenon can be categorized into different categories. At this stage the differentiation thus takes place in the metalinguistic or metasymbolic system itself.

The hypothetical mechanism of the differentiation at that stage cannot be supported by the results of empirical studies as yet. But it can be proposed that the mechanism is related to personal experiences that the same objects or phenomena may be categorized entirely differently by different people and in different contexts. The analysis of such different categorizations leads to the observation that there is more than one possible way for "correct" categorization of representations. In a way, development is reminiscent of the ideas of post-modernists who claim that there are many viewpoints and all of them should be treated as equally correct. Differently from postmodernists, however, construction of representations in different frames of reference does not lead to the universal conclusion that all viewpoints are equally correct. Rather, it is recognized that all viewpoints can be equally correct, but it is necessary first to define all different frames of reference and analyze them before such a conclusion is made.

One of the central questions for any stage theory is always how many stages should be distinguished and why the number of stages is exactly the one proposed. One question is the exact number of stages. Theoretically, it is not possible to define in abstract terms how many stages there should be. It depends on the constraints on the developing system. If there were, for example, a biological organism able to represent through receptors all qualities of the environment, there would be no need for the development of symbols as separate tools. It would be possible to represent every aspect of the environment directly. So the exact number of stages can be found only empirically. But that empirical exploration needs to be constrained theoretically. It is necessary to define the end-stage and to propose an explanation as to why there is no need for further stages. Otherwise we would always have to search for additional stages after the one last identified theoretically so far.

I suggest that the eighth stage is the last stage in representational development because it is not topographically constrained in respect of represented knowledge (all symbols still remain topographically constrained in other ways—they are just symbols). In principle, at this stage it is possible to represent all aspects of the environment, both sensory and nonsensory. That stage of development can be called a systems or functional systems stage of representations. Here it is possible not only to represent nonsensory qualities of the world but also to understand that a world is a functional system where every component or subsystem is or has a potential to come into contact with some other subsystem of the world. Consequently, it is not possible to fully understand anything without explicitly describing the context, the larger system where that particular subsystem belongs. In different systems the same subsystem theoretically must have different characteristics because every system changes when hierarchically included into a larger system or when separated from that larger system (cf. von Bertalanffy, 1968, who essentially proposed the same idea). A stage is defined here as a topographical constraint on what can and what cannot in principle be represented at a certain stage. As there are no topographical constraints on the content of representations any more, there are no further stages either.

Different scholars have proposed that it is possible to differentiate a stage in mental development that has the characteristics as defined here (even though without explicitly describing how or by what mechanism that stage is achieved). Thus, Richards and Commons (1990) suggested that there is a post-formal stage of development that follows the stage of formal operations proposed by Piaget. At that stage one system of logic is applied to the products or operations of another system of logic.

It is very interesting that, according to these authors, it is not possible to formulate developmental conceptions of phenomena before that stage. Formal operations alone are not appropriate because formal operations allow representation of only linear phenomena. Development, however, is nonlinear. These ideas fit well with my theory. Formal operations allow understanding of only linear relations because formal operations are defined in respect to only one abstract frame of reference. But nonlinear transformation requires a description of more frames. The nonlinear transformation is in essence the change of a system from one frame of relationships to the other that qualitatively differs from the first. This idea is very interesting because it may explain why most of modern psychology is a-developmental in essence, why even the possibility that the idea of general stages can be correct is explicitly abandoned as impossible by many researchers. It has been even suggested that there is *evidence against stages* (e.g., Brainerd, 1993). A system view definitely rejects the idea that such evidence can be found. It does not follow, of course, that stages necessarily must exist. Only empirical evidence for stages can prove it. There can be evidence against particular stage theories, but there can be no evidence against the idea of stages as such. Systems view predicts that stages may exist where an appropriate frame of description is proposed. In some other frame it is possible to see all changes as continuous, uninterrupted, and quantitative. Thus, it is possible that modern developmental psychology does not take development seriously because most psychologists think about development in terms of the previous, formal-logical system of representation rather than in a system frame of thinking.

It is better to understand the essence of systems of representations that can be constructed in this stage when system representations are compared to formal-logical linear representations acquisition, which became possible at the previous stage. One domain of knowledge where human culture has developed systematic understanding of the world is ecology. It is increasingly understood that one and the same thing may be useful and dangerous at the same time. Deodorants that contain freons, for example, can be understood as useful if culture requires that humans must not smell naturally. Using deodorants helps to avoid that problem. Scientists found however, that freons destroy the ozone layer of the atmosphere, which might be one way to climate catastrophes. So, the same deodorant becomes dangerous to an ecologically educated person. In different studies on the development of ecological knowledge it has been found that systemic understanding of relationships in the environment is a late development; it only emerges after the age of 10 to 12 years (Brody, 1994; Chandler & Boutilier, 1992; Maurice-Naville & Montangero, 1992).[5] Interesting observations have been made by Brody. He found different misconceptions about ecological crises in adolescents. Some participants thought that anything natural is not pollution; others suggested that biodegradable materials are not pollutants, and so on. Such statements can be interpreted as examples of classically defined categories—if an object belongs to one category, then it does not belong to the other. If biodegradable materials are natural, then they cannot be nonnatural pollutants. It is not represented in such categories that under some conditions, in some specific contexts the same category may change. If the amount of biodegradable material exceeds the available resources of degradation in the environment, everything may become pollutant.

With the differentiation of abstract frames of reference in a representational system, a qualitatively novel way of categorization is also acquired. Now it becomes possible to categorize classically things and phenomena into more than one category. With the explicit definition of in what sense, in what system of relationships a thing or phenomenon is classified, the same thing can appear simultaneously in different, even in the classical sense, mutually exclusive categories.

In sum, at the eighth stage of representational development the topographical constraints on the information that can be represented disappears. As it becomes possible to analyze the same things simultaneously in more than one abstract frame of reference, it becomes possible to explain all aspects of the world. It becomes possible to describe the world systemically. It can be stressed here that a stage is described by topographical constraints, by a *potential* that can be realized in the stage. Whether that potential will be realized depends on the interaction of culturally defined possibilities and biologically determined constraints. Sometimes there is no required information available in the immediate cultural context, and sometimes the characteristics of the nervous system do not allow the use of opportunities created by the social–cultural environment.

THE DEVELOPMENT OF THE SEMIOTICALLY MEDIATED MIND: THE CASE OF DRAWING

The development of representations describes only partly the development of the mind in general. Representational development can be understood as a core that underlies mental development in whatever aspect it is studied. Next I describe how potential created by the representational development is realized in the development of one activity, drawing. Drawing is usually considered to be a "nonverbal" activity, one that requires only visual–motor coordination. I propose that drawing is not "nonverbal," but rather an example of semiotically mediated thought realized through drawings.

According to my theory, some mental operations and corresponding planned activities depend on the use of symbols that direct attention and perform necessary analyses of the situation to reach the expected goal. Symbols must always be used when there is no direct way to perceive required changes. Drawing is clearly the case—it is physically impossible to observe in a natural environment how an object can be transformed into a picture of itself. There is no way to acquire from direct sensory experience a knowledge about how to represent an object with a picture. Thus, there must be some mental tool with the help of which it can be decided what particular visual characteristic of an object must underlie visual-motor coordination in drawing activity. I propose that the mental tool that enters into the mental system underlying the drawing activity is symbolic representation. If my suggestion is correct, then there should be evidence that verbal abilities are involved in drawing performance. The amount of such evidence is amazingly large. I have reviewed that evidence elsewhere (Toomela, 2002). Briefly, several scholars have proposed that drawing can be understood as a form of language; results of empirical studies demonstrate that knowledge formulated in language has a direct impact on drawing performance; there is evidence that drawing performance is influenced by the type of verbal instruction given to children; there is evidence that verbalization is involved in planning drawing; and finally, there is evidence that the relationship between drawing performance and verbal IQ may be stronger than between drawing performance and nonverbal or performance IQ. In addition, I conducted a study where it was empirically demonstrated that drawing ability can be understood as a system of mental components. That system includes not only visual–spatial, motor, and memory but also verbal components (Toomela, 2002). So, there is a lot of evidence to support the idea that drawing is semiotically mediated. If the theory of representational development, described above, is correct, then drawing development should proceed by stages that are structurally similar to the stages of representational development.

First it is necessary to define what kind of visual analysis can be performed at different stages of the development of symbolic representations. Characteristics of drawings that can be supported by such symbolic analysis of the visual world can be proposed on that basis. The picture that emerges from the analysis of developmental stages described above is as follows:

Syncretic symbols can systematically differentiate only very general "places in situations"; no specifically visual analysis can be supported at that first stage of symbol development. If drawing development really reflects the development of symbolic representations, then first drawings should also be nonrepresentational. The structure of a drawing cannot be similar to the visual structure of the object.

Prototypical symbols refer to basic-level categories that are defined visually by shape. Correspondingly, drawings guided by prototypical symbols should depict prototypical categories where object-specific but not relational properties of objects can be depicted as well. It can also be hypothesized that such drawings do not encode the model's three dimensionality because by definition basic-level categories should represent the most informative attributes of objects. Most such informative or "canonical" views are two-dimensional (Cutzu & Edelman, 1994).

Exemplar symbols also encode relational properties of objects and relations between objects as well as object categories and object-specific properties. In drawing development, correspondingly, it can be expected that drawings of single models should attempt to represent the three-dimensional nature of the model. The relational characteristics of objects and relations between objects should also appear in drawings at this stage. It cannot be expected, however, to find drawings where spatial relations are depicted visually realistically, in correspondence with the retinal image. The reason for this limitation is the fact that in the course of depicting a three-dimensional space on a two-dimensional surface, at least one spatial property—area, direction, distance, or shape—must be distorted (Liben & Downs, 1989, 1992). Such a distortion requires abstract representation of the system of spatial relationships because experiences with concrete objects cannot be informative regarding how to distort spatial properties of objects in pictures. Abstract frames can be constructed at the next stage of representational development.

Symbols for classically defined categories allow the construction of abstract frames of reference for every sensory modality. For vision, such an abstract frame is the theory of perspective. In that abstract theory, space properties are abstracted from sensory reality and recoded in a system of symbols. In drawing development, correspondingly, visually realistic drawings that structurally reproduce the retinal presentation of visual objects should become possible.

Finally, *systemic symbols* allow differentiation of abstract contexts in which an object is categorized. The same object can be categorized into different categories, but objects from different categories also can now be categorized into one category. Drawings are also objects that can be categorized. Actually, the descriptions of drawings that should characterize different stages of representational development can be understood as definitions of categories of drawings. If a drawing is visually realistic, then it belongs to one category; if it represents only basic-level prototypes, it belongs to another category. Systemic symbols allow recategorization of all drawings. For example, it becomes possible to categorize them all as "art." Consequently, in principle every sign or scribble made on paper can be categorized as art or representative drawing now. But such categorization must be supported by explicit theory as to why or how any mark on paper can be understood as a representation of something else. There are many such theories that justify abstract or cubistic art, for example. Many famous artists, such as Wassily Kandinsky, Fernand Léger, Georges Braque, and Pablo Picasso, revolutionized art and presented their theories that visual arts must not be visually realistic (see Harrison & Wood, 1992, for numerous examples of such theories).

Evidence from many studies of drawing development indeed suggest that drawing ability develops as proposed above. A detailed review of such studies is beyond the scope of the present chapter, however, so I will give examples from only two studies I have conducted. Examples of characteristic drawings for each stage are shown in Figure 9.1.

In a study of the development of drawing of cubes and cylinders in which drawings from more than 3000 participants were analyzed (Toomela, 1999) it was found that drawing development proceeds over stages that correspond exactly to the theory I described above. *Scribbles* were found already in 2-year-old children. These children used approximately the same irregular scribble or closed form to represent both a cube and a cylinder. It is not possible to understand without observing the actual drawing situation which of the drawings represents a cube and which represents a cylinder (or a doll, or a flower, the drawing of which I describe in the next section). Thus, children's first drawings can be understood as symbols for a "place in a situation,"; scribbles just denote "I drew something here." At the next stage, which I called *single units*, cubes were drawn as rectangles and cylinders as regular circles, extended rectangles, or ovals. These units correspond to the most informative two-dimensional views of the models. This study does not allow one to determine whether a cube or a cylinder in general, a prototypical depiction of the models, was drawn as my theory predicts. At the third stage, the stage of *differentiated figures*, drawings differentiated into parts that represented extendedness of the models in three dimensions, depicting different faces of the models. The relationship between the faces, however, was not visually realistic. That result, again, is in accordance with the theory presented here. Finally, the fourth stage, *integrated wholes*, was characterized by visually realistic three-dimensional depictions of the models. This last stage, which would correspond to the stage of *systemic symbols*, was not differentiated in this study. Actually the method of the study where participants were asked to "draw exactly the model" would not be appropriate for that. The last stage can theoretically be identified in the analysis of the participants explicit theories of the art.

It is important that, even though the study was cross-sectional, it was possible to demonstrate that the stages appear in an invariant order. Scribbles were observed already among the youngest children, single units were *never* observed before the age of 2 years and 6 months; differentiated figures were *never* observed before the age of 3 years and 10 months; and integrated wholes were *never* observed before the age of 7 years and 11 months. It was also found that even many adults in the study did not reach the stage of integrated wholes in their drawings. That result does not contradict the idea of stages that are characterized by a potential that is constrained topographically. The stage does not guarantee that its potential is realized in every field of knowledge or every possible kind of mental operation.

In another study with about 1000 participants, the development of drawing of a doll, and a colored cube was explored (Toomela, 2001). Drawings of a cube or

Figure 9.1
Stages of drawing development and stages of word meaning development

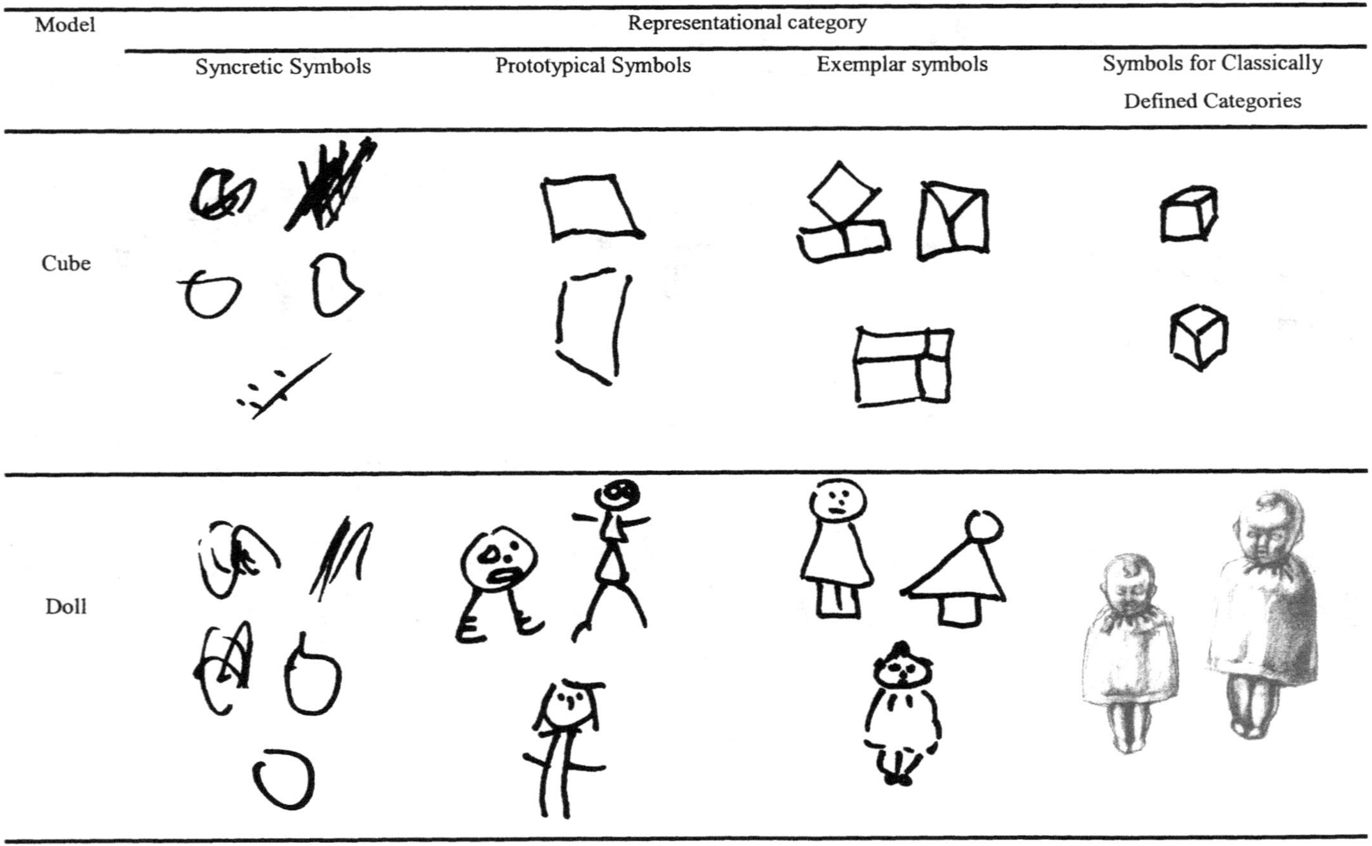

Model	Representational category			
	Syncretic Symbols	Prototypical Symbols	Exemplar symbols	Symbols for Classically Defined Categories
Cube				
Doll				

a cylinder painted with only one color cannot be informative regarding whether children draw at the second-stage prototypes or exemplars, whether they draw a cube or the cube in front of them at the moment. In this study the models were such that it was possible to determine whether drawings represent a prototype or the exemplar. The most informative in that respect was the doll. The model of the doll was unusual; its hands were not visible, it did not have hair, and its legs were melted together. I hypothesized that if some characteristic of the model is missing in the drawing, then the reason might be that it was memory or performance failure. When participants, however, add features that do not characterize the model, the only source of them can be an internal representation. If attributes are added by children, then they have drawn a prototype.

The results, again, are in full agreement with the idea that drawing development is supported by the development of symbolic representations. Again the youngest children in the study drew only scribbles. By analysis of drawings alone it was not possible to determine whether marks on the paper represent a cube, a doll, or something else. The age periodization was exactly the same as in the first study of drawing development, described above. It was found that children after the stage of scribbles indeed produced dolls that *all* had more attributes than the model. They added hands, toes or fingers, hair, or other attributes, and they also separated the legs that were melted together on the model. These drawings never appeared before age 2 years 6 months. The next stage was never observed before the age of 3 years 10 months. At that stage children represented only those attributes that also characterized the model. They drew the exemplar, the model, but the drawing was not as yet visually realistic, and the three-dimensionality of the model was not depicted. Finally, after the age of 8 years some participants were able to draw the model visually realistically.

In sum, development of drawing proceeds over stages that were identified on the basis of symbol development, on the basis of the development of word meaning. Even more, stages of drawing development are related to the same specific ages as the stages of representational development. Thus, it can be concluded that drawing is truly a cultural ability, one that develops in persons only in the social–cultural context. Children acquire a hierarchy of symbol representation in the process of social interaction and use these representations as tools for guiding mental operations—they develop a semiotically mediated mind. Drawing is an example of semiotically mediated abilities.

CONCLUSIONS

Development can be defined in different ways. Some views on development are based on limited, usually implicit, understanding of causality and explanation. In these views causality is understood as a linear cause → effect relationship. According to such views, nothing qualitatively novel can emerge because no mechanism that would lead to nonlinear qualitative changes can be represented if causality is defined as linear. The other view, called here the *theory of functional systems*, assumes that exhaustive explanation can be reached only when different aspects of a thing or phenomenon under study are complementarily described. It is necessary to describe components of the system, specific relationships between those components, and how that system has been constructed or how it has developed.

Next, an analysis of the human mind following the principles of the theory of functional systems was presented in this chapter. It was first suggested that the development of representations proceeds over two general stages. First an ability develops to represent everything in the sensory environments, after that, these sensory representations are hierarchically related to symbols that allow the processing of information about the same sensory phenomena in a qualitatively different way. Nonsensory attributes of the world can be represented only when sensory information is also processed with symbols. It was also suggested that symbols are in essence cultural and can develop only in the social–cultural environment. Next it was suggested that both of these very general stages of development can be differentiated further. It was proposed that sensory representations develop over three general stages, and symbols develop over five additional stages of representational development. All that analysis emphasizes that for understanding mental development it is absolutely necessary to understand not only whether some task is performed or a problem is solved but also how or by what mental mechanisms goals are reached. The same task can be solved in different ways, some of which are developed genetically (from *genesis*, not from *gene*) earlier than the others.

Finally the development of drawing ability was analyzed. It was proposed that drawing ability is a semiotically mediated ability, an ability for which the mental system must include symbols. It was demonstrated that the stages of symbol development indeed allowed construction of a theoretical schema of drawing development. That theoretical schema corresponds to the changes observed in the large-scale studies of drawing development. Thus, development of drawing is structurally identical to the development of symbols.

There are some interesting issues that remain beyond the scope of this chapter. First, the theory of mental development presented here allows a better understanding of the adult mind. In modern psychology, there are different competing theories on conceptual structure or on the structure of memory, for example. There is no single domain in psychology where only one theory can be found. It might be possible that instead of opposing these different theories it would be feasible to treat them as complementary. Theoretically, the mental system is heterogeneous and it is possible to identify mental operations that belong to different stages in all persons. Consequently, different competing theories—that all are supported by numerous empirical studies—may describe different developmental levels within the system of the adult mind.

Another interesting direction where this theory can be moved is connection of the theory of mental development in ontogenesis with the cultural phylogenesis. Even though the idea of recapitulation is rejected in modern psychology, it can be revived again. One line of evidence for recapitulation can be based on empirical data. Analysis of the development of visual arts in culture exactly follows the same stages identified in the ontogenesis. First scribbles and regular patterns with idiosyncratic meaning emerged in culture. Next, about 40,000 years ago humans began to create drawings of prototypical animals, after which depictions of situations emerged. Such depictions are still visually unrealistic. About two millennia ago a visually realistic art developed in Hellenistic Greece. That form of art disappeared with the decline in all areas of thought after the collapse of the Roman Empire and emerged again with the Renaissance. Finally, in the second half of the nineteenth century, a new form of art emerged. Step-by-step, visual arts moved away from visually realistic pictures to the expression of mental states with an almost infinitive variety of forms. That development was accompanied by explicit theories as to why art must not follow visual realism. About a half a century ago, artists realized that absolutely everything can be an object of art.

Another line of support for the idea of recapitulation is purely theoretical. Both phylogenesis and ontogenesis of the mind begin from the structurally identical state, an ability to respond to individual sensory attributes. The mechanism of development is also exactly the same. Both culture and an individual can develop only in one way—through constructing representations on the basis of active interaction with the environment. It is also noteworthy that culture can develop only through individuals—all novelty in culture is first created by a single person. There are no novel ideas that emerge in all people simultaneously. Consequently, if mental development begins from structurally the same mental state and proceeds by the same general mechanism, it should be possible to see recapitulation of mental phylogenesis in mental ontogenesis. It must be stressed here that such recapitulation concerns stages, and only stages—topographical constraints on the mental operations—not exact ways how the potential of a stage is realized dynamically.

NOTES

Acknowledgment: This work was supported by the Estonian Science Foundation Grant No. 3988.

1. The issue of how theories of categories and conceptual structure, mainly studied in adults, are connected to the theory of representational development, is too complicated to be analyzed in detail in this chapter. There are several theories of conceptual structure (cf. Komatsu, 1992). Usually these theories are contrasted as if only one of them can be correct. This assumption, however, may be entirely wrong. I believe that instead of opposing these theories, it can be assumed that, because mental structure is developmentally heterogeneous, all or at least many of these theories can be simultaneously correct. They simply should be applied to different developmental levels or stages. If my suggestion is correct, then another reason emerges why cognition must be studied developmentally. If there are different conceptual structures, and if these structures are developmentally hierarchically ordered, then conceptual structure can be understood fully only in developmental studies.

Otherwise later developing categories may cause changes in earlier developing categories because inclusion of a component to a higher-level structure is always related to the change of properties of elementary components. When whales, for example, are categorized into a superordinate category of mammals together with bears and humans, then the basic level category of fish changes—the whale is not a big fish any more.

2. Kubovy and Van Valkenburg (2001) demonstrated that objecthood can be represented not only in visual but also in auditory modality. Following their way of analysis, it can be suggested that objects can be represented in every sensory modality.

3. Motor movements are, on the one hand, related to the ways in which humans interact and use the objects. In that sense, motor movements are related to the relationships of the objects with other objects. On the other hand, however, motor movements are directly represented in a sensory proprioceptive system. So similarity in motor movements at that stage of development is mentally encoded in a proprioceptive system and is not directly related to functional relationships between objects in the environment. Motor movements in that sense are no more than another set of individual sensory attributes.

4. Chapman and Lindenberger's (1992a, 1992b) studies are relatively exceptional in developmental psychology. The usual way of thinking is that if children can solve problems with certain structure, then they do "have" that form of thinking. Researchers who have demonstrated early competence always have changed tasks by "stripping away *unnecessary* processing demands and *removing complexity*" (Wellman & Gelman, 1992, p. 367, my emphasis). It is hard to understand how the authors knew what are "unnecessary processing demands" and how they proved that after "removing complexity" the task is solved in qualitatively the same way. Actually there is a lot of evidence that processing demands and complexity are directly related to how problems are solved. It is obvious that addition and subtraction can be performed by counting fingers and other body parts when numbers involved are small, usually below 10 or 20. I believe it would be very hard even for the most dedicated supporter of the early competence view to demonstrate that the task $1,000,000,497 + 1,232,789,001 = ?$ can be performed in the same way. Would developmental psychologists take the idea of development seriously and follow the path taken by Chapman and Lindenberger (and, fortunately, by several others), there would be much less "innate knowledge" in theories of children's mind.

5. Results of these studies are partly interpreted differently from my account. Chandler and Boutilier (1992) suggest that their results disagree with the idea that there is a stage of postformal system reasoning that develops after the stage of formal operations. They proposed that these two kinds of thinking develop in parallel. Maurice-Naville and Montangero (1992), in turn, found some evidence of thinking analogous to system thinking already in 8- to 9-year-old children. Both of these studies, however, did not study empirically *how* correct answers were produced. They described thinking development only in terms of correct or noncorrect verbal or pictorial answers to questions. They did not consider the possibility that correct answers to questions about systemic relationships can be based on different mental mechanisms. It is possible, for example, just to memorize from school the relations between components of the food cycle to perform correctly in a dynamic system reasoning task used by Chandler and Boutilier. It has to be concluded again that developmental studies must not only ask *what* tasks can be performed; in addition, such studies must always ask *how* the tasks are performed. No developmental claim can be valid without describing how tasks are performed.

REFERENCES

Aristotle (1941a). Metaphysics. In R. McKeon (Ed.), *The basic works of Aristotle* (pp. 681–926). New York: Random House.

Aristotle (1941b). Organon. In R. McKeon (Ed.), *The basic works of Aristotle* (pp. 1–212). New York: Random House.

Artman, L., & Cahan, S. (1993). Schooling and the development of transitive inference. *Developmental Psychology, 29*(4), 753–759.

Baldwin, D. A., & Markman, E. M. (1989). Establishing word-object relations: a first step. *Child Development, 60,* 381–398.

Baldwin, J. M. (1906). *Thought and things. A study of the development and meaning of thought or genetic logic.* London: Swan Sonneschein & Co.

Bara, B. G., Bucciarelli, M., & Johnson-Laird, P. N. (1995). Development of syllogistic reasoning. *American Journal of Psychology, 108*(2), 157–193.

Barrett, M. (1995). Early lexical development. In P. Fletcher & B. MacWhinney (Eds.), *The handbook of child language* (pp. 362–392). Oxford: Blackwell.

Behrend, D. A. (1990). The development of verb concepts: children's use of verbs to label familiar and novel events. *Child Development, 61,* 681–696.

Bem, S., & Looren de Jong, H. (1997). *Theoretical issues in psychology.* London: Sage.

Bloom, P. (1990). Subjectless sentences in child language. *Linguistic Inquiry, 21*(4), 491–504.

Bloom, P. (1993). Grammatical continuity in language development: the case of subjectless sentences. *Linguistic Inquiry, 24*(4), 721–734.

Borer, H., & Wexler, K. (1992). Bi-unique relations and the maturation of grammatical principles. *Natural Language and Linguistic Theory, 10,* 147–189.

Brainerd, C. J. (1993). Cognitive development is abrupt (but not stage-like). *Monographs of the Society for Research in Child Development, 58*(9), 170–190.

Braunwald, S. R. (1995). Differences in the acquisition of early verbs: evidence from diary data from sisters. In M. Tomasello & W. E. Merriman (Eds.), *Beyond names for things. Young children's acquisition of verbs* (pp. 81–111). Hillsdale, N.J.: Lawrence Erlbaum.

Brody, M. J. (1994). Student science knowledge related to ecological crises. *International Journal of Science Education, 16*(4), 421–435.

Cardon, L. R., Fulker, D. W., DeFries, J. C., & Plomin, R. (1992). Continuity and change in general cognitive ability from 1 to 7 years of age. *Developmental Psychology, 28,* 64–73.

Chandler, M. J., & Boutilier, R. G. (1992). The development of dynamic system reasoning. *Human Development, 35,* 121–137.

Chao, S.-J., & Cheng, P. W. (2000). The emergence of inferential rules: the use of pragmatic reasoning schemas by preschoolers. *Cognitive Development, 15,* 39–62.

Chapman, M., & Lindenberger, U. (1992a). How to detect reasoning–remembering dependence (And how not to). *Developmental Review, 12,* 187–198.

Chapman, M., & Lindenberger, U. (1992b). Transitivity judgments, memory for premises, and models of children's reasoning. *Developmental Review, 12,* 124–163.

Cole, M. (1996). *Cultural psychology. A once and future discipline.* Cambridge, Mass.: The Belknap Press of Harvard University Press.

Cutzu, F., & Edelman, S. (1994). Canonical views in object representation and recognition. *Vision Research, 34,* 3037–3056.

Davidoff, J., & Mitchell, P. (1993). The color cognition of children. *Cognition*, *48*, 121–137.

Eisenberg, S. L., & Cairns, H. S. (1994). The development of infinitives from three to five. *Journal of Child Language*, *21*, 713–734.

Epstein, H. T. (2001). An outline of the role of brain in human cognitive development. *Brain and Cognition*, *45*, 44–51.

Fenson, L., Dale, P. S., Reznick, J. S., Bates, E., Thal, D. J., & Pethick, S. J. (1994). Variability in early communicative development. *Monographs of the Society for Research in Child Development*, *59*(5), Serial No. 242.

Ferreira, F., & Morrison, F. J. (1994). Children's metalinguistic knowledge of syntactic constituents: effects of age and schooling. *Developmental Psychology*, *30*(5), 663–678.

Fulker, D. W., Cherny, S. S., & Cardon, L. R. (1993). Continuity and change in cognitive development. In R. Plomin & G. E. McClearn (Eds.), *Nature, nurture, and psychology* (pp. 77–97). Washington: American Psychological Association.

Gallivan, J. (1988). Motion verb acquisition: development of definitions. *Perceptual and Motor Skills*, *66*, 979–986.

Gigerenzer, G., & Regier, T. (1996). How do we tell an association from a rule? Comment on Sloman (1996). *Psychological Bulletin*, *119*(1), 23–26.

Gogate, L. J., Walker-Andrews, A. S., & Bahrick, L. E. (2001). The intersensory origins of word comprehension: an ecological-dynamic systems view. *Developmental Science*, *4*(1), 1–37.

Gombert, J. E. (1992). *Metalinguistic development.* New York: Harvester Wheatsheaf.

Gombert, J. E. (1993a). Metacognition, metalanguage and metapragmatics. *International Journal of Psychology*, *28*(5), 571–580.

Gombert, J. E. (1993b). Psycholinguistic "meta" is different from linguistic "meta." *Scientia Paedagogica Experimentalis*, *30*(1), 5–18.

Hall, D. G., Waxman, S. R., & Hurwitz, W. M. (1993). How two- and four-year old children interpret adjectives and count nouns. *Child Development*, *64*(6), 1651–1664.

Harrison, C., & Wood, P. (1992). *Art in theory. 1900–1990. An anthology of changing ideas.* Oxford: Blackwell.

Hobhouse, L. T. (1901). *Mind in evolution.* London: MacMillan and Co.

Hudspeth, W. J., & Pribram, K. H. (1990). Stages of brain and cognitive maturation. *Journal of Educational Psychology*, *82*, 881–884.

Hudspeth, W. J., & Pribram, K. H. (1992). Psychophysiological indices of cerebral maturation. *International Journal of Psychophysiology*, *12*, 19–29.

Huttenlocher, J., Smiley, P., & Charney, R. (1983). Emergence of action categories in the child: evidence from verb meanings. *Psychological Review*, *90*(1), 72–93.

Huttenlocher, J., Smiley, P., & Ratner, H. (1983). What do word meanings reveal about conceptual development. In T. B. Seiler & W. Wannenmacher (Eds.), *Concept development and the development of word meaning* (pp. 210–233). Berlin: Springer Verlag.

Hyams, N., & Wexler, K. (1993). On the grammatical basis of null subjects in child language. *Linguistic Inquiry*, *24*(3), 421–459.

Johnston, J. (1984). Acquisition of locative meanings: *Behind* and *in front of. Journal of Child Language*, *11*, 407–422.

Jones, S. S., & Smith, L. B. (1993). The place of perception in children's concepts. *Cognitive Development, 8,* 113–139.

Jones, S. S., Smith, L. B., & Landau, B. (1991). Object properties and knowledge in early lexical learning. *Child Development, 62,* 499–516.

Jorgensen, J. C., & Falmagne, R. J. (1992). Aspects of the meaning of *if . . . then* for older preschoolers: hypotheticality, entailment, and suppositional processes. *Cognitive Development, 7,* 189–212.

Kemler Nelson, D. G., Frankenfield, A., Morris, C., & Blair, E. (2000). Young children's use of functional information to categorize artifacts: three factors that matter. *Cognition, 77,* 133–168.

Kemler Nelson, D. G., Russell, R., Duke, N., & Jones, K. (2000). Two-year-olds will name artifacts by their function. *Child Development, 71*(5), 1271–1288.

Kikas, E. (1998). The impact of teaching on students' definitions and explanations of astronomical phenomena. *Learning and Instruction, 8*(5), 439–454.

Klibanoff, R. S., & Waxman, S. R. (2000). Basic level object categories support the acquisition of novel adjectives: evidence from preschool-aged children. *Child Development, 71*(3), 649–659.

Koffka, K. (1935). *Principles of Gestalt psychology.* London: Routledge & Kegan Paul.

Köhler, W. (1947). *Gestalt psychology. An introduction to new concepts in modern psychology.* New York: Mentor Books.

Komatsu, L. K. (1992). Recent views of conceptual structure. *Psychological Bulletin, 112,* 500–526.

Kubovy, M., & Van Valkenburg, D. (2001). Auditory and visual objects. *Cognition, 80,* 97–126.

Lakoff, G., & Johnson, M. (1999). *Philosophy in the flesh. The embodied mind and its challenge to western thought.* New York: Basic Books.

Landau, B., Smith, L., & Jones, S. (1998). Object shape, object function, and object name. *Journal of Memory and Language, 38,* 1–27.

Landau, B., Smith, L. B., & Jones, S. S. (1988). The importance of shape in early lexical learning. *Cognitive Development, 3,* 299–321.

Landau, B., Smith, L. B., & Jones, S. S. (1992). Syntactic context and the shape bias in children's and adult lexical learning. *Journal of Memory and Language, 31,* 807–825.

Leont'ev, A. N. (1981). *Problemy razvitija psihiki.* Moscow: Izdatel'stvo Moskovskogo Universiteta.

Lewin, K. (1935). *A dynamic theory of personality. Selected papers.* New York: McGraw-Hill.

Liben, L. S., & Downs, R. M. (1989). Understanding maps as symbols: the development of map concepts in children. In H. W. Reese (Ed.), *Advances in child development and behavior* (Vol. 22, pp. 145–201). San Diego: Academic Press.

Liben, L. S., & Downs, R. M. (1992). Developing an understanding of graphic representations in children and adults: the case of GEO-graphics. *Cognitive Development, 7,* 331–349.

Livingstone, M., & Hubel, D. (1988). Segregation of form, color, movement, and depth: anatomy, physiology, and perception. *Science, 240,* 740–749.

Lucariello, J., Kyratzis, A., & Nelson, K. (1992). Taxonomic knowledge: what kind and when? *Child Development, 63,* 978–998.

Luria, A. R. (1969). *Vyshije korkovyje funktsii tsheloveka i ikh narushenija pri lokal'nykh porazenijakh mozga. (Higher cortical functions in man and their disturbances in local brain lesions.)*. Moscow: Izdatel'stvo Moskovskogo Universiteta.

Luria, A. R. (1974). *Ob istoricheskom razvitii poznavatel'nykh processov. Eksperimental'no-psikhologicheskoje issledovanije*. Moscow: Nauka.

Luria, A. R. (1979). *Jazyk i soznanije*. Moscow: Izdatel'stvo Moskovskogo Universiteta.

Markman, E. M. (1990). Constraints children place on word meanings. *Cognitive Science, 14*, 57–77.

Markovits, H. (1993). The development of conditional reasoning: a Piagetian reformulation of mental models theory. *Merrill-Palmer Quarterly, 39*(1), 131–158.

Markovits, H., & Vachon, R. (1990). Conditional reasoning, representation, and level of abstraction. *Developmental Psychology, 26*(6), 942–951.

Maurice-Naville, D., & Montangero, J. (1992). The development of diachronic thinking: 8–12-year-old children's understanding of the evolution of forest disease. *British Journal of Developmental Psychology, 10*, 365–383.

McCrae, R. R. (2000). Trait psychology and the revival of personality and culture studies. *American Behavioral Scientist, 44*(1), 10–31.

Merriman, W. E., Scott, P. D., & Marazita, J. (1993). An appearance-function shift in children's object naming. *Journal of Child Language, 20*, 101–118.

Mervis, C. B., & Rosch, E. (1981). Categorization of natural objects. *Annual Review of Psychology, 32*, 89–115.

Morris, A. (2000). Development of logical reasoning: children's ability to verbally explain the nature of the distinction between logical and nonlogical forms of argument. *Developmental Psychology, 36*(6), 741–758.

Munro, D. (1992). Process vs structure and levels of analysis in psychology. Towards integration rather than reduction of theories. *Theory and Psychology, 2*, 109–127.

Nelson, K. (1988). Where do taxonomic categories come from? *Human Development, 31*, 3–10.

Nelson, K. (1995). The dual category problems in the acquisition of action words. In M. Tomasello & W. E. Merriman (Eds.), *Beyond names for things. Young children's acquisition of verbs* (pp. 223–249). Hillsdale, N.J.: Lawrence Erlbaum.

Nelson, K. (1996). *Language in cognitive development*. Cambridge: Cambridge University Press.

Nelson, K., Hampson, J., & Shaw, L. K. (1993). Nouns in early lexicons: evidence, explanations and implications. *Journal of Child Language, 20*, 61–84.

Olguin, R., & Tomasello, M. (1993). Twenty-five-month-old children do not have a grammatical category of verb. *Cognitive Development, 8*, 245–272.

Oviatt, S. L. (1982). Inferring what words mean: early development in infants' comprehension of common object names. *Child Development, 53*, 274–277.

Pavlov, I. P. (1927). *Lekcii o rabote bol'shikh polusharii golovnogo mozga*. Moscow: Gosudarstvennoje Izdatel'stvo.

Pavlov, I. P. (1951). *Dvatcatilet'nii opyt ob'jektivnogo izuchenija vyshei nervnoi dejatel'nosti (povedenija zhivotnykh)*. Moscow: Medgiz.

Richards, F. A., & Commons, M. L. (1990). Postformal cognitive-developmental theory and research: a review of its current status. In C. N. Alexander & E. J. Langer (Eds.), *Higher stages of human development* (pp. 139–161). New York: Oxford University Press.

Richardson, K. (1992). Covariation analysis of knowledge representation: some developmental studies. *Journal of Experimental Child Psychology, 53*, 129–150.

Roberts, B. (1992). The evolution of the young child's concept of word as a unit of spoken and written language. *Reading Research Quarterly, 27*(2), 125–138.

Roberts, K. (1995). Categorical responding in 15-month-olds: influence of the noun-category bias and the covariation between visual fixation and auditory input. *Cognitive Development, 10*, 21–41.

Roberts, K., & Jacob, M. (1991). Linguistic versus attentional influences on nonlinguistic categorization in 15-month-old infants. *Cognitive Development, 6*, 355–375.

Rosch, E. (1978). Principles of categorization. In E. Rosch & B. B. Lloyd (Eds.), *Cognition and categorization* (pp. 27–48). Hillsdale, N.J.: Lawrence Erlbaum.

Siegler, R. S. (1994). Cognitive variability: a key to understanding cognitive development. *Current Directions in Psychological Science, 3*, 1–5.

Siegler, R. S. (1996). *Emerging minds. The process of change in children's thinking.* New York: Oxford University Press.

Siegler, R. S., & Crowley, K. (1991). The microgenetic method. A direct means for studying cognitive development. *American Psychologist, 46*, 606–620.

Sloman, S. A. (1996a). The empirical case for two systems of reasoning. *Psychological Bulletin, 119*(1), 3–22.

Sloman, S. A. (1996b). The probative value of simultaneous contradictory belief: reply to Gigerenzer and Regier (1996). *Psychological Bulletin, 119*(1), 27–30.

Smiley, S. S., & Brown, A. L. (1979). Conceptual preference for thematic or taxonomic relations: a nonmonotonic age trend from preschool to old age. *Journal of Experimental Child Psychology, 28*, 249–257.

Smith, L. B., Jones, S. S., & Landau, B. (1992). Count nouns, adjectives, and perceptual properties in children's novel word interpretations. *Developmental Psychology, 28*(2), 273–286.

Stockman, I. J., & Vaughn-Cooke, F. (1992). Lexical elaboration in children's locative action expressions. *Child Development, 63*, 1104–1125.

Thatcher, R. W. (1991). Maturation of the human frontal lobes: physiological evidence for staging. *Developmental Neuropsychology, 7*, 397–419.

Thatcher, R. W. (1992). Cyclic cortical reorganization during early childhood. *Brain and Cognition, 20*, 24–50.

Thatcher, R. W. (1994). Cyclic cortical reorganization: origins of human cognitive development. In G. Dawson & K. W. Fischer (Eds.), *Human behavior and the developing brain* (pp. 232–266). New York: Guilford Press.

Thatcher, R. W., Walker, R. A., & Gindice, S. (1987). Human cerebral hemispheres develop at different rates and ages. *Science, 236*, 1110–1113.

Theakston, A. L., Lieven, E. V. M., Pine, J. M., & Rowland, C. F. (2001). The role of performance limitations in the acquisition of verb-argument structure: an alternative account. *Journal of Child Language, 28*, 127–152.

Thompson, D. R., & Siegler, R. S. (2000). Buy low, sell high: the development of an informal theory of economics. *Child Development, 71*(3), 660–677.

Tomasello, M. (1992). *First verbs: a case study of early grammatical development.* New York: Cambridge University Press.

Tomasello, M., & Akhtar, N. (1995). Two-year-olds use pragmatic cues to differentiate reference to objects and actions. *Cognitive Development, 10*, 201–224.

Tomasello, M., & Olguin, R. (1993). Twenty-three-month-old children have a grammatical category of noun. *Cognitive Development, 8*, 451–464.

Toomela, A. (1996a). How culture transforms mind: a process of internalization. *Culture and Psychology, 2*(3), 285–305.

Toomela, A. (1996b). What characterizes language that can be internalized: a reply to Tomasello. *Culture and Psychology, 2*(3), 319–322.

Toomela, A. (1999). Drawing development: stages in the representation of a cube and a cylinder. *Child Development, 70*(5), 1141–1150.

Toomela, A. (2000a). Cultural-Historical psychology: three Levels of Analysis. *Dissertationes Psychologicae Universitatis Tartuensis, 7*. Tartu: University of Tartu.

Toomela, A. (2000b). Stages of mental development: where to look? *Trames, 4*(1), 21–52.

Toomela, A. (2001). Developmental stages in children's drawings of a cube, and, a doll. *Unpublished manuscript.*

Toomela, A. (2002). Drawing as a verbally mediated activity: a study of relationships between verbal, motor, and visual-spatial skills and drawing in children. *International Journal of Behavioral Development, 26*, 234–247.

Toomela, A. (in press). Culture as a semiosphere: on the role of culture in culture-individual relationship. In I. E. Josephs & J. Valsiner (Eds.), *Dialogicality in development.* Westport, Conn.: Ablex.

Tulviste, P. (1988a). *Kul'turno-istoricheskoje razvitije verbal'nogo myshlenija.* Tallinn: Valgus.

Tulviste, T. (1988b). The development of language awareness in children. (A survey of investigations). *Soviet Psychology, 26*, 59–83.

Tulviste, T. (1993). The function of differentiating between a word and its referent. *Journal of Russian and East European Psychology, 31*(2), 27–39.

Valian, V. (1991). Syntactic subjects in the early speech of American and Italian children. *Cognition, 40*, 21–81.

Valian, V., Hoeffner, J., & Aubry, S. (1996). Young children's imitation of sentence subjects: evidence of processing limitations. *Developmental Psychology, 32*(1), 153–164.

von Bertalanffy, L. (1968). *General systems theory. Foundations, development, applications.* New York: George Braziller.

Vosniadou, S. (1992). Knowledge acquisition and conceptual change. *Applied Psychology: An International Review, 41*, 347–357.

Vosniadou, S., & Brewer, W. F. (1992). Mental models of the earth: a study of conceptual change in childhood. *Cognitive Psychology, 24*, 535–585.

Vygotsky, L., & Luria, A. (1994). Tool and symbol in child development. (Originally written in 1930). In R. van der Veer & J. Valsiner (Eds.), *The Vygotsky reader* (pp. 99–174). Oxford: Blackwell.

Vygotsky, L. S. (1926). *Pedagogicheskaja psikhologija. Kratkii kurs.* Moscow: Rabotnik Prosveschenija.

Vygotsky, L. S. (1929). *Pedologija podrostka.* Moscow: Izdanije Bjuro Zaochnogo Obuchenija pri Pedfake 2 MGU.

Vygotsky, L. S. (1935). *Umstvennoie razvitije detei v processe obuchenija.* Moscow-Leningrad: Gosudarstvennoje Uchebno-pedagogicheskoje Izdatel'stvo.

Vygotsky, L. S. (1967). *Voobrazhenije i tvorchestvo v detskom vozraste.* Moscow: Prosveschenije.

Vygotsky, L. S. (1984a). Pedologija podrostka. (Originally published in 1930–1931). In D. B. El'konin (Ed.), *L. S. Vygotsky. Sobranije sochinenii. Tom 4. Detskaja psikhologija* (pp. 5–242). Moscow: Pedagogika.

Vygotsky, L. S. (1984b). Problema vozrasta. (Originally written in 1932–1934). In D. B. El'konin (Ed.), *L. S. Vygotsky. Sobranije sochinenii. Tom chetvjortyi. Detskaja psikhologija* (pp. 244–268). Moscow: Pedagogika.

Vygotsky, L. S. (1994). The problem of the cultural development of the child. (Originally published in 1929). In R. van der Veer & J. Valsiner (Eds.), *The Vygotsky reader* (pp. 57–72). Oxford: Blackwell.

Vygotsky, L. S. (1996). *Myshlenije i rech. (Thinking and speech. Originally published in 1934).* Moscow: Labirint.

Waxman, S. R., & Hall, D. G. (1993). The development of linkage between count nouns and object categories: evidence from 15-month-old to 21-month-old infants. *Child Development, 64*(4), 1224–1241.

Waxman, S. R., & Klibanoff, R. S. (2000). The role of comparison in the extension of novel adjectives. *Developmental Psychology, 36*(5), 571–581.

Waxman, S. R., & Markow, D. B. (1998). Object properties and object kind: Twenty-one-month-old infants' extension of novel adjectives. *Child Development, 69*(5), 1313–1329.

Wellman, H. M., & Gelman, S. A. (1992). Cognitive development: foundational theories of core domains. *Annual Review of Psychology, 43*, 337–375.

Wellman, H. M., & Gelman, S. A. (1998). Knowledge acquisition in foundational domains. In D. Kuhn & R. S. Siegler (Eds.), *Handbook of child psychology, 5th ed., Vol. 2: Cognition, perception, and language* (pp. 523–573). New York: John Wiley & Sons.

Werner, H. (1948). *Comparative psychology of mental development.* New York: International Universities Press.

Werner, H. (1978). The concept of development from a comparative and organismic point of view. In S. S. Barten & M. B. Franklin (Eds.), *Developmental process. Heinz Werner's selected writings Volume 1. General theory and perceptual experience* (pp. 107–130). New York: International Universities Press.

Wundt, W. (1897). *Outlines of psychology.* Leipzig: Wilhelm Engelman.

10. Constructing Knowledge Beyond the Senses: Worlds Too Big and Too Small to See

Eve Kikas

Everyone—animals, children, and adults from different societies—uses senses to acquire knowledge of the world. In addition, people have created tools for improving and extending their senses. Both material and mental (psychological) tools mediate this knowledge (Vygotsky, 1931/1983; Wertsch, 1998). Different apparatuses (e.g., microscope, telescope) have been built for detecting phenomena that we cannot observe due to the lack of the abilities of the senses. Psychological tools—language, schemes, diagrams, models, and theories—also help to see beyond the senses—to "see" tiny and huge things. No one has ever seen what the solar system looks like, but theory makes it visible (Toomela, in press). Thus, models and theories enable us to see even further than apparatuses.

New tools help to develop still better tools (Wertsch, 1998). New theories develop through systematic observations and theorizing and because of new material and mental tools. Contemporary societies have more powerful instruments than did earlier ones; some societies have better tools than others. Not all people and quite a few children use these tools. Since the understanding of the world beyond the senses depends on cultural tools, it is understandable that conceptions of children and people from different societies may be quite different. The understanding depends on what kinds of tools are available and comprehensible at the moment. The ways to describe, understand, and explain different phenomena and make predictions are contained in myths and in traditional and western science. Usually some theories are privileged, one paradigm dominates in each moment, but there is generally no universally accepted single scientific theory or explanation (see also Kuhn, 1962).

This chapter deals with the problems of the development of a child's understanding of the world beyond the senses. As outlined, different signs and mediation of information with the help of signs becomes extremely important in constructing and understanding this world. It is argued that just culture and schooling play a crucial role here. Examples are given from two fields: astronomy and the molecular structure of matter.

CONSTRUCTING KNOWLEDGE BEYOND THE SENSES: BEFORE SCHOOL

Initial Beliefs

It is widely accepted now that the human infant, as the young of other species, is equipped with biologically specified knowledge and with certain perceptual and conceptual structures to interpret and interrelate pieces of the world (Gopnik & Meltzoff, 1997; Spelke, 1991). These structures constrain to what and how a child pays attention. He/she gathers data in accordance with these constraints. Vosniadou (1994a) refers to several nonconscious epistemological and ontological beliefs that constrain the way both younger and older children interpret the world beyond the senses. Ontological beliefs that constrain the understanding of gravity and the concept of spherical earth are (1) space is organized in terms of directions of up and down with respect to a flat ground, and (2) unsupported objects fall in a downward direction. An epistemological belief that constrains both the understanding of the microworld (molecular structure of matter) but also astronomical phenomena states that things are as they appear to be (cf. Albanese & Vincentini, 1997; Piaget & Inhelder, 1941/1974). Chi and her colleagues (Chi, 1992; Reiner, Slotta, Chi, & Resnick, 2000) argue that children and novices apply a substance-based view when reasoning about abstract concepts like heat or force, adding material properties to these constructions. This can also be thought of as a belief that constrains understanding of several physical phenomena.

Explanations, Not Mere Descriptions

There is also a high degree of agreement among researchers that children's first concepts enable explanations that go beyond appearances. In general, people's explanations provide a conceptual framework that would give the feeling of understanding. Therefore, both adults and children actively search for explanations (Brewer, Chinn, & Samarapungavan, 2000). Children explore the world but also frequently ask questions like "why?" or "how?" Wellman, Hickling, and Schult (1997) analyzed children's spontaneous speech recorded from the *Child Language Data Exchange System* database. They found explanations and requests for explanation in children as young as 2 years. Children not only describe but also explain phenomena, but these explanations differ from those of adults'. While functional and intentional explanations are widespread in children, adults give more causal-mechanical explanations (Brewer, Chinn, & Samarapungavan, 2000; Piaget & Inhelder, 1941/1974).

Theories Versus Pieces of Knowledge

The question of how consistently children use their concepts across contexts and tasks is answered differently by various researchers. Empirical studies have shown that even infants understand some general principles of physics and psychology (Gopnik & Meltzoff, 1997; Spelke, 1991). Several researchers refer to these as (naive) theories, the purpose and structure of which are more or less similar to scientific theories. They stress that infants' first theories have to do with fundamental aspects of the world we live in: physical objects and people (Gopnik & Meltzoff, 1997; Gopnik & Wellman, 1994). Other phenomena (e.g., biological, chemical, or astronomical) must thus be described in the terms of these domains, specific theories differentiate later from the first ones. In each stage of life, theory guides the acquisition of new knowledge in the area. Development occurs in the form of conceptual change (a formulation of successive naive theories) due to the child's increased knowledge of the domain (Carey, 1985; Gopnik & Wellman, 1994).

Vosniadou and coworkers (Vosniadou, 1994b; Vosniadou & Brewer, 1992, 1994) have studied astronomical concepts that children of different age and cultures possess. They argue that children first develop initial models, which are based on epistemological and ontological beliefs and observations and are consistently used to explain different phenomena. Observing the seemingly flat surface of the planet earth, children develop their initial model of the flat earth, which could be either rectangular or disc, and which is supported by something (e.g., ground or water). In accordance with this model, the day/night cycle is explained either by the sun moving far away or behind mountains, by something (clouds, moon, darkness) covering the sun or of the sun switching off.

Other researchers, however, stress that attribution of theory structure to the child's domain-specific knowledge is quite problematic. The child's theories (better to say, explanations) are implicit, individual, unshared with others, and not tested in experiments (Brewer, Chinn, & Samarapungavan, 2000; Caravita & Hallden, 1994; Neslon, 1996). Several studies with older children give evidence for fragmented knowledge (DiSessa, 1988; Rowlands, Graham, & Berry, 1999). DiSessa (1988) proposed an alternative view, according to which naive (physics) knowledge consists of a fragmented collection of ideas—phenomenological primitives or p-prims—that are loosely connected, having none of the commitment or systematicity that one attributes to theories.

The Role of Culture and Language

Culture and language were not central in the Piagetian theory but also in domain-specific conceptual change theories. The child is considered as an active subject, constructing his/her understanding more or less by oneself (Spelke, 1991). Nelson argues that "the attribution of 'theories' to the pre-schooler obscures the problems of integrating an experientially derived organization with a cultural system of knowledge" (1996, p. 256). Nelson (1986, 1996) analyzes the formation of scripts, showing how parents help the child to structure the world and acquire the models of events. But parents also help to connect words with categories. Vygotsky has shown explicitly how culture and language guide development; he analyzed the development of everyday and scientific concepts, besides other topics (Vygotsky, 1934/1997; see also Van der Veer & Valsiner, 1994).

Vygotsky (1934/1997) argued that the child's first—everyday (spontaneous)—concepts develop from concrete perceptible instances and are vague and depend on their referents and contexts. The development of everyday concepts proceeds through several stages. Syncretic concepts (unorganized congeries, heaps) are vague and highly unstable; the bonds between concepts are subjective, not real. At first they are developed randomly; later they are organized according to the static fragmented visual field. The next stage of concepts—complexes—are formed according to the visual field. The same perceptual attributes of objects are the basis of both bonds between complexes and between perceived objects. Words have not differentiated from things but are tightly connected to the immediate sensory experience; language is understood and used exclusively as a direct reflection of reality (see also Vygotsky & Luria, 1994). In addition, Vygotsky stresses that it is an adult who supplies a child with the word that must be filled with meaning—content. He states "Complexes corresponding to word meanings are not spontaneously developed by the child: The lines along which a complex develops are predetermined by the meaning a given word already has in the language of adults" (1997, p. 120). So, the child receives the elements of his complexes from adults, in a ready-made form, from the speech of others. Vygotsky refers to the highest level everyday concepts as *pseudoconcepts*. These may be words heard from adults and frequently even used similarly to adults. Adults usually think that a child has the same meaning for a word as they do. Vygotsky argues that pseudoconcepts predominate over all other complexes in the preschool child; however, frequently they are used by older children too (see below).

Examples from the Area of Astronomy

The results of our empirical studies show that young children do not abstract beyond appearances by themselves and that they are quite inconsistent in their answers to different questions about the same phenomena. The following examples are from a longitudinal study carried out in Estonia (unpublished data). As part of a larger project, we studied the concepts of the earth and gravity and how they changed during one year in a class of first and second-year kindergartners. The same children were interviewed twice at a one-year interval (132 children, mean age 34.4 months, minimum 21 months, maximum 48 months at the time of the first interview). We assumed that children of this age are just beginning to develop the understanding of these phenomena, so we hoped to determine their initial understanding (or even initial models) of the earth and gravity. The questions for the interview were developed based on earlier research (see Baxter, 1995; Vosniadou & Brewer, 1992).

One of the questions was "What is the shape of the earth?" which in Estonian sounded like "What is the shape of the earth where all people live?" The difficulty with the wording of this question is due to the fact that the Estonian word "earth" is "earth-sphere," that is the Estonian word for earth already contains reference to its shape. It would be misleading to use the word "maa" ("earth") alone because it has several meanings, including "ground" "land," and "country." If a child said that the earth was round, she/he was shown a ping-pong ball and a disk of similar size and asked: "Is it round like this or this?" The majority of children (111 first year and 71 second year) could not answer this question. In addition, several children (19 and 37 in the first and second year, respectively) gave descriptions that did not contain reference to shape (e.g., green, white, big, with stones). In the second interview a year later, ten children said that the earth was edged or straight. But nobody talked about the flat earth. Some of these young children, however, used the words "round"or "ball-like" to describe the shape of the earth (2 and 14 first and second year, respectively; two of the 14 second year kindergartners were the same as the year before); also, some (1 and 11) of these chose a ball as a model of the earth.

The answers to the question, "If you walked for many days in a straight line, where would you end up?" also showed that young children did not abstract beyond their daily experience. Many children (81 and 56 first year and second year, respectively) did not answer the question. Others (40 and 56) named places close to home (kindergarten, shop and back) or talked about the countryside (where grandmother lives) and well-known foreign countries (10 and 18). Only two second-year children referred to the edge of the earth.

With the fourth question, "Is it possible to fall down from the earth?" we wanted to check if a child thought that the earth had an edge. If a child answered "yes," we asked "Where?" (cf. Vosniadou & Brewer, 1992). Although many children (67 and 55) said that it was possible to fall down from the earth, only one child in each group referred to the edge. Others talked about falling into a hole (11 and 34), and some (9 and 6) gave anthropocentric answers ("where I want").

We also analyzed the answers to all the four questions together and looked for the models children might possess. Of ten children who said that the earth was straight and of four who chose a disk, nobody talked about the edge and the possibility of falling down. So it seems that they had not abstracted their concept of the earth beyond experience and had not abstracted any initial model on their own.

Vosniadou and her colleagues (Diakodoy, Vosniadou, & Hawks, 1997; Vosniadou, 1994a, 1994b; Vosniadou & Brewer, 1992, 1994) argue that children in different cultures initially develop similar flat models of the earth. In addition to the belief about fixed up and down directions, they stress that children presuppose that the ground is flat. Vosniadou and Brewer state, "The flat earth mental model is consistent with everyday experience and is not influenced by culturally accepted, scientific model of a spherical earth" (1994, p. 125). According to Vosniadou and associates, cultural myths and models influence not only the development of later models (synthetic models, see below), but also the understanding of what supports the earth. Actually, the youngest children Vosniadou and her colleagues have studied were 6-year-olds. In the United States sample, of 60 children only one first-grader had a rectangular and one third-grader possessed a disk-model of the earth (Vosniadou & Brewer, 1992). However, this model was more widespread in Indian and Samoan 6- to 9-year old children (Vosniadou, 1994b). These results together with ours indicate that possibly even this seemingly initial model is not developed by observation only. Just as in the Indian tradition, it is believed that the earth is like a disk floating in the ocean and children take this notion from their culture. Accordingly, children learn about the flat earth with an edge around it from adults.

Due to language peculiarities, in Estonia children take the word "sphere" to refer to the shape of the earth very easily. It does not mean, however, that children have conceptual models of a spherical earth and that they understand the principles of gravity. These children's concepts are actually pseudoconcepts—words taken from adults but filled with different meaning (Vygotsky, 1997) or synthetic models (Vosniadou, 1994a). As Vosniadou (1994a) argued, ontological beliefs constrain children's understanding tremendously. It seems that such young children do not have any kind of initial model described by Vosniadou but they rely heavily on the perceptible and depend on context (cf. Vygotsky, 1997). Also, they take the words from adults but fill them with different meaning. The word "earth-sphere" may inhibit the development of a flat model but it encourages the development of some specific synthetic notions (e.g., that people live on the top of the sphere, the sphere is a bit flattened).

CONSTRUCTING KNOWLEDGE BEYOND THE SENSES: SCHOOL YEARS AND EDUCATION

Theories and Conceptual Change

When children enter school, they have already acquired a substantial amount of information about the physical and social world. This knowledge influences what children learn in school and how they interpret the information taught (Driver, Squirer, Rushworth, & Wood-Robinson, 1995; Schnotz, Vosniadou, & Carretero, 1999). Starting from the paper by Posner, Strike, Hewson, and Gertzog (1982), conceptual change has been an ideal model of science learning (see Glynn & Duit, 1995). According to the model, science learning means successive changes in students' concepts and/or theories. It is presumed that students come to science class with well-articulated naive concepts: get new—contradictory to these conceptions—information, which leads to cognitive conflict, the resolution of this results in learning. Students learn scientific concepts by becoming dissatisfied with their own concepts as a result of the teacher showing them contradictory evidence.

Researchers stress that conceptual change in children is often similar to changes in the history of science. Younger children possess theories that resemble historically earlier (medieval or even antic) scientific theories (e.g., Carey, 1985; Chi, 1992). The process of learning is analogous to the process of changing scientific theories in history (cf. Posner et al., 1982; Kuhn, 1962). Although theories change when a lot of contradictory evidence has been collected, students change their concepts when they are shown confronting examples (which they observe in experiments or are shown by teachers).

It is quite questionable, one possibility is that students themselves invent new theories but there are also other possibilities from which theories can be acquired or why children's theories differ from the theories of adults (see below and Chinn & Brewer, 1993, 2000). Also, motivational beliefs about the self and learning may hinder learning (Pintrich, 1999). Conceptual change approaches stress the active child as responsible for constructing new knowledge (theories) but pay little emphasis on the ways culture (through the ways teaching/learning is organized in the classroom, through the teacher's language use, etc.) influences the development of concepts (cf. Valsiner, 1994).

Cultural Tools Specific to the Classroom

Learning about the world beyond the senses occurs through the medium of verbal instruction. Abstract, out-of-empirics content of knowledge taught in school demands the use of a new type of psychological tools (signs); students study a new type of—scientific—concepts (Vygotsky, 1997). Wertsch refers to this as decontextualization of cultural tools, "the process whereby the meaning of signs become less and less dependent on the unique spatiotemporal context in which they are used" (1985, p. 33). Scientific concepts are defined in relation to each other and are connected with referents only indirectly through their integrated syntactic networks. These concepts do not directly refer to objects but to everyday concepts; they are generalizations of generalizations in which perceptual and other features are recombined into new, supposedly more informative, structures (e.g., from the point of view of contemporary western astronomical theory the sun is one of the stars). It should be stressed that Vygotsky did not consider scientific concepts only as those used in exact or natural science; according to him, scientific concepts are those that are mediated by signs and that belong to logical and hierarchical structure. Thinking in scientific concepts does not depend on the immediate reflection of reality; in this process, linguistic units are abstracted from their communicative contexts and become objects of reflection. Scientific thinking often uses the same linguistic terms as everyday thinking, but everyday language does not reflect the same logical structures.

Vygotsky stresses that scientific concepts are not acquired via memorization alone. Their development takes time and starts, not ends, with learning the term: "Memorizing words and connecting them with objects does not in itself lead to concept formation; for the process to begin, a problem must arise that cannot be solved otherwise than through the formation of new concepts" (1997, p. 100). He argues that the internalization of the real concept proceeds through the stage of pseudoconcept that serves as a connecting link between thinking in complexes and thinking in concepts. It means that at first the child uses the word, learned in school, but its meaning differs from the real scientific meaning. Only after some time, if the child has had a necessity to use it to solve new problems can he fill it with real meaning. To become internalized (to become understood), scientific concepts must be backed up with everyday examples.

Difficulties with Constructing the Knowledge about the World Beyond the Senses

Cultural tools have both affordances and constraints (Valsiner, 1994; Wertsch, 1998). On the one hand, new scientific theories are developed to overcome some problems (either theoretical or empirical) in the earlier theories. Usually, they are more powerful in the sense that they explain a wider range of phenomena and enable new predictions (Chinn & Brewer, 2000; Kuhn, 1962). On the other hand, they constrain understanding in the sense that their usage demands better preliminary knowledge of the content and the procedures (i.e., the ways to use new tools), also constraining the group of people who take them seriously. New theories expand with difficulty even among scientists themselves, which is one of the reasons Kuhn (1962) called theory changes "revolutions." As Toomela (in press) stresses, it is not so much the lack of time but the complexity of the reorganization of existing meaning-systems that inhibits the understanding and internalization of new ideas. The reorganization of the conceptual system needs new knowledge, but it also needs the abilities to think and memorize and the willingness to accept the new idea as possibly correct.

Chinn and Brewer (1993, 2000) analyze different ways by which people modify their knowledge in response to anomalous data that contradict the knowledge already possessed. They have found eight possible responses: ignoring data, rejecting data, uncertainty about data, excluding data from the domain of the current theory, holding data in abeyance, reinterpreting the data, peripheral theory change, and theory change. So, theory change is only one possibility, along with seven other ways, and occurs rarely. Chinn and Brewer show that all these possibilities are used in different areas like science, magic, and religion, but also by both nonscientist adults and children. These are efficient ways to deal with the large amount of ambiguous and messy information in today's world. But the same processes work in classrooms and inhibit the understanding of the material taught in school.

When students learn new information that is somehow inconsistent with their previous knowledge, they may respond in any one of these eight ways, only the last of which is the desired response. It is especially easy *not to change* one's knowledge if new information is ambiguous and there is no time to discuss and think about it (Chinn & Brewer, 2000). Frequently, learning leads to the development of pseudoconcepts (cf. Vygotsky, 1997). Students may acquire verbalisms (Vygotsky, 1997) or inert or rote memorized knowledge (Vosniadou, 1994a), or they may exclude data (Chinn & Brewer, 1993, 2000). Most frequently, however, students develop synthetic concepts. In synthetic concepts, new, learned in-school information, is reinterpreted to fit with everyday experience (cf. reinterpreting data or peripheral theory change, Chinn & Brewer, 1993, 2000). A lot of research has shown students' (and adults') synthetic conceptions (also called "misconceptions" or "alternative frameworks") (Driver, Squirer, Rushworth, of Wood-Robinson, 1995; Garnett, Garnett, & Hackling, 1995; Glynn & Duit, 1995; Schnotz, Vosniadou, & Carretero, 1999).

What really happens depends also on the teaching methods used in the classroom. Different methods offer different advantages and constraints. Traditional methods constrict the material learned in school, leading more frequently to the compartmentalization of school and everyday knowledge (Chinn & Brewer, 1993). The emphasis is on quantitative and inductive reasoning (Ploetzner & VanLehn, 1997; Smith, Maclin, Grosslight, & Davis, 1997). School and life (theoretical and empirical contexts) become separate, so it is difficult to understand the new knowledge and to back it up with one's own experiences (see also Caravita & Hallden, 1994). Alternative methods stress more the connections between school and everyday life, trying to build scientific knowledge on the preliminary one (Glynn & Duit, 1995; Schnotz, Vosniadou, & Carretero, 1999; Smith, Maclin, Grosslight, & Davis, 1997).

Examples from the Area of Astronomy

Children observe the changes in light and temperature during the day and night and during the seasons of the year. They see the sun moving in the sky and hear explanations such as "It is time to go to bed, the sun is sleeping already." Based on these observations, they have developed explanations of the reasons for these changes. In school, the heliocentric theory is taught, and the changes are explained according to this theory.

In an earlier investigation, we studied students' concepts of the day/night cycle and seasonal changes at two different times: at two months (fifth grade) and at four years (ninth grade) after students had learned the topics by traditional teacher-centered methods (Kikas, 1998a). It was found that students remembered the explanations very well two months after having learned the topic in school; they even used the textbook's wordings quite exactly. However, the picture had changed four years after learning the topic. Ten (of 20) students started with everyday or personal explanations (e.g., day/night alternate because we must rest; seasons change because there is snow and it is cold). After several questions from the experimenter, children tried to give causal physical explanations that showed they had actually reverted to synthetic concepts. Namely, students connected the changes with the revolving sun. For example, one girl argued: "The earth goes around . . . no, I think it was the sun that turned around the earth and . . . I don't remember it any more. We studied it a long time ago" (Kikas, 1998a, p. 451). But two students gave everyday explanations: seasons change because in winter there is a cold northern wind and snow is cold. These answers are similar to younger students' answers from other studies (Baxter, 1995). So we could conclude that children had really acquired *verbalisms* that afterward reverted to synthetic concepts. If newly learned knowledge is not integrated with the preliminary one, it is forgotten as soon as there is no use for it anymore.

These results differ from those of similar studies in other countries, which have shown that students do not know terms and explanations even shortly after learning them in school. For example, Diakidoy and Kendeou (2001) compared the effectiveness of two instructional approaches (standard, textbook-based vs. experimental, which took into account students' preconceptions) in facilitating fifth graders' conceptual change in astronomy. They found that the standard instruction did not lead to improvements in astronomy tests. The differences between studies may be explained by the fact that the Estonian textbook covered the material more thoroughly, but also the teacher devoted much more time to checking students' knowledge in the classroom.

Besides traditional teacher-centered methods, alternative student-centered methods have been used. Diakidoy and Kendeou (2001) proved the advantage of this approach as compared with the traditional method. Still, even after learning the topic by the experimental method, many fifth graders had difficulties with understanding how it was possible to live on the bottom part of the spherical earth. This is where the ontological belief that space is organized in fixed up and down directions hinders understanding tremendously. However, using nontraditional teaching methods may lead to worse factual knowledge without gaining real understanding, where more empirical, everyday concepts remain dominant (see, for Waldorf schools, Kikas, 1998b, 2000).

Examples from the Area of Molecular and Submolecular Structure of Matter

Everyday life provides children with many opportunities for interacting with different materials and for observing their properties and changes. But several molecular and submolecular processes are beyond the range of the sensitivity of material tools; several of these processes cannot be directly seen even with the help of the most powerful apparatuses. Cultural tools—theories, explanations, models—make these phenomena visible, however. Scientists use mathematical formulas and complex theoretical structures in their descriptions and explanations. In addition, informal reasoning plays an important role in scientific thinking, both in creating the new knowledge and in understanding existing theories (Kuhn, 1962; Tweney, 1991). Analogy is one of the ways of creating knowledge about various phenomena, including molecular structure of matter (Gentner, Brem, Ferguson, Markman, Levidow, Wolff, & Forbus, 1997). In analogical reasoning, the information from one well-known domain is transferred to a new domain. Scientists use analogies in their informal reasoning. For example, they make materialistic models (i.e., they add materialistic features to various processes like light, electric current, heat) to gain an intuitive understanding of the topic (Reiner, Slotta, Chi, & Resnick, 2000). They abandon these ideas, however, for more abstract representations if needed. Alchemists also relied on analogies as a guide to truth. These analogies, however, were unconstrained from the point of view of contemporary science (Gentner et al., 1997).

Analogy is also used by children and adults to gain understanding about molecular and submolecular processes, based on well-known observable phenomena. Epistemological belief that things are as they appear to be constrains the development of conceptions here (see earlier and Vosniadou, 1994a). Based on this proposition, people use analogy with the macroworld to understand microscopic phenomena; they consider the microscopic world as totally isomorphic to the macroscopic one, except for scale. So, students develop *synthetic conceptions* that describe microscopic processes in terms of perceptual macroscopic entities. For example, students believe that molecules melt when substance melts, that an atom has the color of its substance, that the chemical bond is a physical entity (Albanese & Vincentini, 1997; Boo, 1998; Driver, Squirer, Rushworth, & Wood-Robinson, 1995).

In other words, it means that decontextualized signs are interpreted in a context-specific way. People do not make sense of indirect and abstract chains of new—scientific—concepts; instead they simply put theoretical microscopic entities taught in school among other perceptible things in the macroscopic world. Microscopic theoretical concepts are taken as a new kind of object one can see and touch and these concepts are understood in analogy to the everyday macroscopic world. Scientific concepts are hence understood structurally equivalently to everyday concepts. Brewer, Chinn, and Samarapungavan (2000) refer to the application of macro properties to micro entities as a specific type of explanation, characteristic to children. It is not used only by children, however, but by lay adults as well (Albanese & Vincentini, 1997).

Smith, Maclin, Grosslight, and Davis (1997) compared the impact of two forms of instruction on the development of students' concepts of matter. The standard approach aimed to develop a formal understanding, the other instruction engaged students in explicit reasoning about their preliminary conceptions and used a variety of models to build relations between scientific and everyday concepts. In the latter approach, the importance of informal, qualitative, as well as quantitative, reasoning was stressed. In developing the alternative curriculum, Smith and associates proceeded from the novice-expert research, which had shown that experts used qualitative reasoning, models, and analogies before starting to solve the problem mathematically (Chi, Feltovich, & Glaser, 1981). As expected, Smith and associates proved the advantage of the alternative method in restructuring students' preliminary conceptions of matter. But perhaps of more theoretical interest is their analysis of difficulties in the learning process. They write: "although they /students/ sometimes showed clear signs of being exhilarated by open-ended classroom debates, at other times they were frustrated when the teacher would not simply tell them the right answer or when they had to wrestle with a conceptual confusion" (1997, p. 386). It was shown that qualitative restructuring takes time and mental effort, and that even with alternative, well-designed instruction, students' factual knowledge improved more than their conceptual knowledge.

The Usefulness of Synthetic Concepts

One question is whether it is necessary and reasonable at all to *change* conceptions (cf. Chi, 1992; Mortimer, 1995). In reality, instead of being changed, naive concepts stay alive and frequently coexist besides the new concepts. In spite of strong efforts to improve teaching methods, students do not acquire scientific understanding and theories in several, if not all, the domains. Some researchers talk about the possibility of plural conceptual systems, each appropriate for specific social settings, saying that conceptual development is not replacement of "incorrect" with "correct" conceptions, but different contextual activation of alternative representations (e.g., Caravita & Hallden, 1994; Chi, 1992; Moritmer, 1995). Caravita and Hallden write that "the aim of learning, science for example, is not to abandon old ideas in favour of new ones, but rather to extend our repertoire of ideas about the physical and cultural world, to refine their organization and coherence" (1994, p. 106). A successful result of learning should be "an extension of conceptions held by a learner about the world, sometimes resulting in reorganization of already existing knowledge" (ibid.). In this case, however, individuals should become aware of their earlier concepts, learn new knowledge, and become able to distinguish between different contexts and learn which concepts are useful in which situations and activities (cf. Mortimer, 1995). The studies show that this ideal has not been reached either. Students lack meta-conceptual awareness about their knowledge even after learning the topic; only experts in the field show a higher level of awareness (Chi, Feltovich, & Glaser, 1981).

Abstract scientific concepts liberate people from the limitation of the senses, but time and effort, specific abilities, and knowledge are needed to understand them. These are possessed and used by experts in specific fields but not by novices and children. Synthetic conceptions are "compromises" between scientific and everyday concepts (Vosniadou, 1994a, 1994b; Vygotsky, 1997) and they are useful for several reasons. First, they are reminiscent of scientific concepts on the surface, giving an impression that the student has "gained" the knowledge taught in school, which in turn enables him/her to be successful in school (cf. Vygotsky, 1997). Second, as scientific knowledge is reinterpreted to fit with everyday experience, synthetic concepts still enable the student to use earlier everyday explanations outside of school (cf. Mortimer, 1995; Vygotsky, 1997). As learners feel no dissatisfaction with these concepts, it is unrealistic to expect them to give them up in favor of new, school concepts, and it is no surprise that they survive well into adulthood (cf. Chinn & Brewer, 1993; Toomela, in press). Synthetic concepts enable learners to interpret the phenomena, giving them the feeling of understanding.

CONCLUSIONS

Constructing knowledge beyond the senses—knowledge about the worlds too big and too small to see—is mediated with material and mental tools. Material tools like microscopes or telescopes broaden the range of observable phenomena, but models and theories enable us to "see" even further. In these theories, the knowledge gained during earlier generations is also accumulated.

To understand this mediated-by-signs knowledge is much more complicated and time-consuming than understanding the visible world. From early on, adults help children construct this knowledge. On the one hand, the child is an active subject, constructing his/her knowledge, including the knowledge about tiny and huge objects. Children ask questions, look for explanations, carry out experiments, and observe phenomena. In addition, various initial beliefs constrain their understanding, helping to make sense of the phenomena. Many researchers stress this side of the child's development (Carey, 1985; Piaget & Inhelder, 1974; Vosniadou, 1994a). On the other hand, adults supply children with words; they answer children's explorative questions and construct their environments. Talking about the world beyond the senses starts very early. Much less emphasis has been paid to this side of development (but see Nelson, 1996). Sometimes it seems that children are alone in the world, trying to discover everything on their own. Based on empirical data, we showed that even a child's first concepts about the world beyond the senses are culturally bound and influenced by the language used by adults. Even the model of the flat earth is culturally mediated, being more frequently used in cultures where this model is still described in myths (cf. Vosniadou, 1994a, 1994b).

As has been shown, children's concepts are reminiscent of earlier scientifically valid concepts. Some researchers, drawing parallels between cultural and onto-genetic development, infer from this that children really construct their knowledge like scientists have done in the course of history (Carey, 1985; Chinn & Brewer, 1993). But there are other possible explanations, for children's and historically earlier scientifically valid concepts being similar. First, just these culturally earlier views are seen in everyday language. For example, the term "force of inertia" is used in everyday language. Such a conceptualization of force was used in the pre-Newtonian impetus theory. According to this theory, force can be possessed, transformed, and dissipated; it can be seen as a kind of impetus-like substance or a property of material objects. This view of force is not valid in the Newtonian theory, but it is widespread among children and nonscientist adults (e.g. Chi, 1992; Rowlands, Graham, & Berry, 1999). Second, historically earlier cultures had fewer and less powerful cultural tools to use to develop explanations. The same is also true for children in contemporary societies.

Learning about the world beyond the senses takes place frequently and systematically in school. This knowledge is mediated by cultural tools—children study scientific concepts, which are generalizations of everyday concepts. Language is used more and more to refer to other concepts, not only to referents themselves. When new information is taught in school, students integrate this new knowledge with their previous knowledge. As Vygotsky (1997) stresses, the normal way of development proceeds through the stage of pseudoconcepts. The development may end on this stage, however; students acquire verbalisms or synthetic concepts. Different teaching methods constrain and afford development differently. Traditional teacher-centered teaching encourages memorizing facts, definitions, and even explanations. These are forgotten after some time, however, and the knowledge is "made" more understandable by learners' forming synthetic concepts (Kikas, 1998a). But if teaching is limited to everyday experiences and observations, conceptual understanding does not develop either (see Kikas, 1998b, 2000 for Waldorf schools). The most effective methods seem to be the experimental ones that concentrate on discussing students' preliminary concepts and on building the new knowledge on these concepts (e.g., Diakidoy & Kendeou, 2001; Smith et al., 1997). In addition, these latter methods take time for informal reasoning, which is frequently used in daily life and also by experts for solving difficult new problems (Chi, Feltovich, & Glaser, 1981).

To conclude, constructing knowledge about the world beyond the senses is complicated and time-consuming. To think about conceptual systems presupposes the development of several psychological functions (memory, deliberate attention, deductive reasoning skills) as well as motivation. Much of the knowledge people possess is the synthesis of visible and verbally learned information. These synthetic concepts are useful, enabling people to be successful both in everyday and school areas.

NOTE

Acknowledgment. This work was supported by the Estonian Science Foundation Grant No. 3993.

REFERENCES

Albanese, A., & Vicentini, M. (1997). Why do we believe that an atom is colourless? Reflections about the teaching of the particle model. *Science and Education, 6,* 251–261.

Baxter, J. (1995). Children's understanding of astronomy and Earth sciences. In S. M. Glynn & R. Duit (Eds.), *Learning science in the schools* (pp. 155–178). Mahwah, N.J: Erlbaum.

Boo, H. K. (1998). Students' understanding of chemical bonds and the energetic of chemical reactions. *Journal of Research in Science Teaching, 35,* 569–581.

Brewer, W., Chinn, C., & Samarapungavan, A. (2000). Explanation in scientists and children. In: F. Keil & R. Wilson (Eds.), *Explanation and cognition* (pp. 279–298). Cambridge, Mass: MIT Press.

Caravita, S., & Hallden, O. (1994). Re-framing the problem of conceptual change. *Learning and Instruction, 4*, 89–111.

Carey, S. (1985). *Conceptual change in childhood*. Cambridge, Mass: MIT Press.

Chi, M. (1992). Conceptual change within and across ontological categories: examples from learning and discovery in science. In: R. Giere (Ed.), *Cognitive models of science. Minnesota Studies in Philosophy of Science, 15* (pp. 129–187). Minneapolis: University of Minnesota Press.

Chi, M. T., Feltovich, P. J., & Glaser, R. (1981). Categorization and representation of physics problems by experts and novices. *Cognitive Science, 5*, 121–152.

Chinn, A., & Brewer, W. F. (2000). Knowledge change in response to data in science, religion and magic. In K. Rosengren, C. Johnson, & P. Harris (Eds.), *Imagining the impossible. Magical, scientific, and religious thinking in children* (pp. 334–371). New York: Cambridge University Press.

Chinn, A., & Brewer, W. F. (1993). The role of anomalous data in knowledge acquisition: a theoretical framework and implications for science instruction. *Review of Educational Research, 63*, 1–49.

Diakidoy, I.-A., & Kendeou, P. (2001). Facilitating conceptual change in astronomy: a comparison of the effectiveness of two instructional approaches. *Learning and Instruction, 11*, 1–20.

Diakodoy, I.-A., Vosniadou, S., & Hawks, J. (1997). Conceptual change in astronomy: models of the earth and of the day/night cycle in American-Indian children. *Learning and Instruction, 12*, 159–184.

DiSessa, A. (1988). Knowledge in pieces. In G. Forman & P. Pufall (Eds.), *Constructivism in the computer age* (pp. 49–70). Hillsdale, N.J.: Erlbaum.

Driver, R., Squirer, A., Rushworth, V., & Wood-Robinson, M. (1995). *Making sense of secondary science: research into science ideas*. New York: Routledge.

Garnett, P. J., Garnett, P. J., & Hackling, M. W. (1995). Students' alternative conceptions in chemistry: a review of research and implications for teaching and learning. *Studies in Science Education, 25*, 65–95.

Gentner, D., Brem, S., Ferguson, R., Markman, A., Levidow, B., Wolff, P., & Forbus, K. (1997). Analogical reasoning and conceptual change: a case study of Johannes Kepler. *The Journal of Learning Sciences, 6*, 3–40.

Glynn, S. M., & Duit, R. (Eds.) (1995). *Learning science in the schools*. Mahwah, N.J.: Erlbaum.

Gopnik, A., & Meltzoff, A. (1997). *Words, thoughts, and theories*. Cambridge, Mass.: MIT Press.

Gopnik, A., & Wellman, H. (1994). The theory theory. In: L. A. Hirschfeld & S. A. Gelman (Eds.), *Mapping the mind: domain specificity in cognition and culture* (pp. 257–293). New York: Cambridge University Press.

Kikas, E. (1998a). The impact of teaching on students' definitions and explanations of astronomical phenomena. *Learning and Instruction, 8*, 439–454.

Kikas, E. (1998b). Pupils' explanations of seasonal changes: age differences and the influence of teaching. *British Journal of Educational Psychology, 68*, 505–516.

Kikas, E. (2000). The influence of teaching on students' explanations and illustrations of the day/night cycle and seasonal changes. *European Journal of Psychology of Education, 15,* 281–295.

Kuhn, T. (1962). *The structure of scientific revolutions.* Chicago: University of Chicago Press.

Mortimer, E. (1995). Conceptual change or conceptual profile change? *Science and Education, 4,* 267–285.

Nelson, K. (1986). *Event knowledge: structure and function in development.* Hillsdale, N.J.: LEA.

Nelson, K. (1996). *Language in cognitive development. Emergence of mediated mind.* New York: Cambridge University Press.

Piaget, J., & Inhelder, B. (1941/1974). *The child's construction of quantities: conservation and atomism.* London: Routledge and Kegan Paul.

Pintrich, P. (1999). Motivational beliefs as resources for and constraints on conceptual change. In W. Schnotz, S. Vosniadou, & M. Carretero (Eds.), *New perspectives on conceptual change* (pp. 33–50). Amsterdam: Pergamon.

Ploetzner, R., & VanLehn, K. (1997). The acquisition of qualitative physics knolwedge during textbook-based physics training. *Cognition and Instruction, 15,* 169–205.

Posner, G., Strike, K., Hewson, P., & Gertzog, W. (1982). Accommodation of a scientific conception: toward a theory of conceptual change. *Science Education, 66* (2), 211–227.

Reiner, M., Slotta, J., Chi, M., & Resnick, L. (2000). Naive physics reasoning: a commitment to substance-based conceptions. *Cognition and Instruction, 18,* 1–34.

Rowlands, S., Graham, T., & Berry, J. (1999). Can we speak of alternative frameworks and conceptual change in mechanics? *Science and Education, 8,* 241–271.

Schnotz, W., Vosniadou, S., & Carretero, M. (Eds.) (1999). *New perspectives on conceptual change.* Amsterdam: Pergamon.

Smith, C., Maclin, D., Grosslight, L., & Davis, H. (1997). Teaching for understanding: a study of students' preinstruction theories of matter and comparison of the effectiveness of two approaches to teaching about matter and density. *Cognition and Instruction, 15,* 317–393.

Spelke, E. (1991). Physical knowledge in infancy: reflections on Piaget's theory. In: S. Carey & R. Gelman (Eds.), *The epigenesis of mind: essays on biology and cognition* (pp. 133–169). Hillsdale, N.J.: Erlbaum.

Toomela, A. (in press). Culture as a semiosphere: on the role of culture in the culture-individual relationship. In I. Josephs & J. Valsiner (Eds.), *Dialogicality in development.* Westpont CT: Ablex.

Tweney, R. (1991). Informal reasoning in science. In J. Voss, D. Perkins, & J. Segal (Eds.), *Informal reasoning and education* (pp. 3–16). Hillsdale, N.J.: Erlbaum.

Valsiner, J. (1994). Social organization of cognitive development. Internalization and externalization of constraint systems. In A. Demetriou, M. Shayer, & A. Efklides (Eds.), *Neo-Piagetian theories of cognitive development: implications and applications for education* (pp. 65–79). London: Routledge.

Van der Veer, R., & Valsiner, J. (Eds.) (1994). *The Vygotsky reader.* Cambridge: Blackwell.

Vosniadou, S. (1994a). Capturing and modeling the process of conceptual change. *Learning and Instruction, 4,* 45–69.

Vosniadou, S. (1994b). Universal and culture-specific properties of children's mental models of the earth. In L. A. Hirschfeld & S. A. Gelman (Eds.), *Mapping the mind: domain specificity in cognition and culture* (pp. 412–429). New York: Cambridge University Press.

Vosniadou, S., & Brewer, W. (1992). Mental models of the earth: a study of conceptual change in childhood. *Cognitive Psychology*, *24*, 535–585.

Vosniadou, S., & Brewer, W. F. (1994). Mental models of the day/night cycle. *Cognitive Science*, *18*, 123–183.

Vygotsky, L. S. (1934/1997). *Thought and language* (revised edition of 1986). Cambridge, Mass.: MIT Press.

Vygotsky, L. S. (1931/1983). Istorija razvitija vyschikh psikhicheskih funktsii [History of the development of higher mental functions]. In *Sobranije sochineniii* (Vol. 3, pp. 5–228). Moscow: Pedagogika.

Vygotsky, L., & Luria, A. (1994). Tool and symbol in child development. In R. Van der Veer & J. Valsiner (Eds.), *The Vygotsky reader* (pp. 99–175). Cambridge: Blackwell.

Wellman, H., Hickling, A., & Schult, C. (1997). Young children's psychological, physical, and biological explanations. *New Directions for Child Development*, *75*.

Wertsch, J. (1985). *Vygotsky and the social formation of mind*. Cambridge, Mass.: Harvard University Press.

Wertsch, J. (1998). *Mind as action*. New York: Oxford University Press.

Afterword: Animals, Brain, Culture, and Children—The Emerging Picture from Complementary Perspectives

Aaro Toomela

The mental development of the child is primarily studied in developmental psychology. This volume, however, attempts to show that child development cannot be fully understood unless evidence from other fields of psychology—comparative psychology, neuropsychology, cultural psychology—is taken into account in studies of individual mental development. There are several questions that developmental psychology alone is not able to answer at all. Basically, mental development results in the interaction of two factors, "components" in terms of the theory of functional systems (see Toomela's chapter on the description of the theory), nervous system, and environment. We also know that there are characteristics of the mind that develop only in healthy human children in a social–cultural environment. Other animals in such an environment as well as human children in a nonhuman environment do not develop such characteristics. Thus, it can be suggested that both the human brain and the human environment are special. Consequently, if our goal is to understand child mental development, we must understand specific characteristics of the human brain and the human environment. This volume as a whole provides an outline of the "big picture," to see how different perspectives in psychology may be truly complementary.

GENERAL THEORY

The first important subject that has been discussed in several chapters in this volume concerns not specific questions but rather the general theoretical background that underlies all scientific enterprises in psychology. **Valsiner** draws attention to the idea that it might be unproductive to search for answers to certain questions. It does not help very much to understand the human mind if the main question is whether animals or children or people from different cultures "have" certain mental abilities or characteristics. Specific examples of this as it concerns child development can be found in chapters by **Nelson**, by **Toomela**, and by **Kikas**: they all demonstrate that externally the same behavior may internally rely on different mechanisms and mental structures. Children's first words are not related to each other; they just "stand for" something in the external sensory environment. The same words are embedded into a complex web of other words in adults. The same word forms thus have different fields of meanings (**Nelson**). Relationships with other words are not only the basis for differentiation in semantic fields but also the basis for differentiation of grammatical classes (**Toomela**). If children learn in school that "earth is a sphere," then it does not necessarily follow that they understand such an expression the same way that educated adults do (**Kikas**).

The same line of thinking can be extended to other fields of psychology. When apes, for example, are able to calculate, it must be demonstrated that psychological mechanism of calculation are the same in humans and apes. **Ardila**, in fact, shows that animal counting mechanisms are based on visual perception and proprioception, whereas humans, in addition to using such counting mechanisms, can count by using symbols (numbers). It can be suggested that the use of symbols for counting extends counting ability to a qualitatively novel level that cannot be found in animals other than humans. Thus, the fact that animals "have" counting ability is not very informative because there are different ways of counting, some of which are available only to humans.

Valsiner goes further and suggests that the main question that should be studied is the question of development, the question of emergence of novel psychological phenomena. Indeed, there are only two possibilities. One possibility is that qualitatively novel psychological phenomena may emerge in the process of the interaction of an individual with the environment. The other possibility is that all psychological phenomena exist already in the beginning of development. Organisms "have" abilities that unfold in time. In the latter case, it is usually suggested that such abilities are biologically determined, they are "innate." Considering the complexity of the mental phenomena, the latter understanding is less plausible. The biological differences between humans and apes, for example, seem to be very small when compared to the differences in their psyches (cf. **Gibson**).

Toomela suggests that it is feasible to make the general theoretical background even more explicit. The goal of psychology seems to be explanation of the mind. Theoretically, there are different understandings of what the explanation is. The implicit definition of explanation that underlies much of mainstream psychology is understanding, according to which explanation means description of linear relationships between causes and effects. Such understanding, however, must deny the idea of development as emergence because emergence of a novel form is in essence a nonlinear event. **Toomela** proposes that satisfactory explanation is more complex; it must include complementary descriptions of qualitatively distinguishable components of the phenomenon, relationships between those components, and description of the development of the phenomenon through the process of differentiation of novel components and following synthesis of those components into a hierarchically higher level whole with new qualities.

There are two more ideas worthy of attention as to the general theoretical back-ground underlying scientific thinking. **Markova** draws attention to the very important fact that scientific ideas are shaped by political ideology, which may hinder the development of some ideas and suppress the expression of other ideas. In totalitarian societies scientists sometimes are forced to use language that obscures ideas. Some other ideas cannot be expressed at all. I believe the same applies to nontotalitarian societies as well. It is politically incorrect, for example, to attribute cognitive differences between sexes to biological factors. When researchers dare to challenge such ideological "truths," they must present long introductions as to why such challenges are necessary at all (cf., e.g., Kimura, 1999). Possible ethnic differences in mental abilities may be another example (e.g., Herrnstein & Murray, 1994).

Finally, several chapters in this volume demonstrate that "historical blindness" is dangerous for scientific thinking. **Valsiner**, **Markova**, **Nelson**, **Toomela**, and **Kikas** all rely heavily on theories that are relatively "old" and relatively forgot-ten. And they all demonstrate that these "old" theories allow insights that are fresh and help to go much beyond "modern" thinking in psychology. It can be sug-gested that there are many brilliant theories in the history of psychology that have been rejected for no good reason—and sometimes replaced by much less powerful ideas.

THE BRAIN AND BEHAVIOR

The Brain

I allow myself to proceed with the assumption that it is worthwhile to rely on the theory of functional systems in the study of the mind (or whatever other phe-nomenon). I suggest, together with **Berry**, that the individual and the social–cultural environment can be distinguished (I would like to stress here that "distinguishing" is not "separating") as "components" of a more complex system. The adult "cultural" mind can be understood as a qualitatively novel phenome-non that emerges in the interaction of these two components. Developmentally, distinguishing the culture and the individual means that each of them has qualitatively different roles in the developing synthesis of the cultural mind. The individual in the beginning of development is characterized by biologically constituted characteristics of the nervous system, the brain. These characteristics of the brain make the development of the cultural mind possible. In this sense, the brain is necessary but not sufficient for human mental development. Such development also requires the possibility to participate actively in the social–cultural environment.

Several chapters in this volume propose what makes the human brain special, as well as what can be considered to be "innate" and what mental characteristic may be emergent in individual development. **Gibson** draws attention to the fact that discontinuities that may differentiate humans from other animals cannot be fine-grained because only about 300 to 400 genes are not shared by humans and apes. She goes further and suggests that the most important specifically human characteristic that may underlie most, if not all, psychological differences may be the size of the human brain, especially the size of the neocortex, the striatum, and the cerebellum (**Ardila** proposes essentially a similar idea). There are no parts of the brain that are specifically human. Some cytoarchitectonic differences have been described, but it is not clear whether these differences are truly qualitative or result from quantitative growth of the brain in evolution. **Toomela** mentions that one important characteristic of all systems is the number of components/elements. The system cannot differentiate when the number of components is small. Thus, even when the most important biologic difference between humans and other animals is just the size of the brain, it does not necessarily follow that the human mind must differ from that of other animals also only quantitatively. The quantity of the brain may be necessary for its qualitative differentiation in the interaction with the environment. Goldberg has given a lot of evidence to support the idea that such differentiation, indeed, takes place in human ontogeny (Goldberg, 1989, 1995; see also **Gibson**).

It seems to be unclear at present whether more specific differences exist in the construction of the brain that differentiate humans from other animals. **Ahmed and Miller**, in essence, suggest that there are such more specific differences. They propose that the evolution of visually realistic art—which is unique to humans!—cannot be explained by the increase in brain size only because some early hominids had bigger brains than anatomically modern humans but still did not have art. They go further and propose that certain abilities are related to asymmetry of the brain. Visual artistic abilities are related to the nondominant parietal lobes and writing to the dominant parietal lobes. So, from their account it follows that even if visual artistic abilities are not related to the evolution of some very specific biological mechanisms that may underlie artistic abilities, then at least these abilities should be related to asymmetrical functioning of the brain. Another candidate for brain differences that may be related to specifically human mental abilities may be the degree of asymmetry of the brain. **Vauclair's** observation that animals seem not to have an asymmetric division of labor between hands is in agreement with this proposition.

There is evidence, however, that biological differences in brain asymmetry by itself are not sufficient for explaining human differences from other animals. First, brain asymmetry characterizes many species, for example, rodents (cf. Kimura, 1999). Second, there have been numerous studies that demonstrate smaller asymmetry of the female brain when compared to the male brain (Kimura, 1999). A less asymmetric brain does not hinder the development of the human mind in any way. Next, **Ardila** gives evidence that increasing asymmetry of the brain may be related to schooling and acquisition of reading. Early hominids may have presented a more bilateral representation of spatial abilities too. Consequently, a high degree of brain asymmetry by itself does not need to be biologically determined.

It might be sufficient to have a big enough brain that had a potential for differentiation into asymmetrically functioning hemispheres. Finally, **Ahmed and Miller** suggest that painting, sculpture, and drawing are possible with injury to every brain area except to the nondominant parietal lobe. They ignore developmental dimension here. There is quite a lot of evidence that brain structures related to acquisition of knowledge and abilities do not necessarily overlap with structures related to their maintenance. Right hemisphere structures may be responsible for acquisition of novel abilities, whereas left hemisphere mechanisms are better for using already acquired knowledge and abilities (Goldberg & Costa, 1981). In sum, it is not clear whether relatively highly asymmetrical functioning of the brain, which characterizes the human brain, is determined biologically. A lot of evidence is in agreement with the idea that such asymmetry results in the process of interaction with the social–cultural environment.

Also, more specifically, **Ahmed and Miller**'s suggestion that artistic abilities may be an example of how biological evolution gave rise to the specifically human ability of visual arts seems not to be sufficiently grounded. To support the idea that drawing ability "is independent of culture"—and, correspondingly, determined biologically—they also present evidence that some autistic children have produced visually realistic art already at the age of 18 months. Again, such findings do not necessarily indicate a biological, noncultural origin of artistic abilities for several reasons. First, 18 months is actually a long time on the developmental scale, and 18-month-old children have had a lot of opportunities to acquire some cultural abilities. Second, in order for such children to draw, they are supplied with tools, pencils, and paper, provided by their social–cultural environment. Third, the fact that autistic children do not communicate almost at all through language does not indicate that they are totally linguistically and socially isolated from the world. They do understand words and language, even though less than healthy children do; they actually do interact socially, even though their ability for reciprocal interactions is limited; and they definitely live in the social–cultural environment (Frith, Morton, & Leslie, 1991; Gillberg, 1990; Sandberg, Nyden, Gillberg, & Hjelmquist, 1993; Tager-Flusberg, 1995). Finally, it is important to keep in mind that autism is a disorder. It is not always appropriate to generalize findings from an unusual population of humans to the usual human being. There is evidence, for example, that brain injury may be related to supranormal performance in some tasks (e.g., Irle, 1987; Kapur, 1996; Toomela, Tomberg, Orasson, Tikk, & Nõmm, 1999). Unusual drawing abilities may result from the interaction of the social–cultural environment with the unusual brain of some autistic children.

Behavior

Behavioral differences between humans and other animals are also informative as to possible biologically determined differences in nervous systems. All authors who discussed comparative issues agree that there is continuity in the human evolution. If we are to assume, as is done in the theory of functional systems, for example, that novelty emerges in the process of differentiation of existing structures, then every developing phenomenon must be in some sense continuous. Discontinuities can emerge only on the basis of continuity.

There are many examples of behaviors that may be specific to humans. **Gibson** argues that basically all humanly unique processes may develop on the basis of two general capacities, fine sensorimotor discrimination and mental construction, which are more developed in humans. These basic abilities allow building hierarchies of functions where every next level opens qualitatively novel abilities. What **Ardila** proposes is essentially similar. According to Ardilla, the brain possesses basic ways of information processing. Culture provides contents to these basic capabilities.

There are differences between the linguistic abilities of animals and humans. For example, animal ability to combine linguistic signs is very limited when compared to even $2^1/_2$ to 3-year-old children (**Gibson**). It can be suggested that such difference in the number of possible combinations may ground qualitatively novel ways of thinking that are unique to humans (cf. **Nelson**, **Toomela**, **Kikas**). **Vauclair** describes other differences in the structure and function of language. Animal signals in nature are wholistic; they are not arbitrary and conventional as human symbols are. In addition, human linguistic signs can be detached or decontextualized from the elements to which they relate, but animal signals cannot. Human signs have mainly a declarative function, whereas animal signs are used mainly as imperatives. **Valsiner** reminds us that language development depends also on external circumstances, on the need to use language. It follows that the simple finding of different "have not's"—animals do not "have" arbitrary and conventional signals, for example—does not necessarily indicate biological differences between humans and apes. Some environmental factors may be decisive instead. Thus, a question for further studies and analyses is whether such differences in language emerge on the basis of differences in brain size alone or are there some language-specific "innate" mechanisms also involved.

Vauclair directs attention to differences in nonlinguistic domains as well. Animals almost lack asymmetric division of labor between hands/limbs. Genuine visuo-gestural representations that are manifested in the use of specific techniques such as weaving exist in humans. Developmental pathways of human and non-human primates in the acquisition of manipulatory behaviors, including the use of tools, are also different. Again, evidence seems to fit more with the idea that such behavioral and cognitive differences emerge in the interaction of an individual with the social–cultural environment; they are not based solely on "innate" mechanisms.

THE SOCIAL–CULTURAL ENVIRONMENT

The chapters that specifically are dedicated to the analysis of the social–cultural environment—**Ardila, Berry, Markova**—do not give us a clear understanding of what definition of culture may be appropriate for understanding the development of the human mind. But they all help us to understand better the functioning of the human environment.

Markova analyzes similarities and differences between Bakhtin's and Lotman's approaches to the functioning of culture. It is important in this context that it is primarily the human language and communication that comprises culture for both of these scholars. The following analysis reveals important differences between these two theoretical schools. Bakhtinian understanding of the functioning of culture is related to the continuous, simultaneous, nondiscrete, and always-changing nature of cultural communication. Lotmanian understanding is related to sequential and discrete opposition of communicators who use a relatively stable code for creating and changing messages.

Markova's chapter leaves an impression that these two views are mutually exclusive. Indeed, at first glance it may seem that stable phenomenon cannot be always-changing, that discrete and nondiscrete are in opposition, and that sequential and simultaneous cannot characterize the same phenomenon. It is not necessarily so. In general terms these oppositions can be related to two complementary aspects of phenomena—structure or system on the one hand and process on the other. Every system can be intrinsically stable and always-changing at the same time. Process means interaction of a system with another system. Properties of the interacting systems change during the interaction. But components of the interaction are distinguishable in principle. They do not become the same (cf. **Toomela**). **Berry** points to a similar idea when he explains how culture can be simultaneously an "independent" variable and an "organismic" variable.

Let's take a dialogical example. When detailed analysis of mother–child interaction demonstrates the seamlessness of dialogical contributions, the nonexistence of discrete units, and the mutual construction of messages, as **Markova** suggests, then I believe there are other layers that can be understood as stable. Many roles of the mother and infant cannot be interchangeable. Mother remain mother for feeding and many other activities. For many years, mother also remains the primary source for cultural knowledge about the world. Mothers, of course, may learn a lot in their interactions with their children, but in almost all cases what children learn and what mothers learn—even in a dialogue with each other—are different. The time factor is important also. Building of linguistic messages takes time. Language, used for/in dialogue, must thus be sequentially organized and discrete. At the same time, the speaker adjusts expressions for a listener and the listener—simultaneously—tunes to the speaker. There are simultaneous and successive aspects in the same act.

Markova's chapter gives several ideas that may contribute to understanding the cultural aspect of human development. I believe one of the most important ideas from her account indicates a question that must be addressed rather than a ready-made answer. Children's minds develop in a dialogue. How can it be that every dialogue is unique and still may lead to the development of relatively universal mental characteristics? At the very general level the answer may lie in the definition of the stage of mental development I proposed—stable characteristics define kinds of possible configurations a system may take ("topographical constraints"), whereas the number of possible combinations within those constraints is almost unlimited ("dynamic possibilities," cf. **Toomela**). But the way from that theoretical idea to understanding every specific aspect of mental development is long. And the question definitely needs specific answers in respect to every mental change we want to understand.

Berry outlines principles that help to understand similarities and differences between cultures. According to his ecocultural approach, there are "cultural universals" together with basic psychological processes shared by all cultures, and behaviors that develop differently as adaptations to specific characteristics of ecological and cultural contexts. Thus, again, a very important question emerges—for understanding human development, universal and unique aspects must be differentiated. In addition, **Berry** also points out how individual and cultural levels of analysis and observation can be related and how they should be differentiated.

There is one idea in **Berry**'s account that needs special attention. He states that the ecocultural approach explicitly rejects the idea that some cultures or behaviors are more advanced or more developed than others. He is certainly correct when such "more developed/ less developed" differentiations are expressions of ethnocentric prejudices. But actually that statement is very fundamental—it denies the possibility that culture can develop (in a sense discussed by **Valsiner**). Description of hierarchically different stages of development is not necessarily ethnocentric in origin. Rather, it is an empirical question. In fact, there is a lot of evidence that cultures may be at hierarchically different levels or stages of development (see Toomela, in press, for a review). **Ardila** also gives some examples. He demonstrates that learning to read and write is related to development of other processes and abilities, such as verbal short-term memory, visual–spatial abilities, and phonological abstraction. As reading and writing are cultural phenomena, it can be conjectured that illiterate cultures may be less developed as a whole. In addition, **Nelson**, **Toomela**, and **Kikas** all demonstrate that symbols develop hierarchically. As symbols are cultural constructions, then it naturally follows that cultures can in principle be at different levels of development. At this moment, **Berry**'s suggestion that cultures cannot develop hierarchically (otherwise cultures with no contact between each other can in principle be at different developmental levels) seems to be insufficiently grounded. The possibility that his position is more ideological than scientific cannot be ruled out.

Another perspective on the role of culture in the development of the individual mind is discussed by **Ardila**. He demonstrates how basic ways of information processing, which humans share with other animals, acquire novel content in the interaction with culture. Rudimentary numerical concepts and spatial abilities, for example, can be found in human ancestors. In humans, however, these processes develop; entirely novel psychological functions emerge on the basis of evolutionally old processes. Ardila provides several examples that demonstrate the role of culture in the development of such basic processes. Thus, on the one hand human mental development is continuous and novel processes develop on the basis of processes shared with evolutionally earlier species. On the other hand, there are processes that are not shared with other species. These processes emerge in a cultural context; culture can be understood as a source or origin of novelty.

CHILD DEVELOPMENT

The views presented in the first three parts of this volume suggest that specifically human individual development is made possible by the interaction of a uniquely plastic and adaptive brain, with "innate" basic processes shared with other animals, and complex social–cultural environment, which gives qualitatively novel content to these processes. The last part of this volume discusses the development—true development, development as hierarchic reorganization of basic abilities—of semiotic abilities, mainly verbal language, and also other processes that emerge because of the development of language.

Nelson adds evidence for the support of the idea that complex semiotic operations are not biologically determined *per se*. She demonstrates that all semiosis is fundamentally social, even when symbols are used individually. Both **Nelson** and **Toomela** also discuss the mechanism by which such development is made possible. In principle, hierarchical change in the structure of the mind emerges in activity, in the process of interaction with the environment. Activity, however, is not always ahead of the mind; it is not *the* determinant of mental development. Rather, earlier developments in mental structure give rise to novel forms of activities that were not available before. These novel abilities, in turn, lead to hierarchical changes in the structure of the mind. Thus, activity and mind are in mutual relationships. So, for example, **Nelson** describes in her slot-filler theory how taxonomies emerge in everyday activities. These taxonomies are linguistic; they are hierarchical systems of symbols. Such hierarchy can develop only when some less developed form of language—indexical in Nelson's/Peircean terms—already exists. Activity leads to the acquisition of indexical signs, and their acquisition, in turn, is the basis for the development of activity. A potential emerges for creating symbols with the help of signs. This potential is realized in linguistic activities so that hierarchical systems of symbols develop. Examples of this kind of development are also discussed by **Kikas**, who demonstrates how the development of mental tools, i.e., symbols, helps to develop even better tools.

Kikas directs attention to some very interesting aspects of symbolic development. She shows how complex the developmental process actually is. Continuity in development acquires novel aspects here. Usual accounts of continuity discuss how developmentally earlier structures change into novel, more complex structures. **Kikas**, however, analyzes evidence of how earlier structures may also hinder development. Already constructed knowledge is relatively stable, and very often children (and adults as well) do not accept novel information. They either ignore novel data, just memorize them without understanding meaning coded in a message, or assimilate novel evidence into a less-developed conceptual structure so that the meaning of the novel messages changes completely. Finally, **Kikas** adds that development is not a passive acceptance of messages. Rather, learning humans are active; they must also be ready to accept views that do not fit their conceptual structure; they must be willing to learn.

Both **Nelson** and **Kikas** discuss two stages in symbol development; "indexical" (Nelson) or "everyday" (Kikas) signs develop first, and "symbols" (Nelson) or "scientific concepts" develop in the hierarchical reorganization of the first level of development. **Toomela**'s account goes further. In the analysis of symbol meaning development in the context of the theory of functional systems, he proposes that five stages of symbol meaning development can be differentiated. Empirical evidence given seems to support that account. It is interesting that **Kikas**' and **Nelson**'s ideas are in agreement with **Toomela**'s approach. The only difference is that according to **Toomela** additional stages should be differentiated.

Finally, all three chapters on child development agree that the development of semiosis should not be understood as a thing in itself, as development isolated from other aspects of mind. On the contrary, development of language is related, for example, to the development of memory (autobiographic memory, **Nelson**), perception and perceptual–motor coordination in activities (drawing, **Toomela**), knowledge (about the world that is not directly available for senses, **Kikas**), and "self" (**Nelson**). All such developments seem not to be possible without using some semiotic system, some kind of language, in addition to the basic ways of information processing humans share with other animals. Thus, insight from developmental psychology allows us to suggest that the human mind may be fundamentally different from the minds of other animals. The main differences should be related to novel ways of information processing, *how* knowledge is constructed and problems are solved, as well as to the content of mind that can be constructed only using those uniquely human mechanisms, especially knowledge about the world that cannot be perceived directly in principle.

THE IDEA OF RECAPITULATION AND RELATIONSHIPS BETWEEN COMPARATIVE PSYCHOLOGY, NEUROPSYCHOLOGY, CULTURAL PSYCHOLOGY, AND DEVELOPMENTAL PSYCHOLOGY

So, it seems the circle is full. We started with the ideas from comparative psychology, which are relevant to a better understanding of the human brain, culture, and child development. Then it appeared that understanding of the human brain and culture is useful for better understanding of animal minds and human ontogenesis. Finally, human ontogenesis leads to novel insights in comparative psychology. It really looks like different perspectives on the study of the mind—comparative psychology, neuropsychology, cultural psychology, and developmental psychology—are complementary rather than isolated fields of knowledge as they are studied by many in the mainstream psychology.

If so, then we must admit—together with **Valsiner** (and **Gibson**, **Ardila**, **Nelson**, **Toomela**, and **Kikas**, in this volume)—that phylogenesis, ontogenesis, and microgenesis are not equivalent, but the three kinds of developmental processes are mutually linked—the question is, how. Perhaps Ernst Haeckel, with his "fundamental law of biogeny"—"ontogeny is recapitulation of phylogeny" (e.g., Haeckel, 1910a)—was right? If what we learn from phylogenesis is helpful for understanding ontogenesis and vice versa, then there must be something fundamentally similar in them. Space limitation does not allow us to discuss that issue in details. But some additional ideas from Haeckel are relevant here (cf. Haeckel, 1910a, 1910b). First, Haeckel *did not* suggest that ontogenesis *exactly* recapitulates phylogenesis. He differentiated between "paligenetic" and "cenogenetic" evolutionary processes, the first related to continuity and the second to uniqueness in development due to "adaptation" to certain conditions of development. Thus, universal and unique are not necessarily mutually exclusive. That idea is actually quite modern. **Berry**, for example, also suggested that there are both universal characteristics of all cultures and unique characteristics as adaptations [!] to unique environmental influences within universals. Second, Haeckel gave reason why recapitulation must be characteristic of development: "The first and most important of these facts is that every man, like every other animal, begins his existence as a single cell (Haeckel, 1910b, p. 733)." Biological evolution begins similarly from a single cell. There is only one direction in which a single cell can develop—it can differentiate into two. Many more cells are necessary for differentiation of bones, muscles, nervous tissue, lungs, kidneys, liver, and so on. It can be said, using more modern terminology, that development is "canalized" by its starting point. **Toomela** just went a step further and proposed that the law of recapitulation characterizes behavioral evolution for the same reason—both phylogenesis and ontogenesis begin similarly from the ability to respond to individual sensory attributes. Even more, the basic mechanism of development seems also to be the same—through constructing representations on the basis of active interaction with the environment.

Thus, different perspectives on the human mind can be analyzed in the same universal background, which is defined by the similar starting point of mental development. That starting point canalizes development. This does not mean, however, that developmental trajectories in different time-scales are identical in every respect. Actually, every individual line of development within the universal constraints is unique. And understanding what is universal and what is idiosyncratic is perhaps one of the most important questions for all truly developmental perspectives on the mind.

CONCLUSIONS

This volume is more than a collection of chapters; it can be treated as a coherent whole where every part and every chapter contribute something unique to the "big picture" of mind and its development. Very briefly, the emerging picture can be described as follows: In the biological evolution, the human brain differentiates from the brains of other animals. The most important difference seems to be the growth of the brain, especially its neocortical areas. The bigger brain becomes more plastic and acquires a potential to differentiate and develop very complex psychic functions in interaction with the social–cultural environment. The most important aspect of this interaction can be connected with the term "dialogue," the active social participation of an individual in a culturally structured environment. Culture can be understood as a source or origin for many psychological functions. What makes the cultural environment special seems to be enormously rich information that is coded in semiotic systems, language. Cultural psychic development is in essence the development toward individual representation of that information. In addition, cultural development is not constrained to individual reconstruction of cultural information. Rather, acquisition of semiotic systems, which seems to proceed over several distinguishable hierarchical stages, becomes a basis for fundamental reorganization of all basic psychological processes humans share with other animals—memory, perception, motor planning, thinking, and feeling.

And finally, it can be concluded that every branch of psychology may benefit from other branches of psychology because, after all, Ernst Haeckel may have been much closer to the truth with his law of recapitulation than is acknowledged in modern psychology. The general direction of mental development, whether phylogenetic, ontogenetic, and maybe also microgenetic, seems to be universal because all these lines of development are constrained by structurally the same starting point that canalizes all of the following developments of the system. Haeckel's message is worthy of attention (Haeckel, 1910b):

Just as all other functions of the body develop in the connection with their organs, so the soul does in connection with the brain. This gradual unfolding of the soul of the child is, in fact, so wonderful and glorious a phenomenon that every mother or father who has eyes to observe is never tired of contemplating it. It is only our manuals of psychology that know nothing of this development: we are almost tempted to think sometimes that their authors can never have had children themselves. The human soul, as described in most of our psychological works, is merely the soul of a learned philosopher, who has read a good many books, but knows nothing of evolution, and never even reflects that his own soul has had a development. (p. 746)

REFERENCES

Frith, U., Morton, J., & Leslie, A. M. (1991). The cognitive basis of a biological disorder: autism. *Trends in Neurosciences, 14*(10), 433–438.

Gillberg, C. (1990). Infantile autism: diagnosis and treatment. *Acta Psychiatrica Scandinavica, 81,* 209–215.

Goldberg, E. (1989). Gradiental approach to neocortical functional organization. *Journal of Clinical and Experimental Neuropsychology, 11*(4), 489–517.

Goldberg, E. (1995). Rise and fall of modular orthodoxy. *Journal of Clinical and Experimental Neuropsychology, 17*(2), 193–208.

Goldberg, E., & Costa, L. D. (1981). Hemispheric differences in acquisition and use of descriptive systems. *Brain and Language, 14,* 144–173.

Haeckel, E. (1910a). *The evolution of man. A popular scientific study. Vol I. Embryology or ontogeny.* London: Watts & Co.

Haeckel, E. (1910b). *The evolution of man. A popular scientific study. Vol II. The evolution of the species or phylogeny.* London: Watts & Co.

Herrnstein, R. J., & Murray, C. (1994). *The Bell curve. Intelligence and class structure in American life.* New York: The Free Press.

Irle, E. (1987). Lesion size and recovery of function: some new perspectives. *Brain Research Review, 12,* 307–320.

Kapur, N. (1996). Paradoxical functional facilitation in brain-behavior research: a critical review. *Brain, 119,* 1775–1790.

Kimura, D. (1999). *Sex and cognition.* Cambridge, Mass.: Bradford Book.

Sandberg, A. D., Nyden, A., Gillberg, C., & Hjelmquist, E. (1993). The cognitive profile in infantile autism—a study of 70 children and adolescents using the Griffiths Mental Development Scale. *British Journal of Psychology, 84,* 365–373.

Tager-Flusberg, H. (1995). "Once upon a ribbit": stories narrated by autistic children. *British Journal of Developmental Psychology, 13,* 45–59.

Toomela, A. (in press). Culture as a semiosphere: on the role of culture in culture-individual relationship. In I. E. Josephs & J. Valsiner (Eds.), *Dialogicality in development.* Westport, Conn.: Ablex.

Toomela, A., Tomberg, T., Orasson, A., Tikk, A., & Nômm, M. (1999). Paradoxical facilitation of a free recall of nonwords in persons with traumatic brain injury. *Brain and Cognition, 39,* 187–201.

Index

www.ingramcontent.com/pod-product-compliance
Lightning Source LLC
Chambersburg PA
CBHW052000270326
41929CB00015B/2734